Narrative(s) in Conflict

Culture & Conflict

Edited by
Isabel Capeloa Gil and Catherine Nesci

Volume 10

Narrative(s) in Conflict

Edited by
Wolfgang Müller-Funk and Clemens Ruthner

DE GRUYTER

ISBN 978-3-11-055564-6
e-ISBN (PDF) 978-3-11-055685-8
e-ISBN (EPUB) 978-3-11-055590-5
ISSN 2194-7104

Library of Congress Cataloging-in-Publication Data
A CIP catalog record for this book has been applied for at the Library of Congress.

Bibliographic information published by the Deutsche Nationalbibliothek
The Deutsche Nationalbibliothek lists this publication in the Deutsche Nationalbibliografie; detailed bibliographic data are available on the Internet at http://dnb.dnb.de.

Cover image: Mark Winfrey/Dreamstime
Typesetting: Konrad Triltsch GmbH, Ochsenfurt-Hohestadt
Printing and binding: CPI books GmbH, Leck
♾ Printed on acid-free paper
Printed in Germany

www.degruyter.com

Table of Contents

Preface by the Editors

Narrative(s) in Conflict presents the results of an international workshop, held with prominent senior scholars and promising junior researchers at Trinity College Dublin in May 2013, to a wider audience. The project was a spin-off of sorts of the cross-disciplinary and comparative research network *Broken Narratives*, organized by the Faculty of Philology and Cultural Studies at the University of Vienna, and situated within the research strand *Identities in Transformation* of the *Trinity Long Room Hub* Arts and Humanities Research Institute, housed at Trinity College Dublin; also our contacts with the *Graduate Centre for the Study of Culture* (GCSC) at the University of Giessen, Germany, proved to be very inspiring.

What has brought this informal network together, is its credo that narrative theory and narratological tools should be regarded as an integral part of cultural analysis (cf. Bal 2009). By choosing exemplary case studies, our workshop tried to analyze the relation between representation and conflict, i.e. between narrative constructions, social/historical processes and cultural *agon*. In order to address this research question properly, it is crucial to state that narratives do not simply and passively mirror conflicts as the conventional 'realism' fallacy suggests. They rather provide a *symbolic matrix* to make sense of a conflict in a way that is accepted by a narrative community; also, they have even a *generative* and *performative* dimension.

Generally speaking, cultures can be seen as a reservoir of different types or templates of narratives that are available for the purpose of formatting and *making* events (cf. White 1973; Rowner 2015; Ruthner 2016). However, narratives are only partly *referential* texts, but rather entail interpretation(s) by choosing a certain plot. From this point of view, one may revert the traditional idea that narratives are simply the *effect* of dramatic events. It is also true that, under certain circumstances, events gain their momentum only through their *emplotment* by pre-existing templates (White 1987).

Storytelling can thus be approached as a central element and technique in and of culture (cf. e.g. Müller-Funk 2008, 2012). Following the tradition of Anglophone cultural studies and Antonio Gramsci (1978), culture is not an innocuous meta-phenomenon beyond power, but the latter is inscribed in the former and shapes it (see Foucault 1980). With regard to our topic, this also means it is a question of power, which narratives are present in a society and which are not. Or, which sorts and formats of narrative are dominant in the uses of the past in a culture, particularly when it comes to cultural memory formation (cf. Erll & Nünning 2008).

https://doi.org/10.1515/9783110556858-001

The *agonistic* model used in our volume implies that culture/s are a battleground for meaning and significance (Fiske 1990: 23), between various actors and stakeholders, within and between narrative communities such as social groups or national collectives, between centres and peripheries, etc. Concurrently, conflict in itself is one of the most important plot devices not only in fiction and drama (Abbott 2008: 55), but social, political, economic, epistemological and other conflicts also inform the polysemy of all cultural texts and vice versa. They run through the narratives as lines of rupture or ambiguity at a textual level (cf. Nünning & Nünning 2016); on the other hand, they can be approached as competing stories at a cultural level as well.

Accordingly, we have placed the case studies of our volume between literary criticism, historiography, and cultural theory, involving disciplines such as cultural sociology, or film and media studies as well. The book thus applies narrative analysis not only to literature and its interpretation, but it goes further than that, pointing at other important functions of narrative production for culture; for instance, in the construction of collective identities and memory. The case studies collected here try to include different countries, cultures, cultural media and genres. In terms of thematic scope and historical focus, they range from early modern times to (German and Austrian) Modernism and international Postmodernism, from the Ottoman Empire and the cultural reactions to it in the South Slavic and Hungarian literatures to post-war trauma, be it in France, Ireland, Japan and the US after World War II, in Bosnia-Herzegovina after the Yugoslav Succession Wars of the 1990s, or in the aftermath of 9/11. Thus, this volume shows narrative activity – to refer to Ansgar and Vera Nünning's central essay – as a symbolic machinery of world-, identity- and conflict-making, in which not only antagonism, but also *caesura* plays an important role.

The latter was also central to the Viennese research project *Broken Narratives* that served as an incentive of sorts for our project as well. The German word *Bruch* namely entails at least two aspects, which can be translated into English as *break*, and as *rupture*, respectively. There is a moment of destruction (broken glass) linked with a temporal aspect: a sudden and often unexpected change, but also an interruption, and finally a halt to a continuous process.

At first glance, it might seem as if narration were the simple opposite of rupture. But narrative and rupture are not in a binary opposition; there is a strong interdependence instead. Narrative is always something that constitutes continuity by connecting disparate elements. Narrative, however, is broken, too, when the rupture is visible as a trace. Thus, to some extent, traditional narratives work in the tricky Hegelian way of *aufheben:* they 'pick up' (and preserve), and they suspend at the same time.

'Broken narratives' have thus a triple meaning. On a semantic level, they refer to a 'real' rupture in history or in a certain historical discourse; they relate to a sudden event, to a dramatic turning point. The second aspect of narrative is an interpretative or even performative one. Because narratives are never a simple reproduction of what has happened, they always include an interpretation of the events they refer to (and create). This, however, entails the (performative) world-making aspect of narratives, which plays a key role in Ansgar and Vera Nünning's essay in this volume. On a structural level, finally, modernist narratives are broken in themselves since they break with the traditional way of storytelling. From James Joyce's *Ulysses* (1922) to Péter Nádas's *Parallel Stories* (2005), there is a programmatic distrust vis-à-vis homogeneity, closure, and linearity.

From this point of view, one can revise the mainstream understanding of broken or conflicting narratives, which regards them deriving from a break, a crisis, the outbreak of a conflict only, e.g. in cases of trauma. In contrast, a broken narrative can be seen as a certain type of storytelling, in which a series, a chain of events will be constructed and interpreted in a dramatic or traumatic sense.

Rupture is associated with conflict, caused by an opposition that can be internal (within one and the same person) and external (between two and more actors). As rupture, conflict is ambivalent; it is experienced as dangerous and creative, as an act of violence and destruction as well as an act of liberation and overcoming of the frozen structures of tradition, as an act of *becoming*.

The philosophy of Heidegger, but also of Nietzsche, had a radical break in mind, namely the destruction of the occidental mainstream of philosophy beginning with Socrates, Plato, and Aristotle. Similarly, many representatives of the (ironically termed: 'classical') avant-garde and modernist movements pushed for the end of traditional aesthetics along with the prevailing definitions of fine arts and literature.

As for this, Wolfgang Müller-Funk – following the Mexican poet Octavio Paz – elaborates in our volume that there is something like a paradoxical *tradition* of rupture and break in 'classical' Modernism. As Paz demonstrates, this tradition of Modernism is undermined by itself, with Postmodernism being the effect of that paradoxical process.

In Postmodernism, however, there is a tendency of moderation; the programmatic turn of destruction has been substituted by deconstruction, which avoids the total break and conflict, suggesting that the idea of *tabula rasa* is an illusion. As one can see in Harold Bloom, Jacques Derrida, and Paul de Man, there is a moment of sublimation and weakening of all the aggressive impulses that go hand in hand with rupture and conflict. Thus, pathos-laden modernist destruction has given way to ironic postmodernist revision. But as Ansgar and Vera Nünning point out, there is a renaissance of narrative concepts in which conflict plays a central role, at least on a political level as in George W. Bush's speeches on the 'War on Terror'.

Conflict and rupture in their narrative embedding also create the frame for other contributions to this volume. In her analysis of the image of the Ottomans in early modern Hungary, Andrea Seidler goes back to the fifteenth and sixteenth centuries, to the fall of Constantinople and the defeat of the Hungarians against the Ottomans in the Battle of Mohács (1526). In this context, the mainstream narrative in Hungary is one of victimization, lamentation, and mourning. Simultaneously, this gives the trauma a new and religious sense by referring to the Old Testament, in which the Jews are seen as a suffering people, punished by God because of their disobedience. In analogy, the Hungarians are seen as God's chosen people who will back his fight against the "savage warriors" and "devils". It is evident that this is a conflicting narrative in the sense that it intentionally creates conflict. Later, in the eighteenth and nineteenth centuries, a shift occurs, and the concept of the enemy is no longer the Ottoman Empire, but Habsburg rule.

Davor Dukić's contribution leads us to the nineteenth century (i.e., the era of nation-building) by interpreting a famous piece of Croatian literature, Ivan Mažuranić's *The Death of Smail-aga Čengić* (1846). The writer, whose counterfeit can be seen on the Croatian 100-Kuna banknotes nowadays, was an admirer of Lord Byron. His modern anti-Turkish narrative tells a historical story, the assassination of a local Turkish commander in Montenegro in 1840. In the epic poem of the Croatian author who never visited Montenegro in his life, however, the Ottoman chief, who seems to have been a justice-loving man, is transformed into a monster – a 'cog' in the repressive regime. This image is embedded in a narrative that suggests the religious enemy is the only one being responsible for the backwardness of the Balkans.

While Seidler and Dukić refer to the first and the second level of conflict narratives, Rüdiger Görner analyses the conflict within the genre of the prose poem, discussing texts by Rimbaud, Turgenev, Rilke, and Trakl. The prose poem can be seen as a hybrid, an in-between. It occupies the place between exterior and interior, plot and impression, narration and intuition. As Görner shows, in Trakl there is in correspondence to the heterogeneous character of this trans-genre, a mixture in time as well, between past and present.

Also António Sousa Ribeiro occupies himself with questions of genre. He discusses Karl Kraus's hostility towards the novel and the realistic effect of storytelling by contrasting it with the purely fictional character of satire. But, as Sousa Ribeiro can show with reference to Lukács and Bakhtin, Kraus's satires have also a narrative structure as a "significant device for the projection of conflict and for the structuring of the violent gesture which is inherent to the very definition of satire". There is no doubt that Kraus's satires are conflict-generating, "civilized forms of the cannibal", but also part of the "laboratory of the experimental".

Nicola Creighton's reflections on Carl Einstein locate the art historian's project within the discourse of modernism, using the concept of ekphrasis to test his ideas about producing a completely new history of the arts. What he has in mind is a consequent rupture within the discipline. Its new historiography is planned in analogy with Cubism. Just as this movement is dethroning and decentering the subject, and questioning the construction of space in art, Einstein's intention is to subvert the traditional narrative of art history, especially the idea of comparability. Instead, art is to be seen as a "human activity" (Nietzsche); the subject matter of art history not being objects, but "configured vision".

Dorothea Depner's text is a case study between history and literature, discussing the works of two Irish authors, Francis Stuart's *The Pillar of Cloud* (1948) and Hugo Hamilton's *The Last Shot* (1991). Both writers had an intensive contact to Germany, Stuart especially during World War II. After the war and the victory of the Allies, this kind of narrative with a certain pro-German tendency came under pressure. Accordingly, the key element in this self-legitimization becomes "elsewhere", which also implies a symbolic nowhere-land. Depner shows how the two books' "conflicting narratives", the one of the older author and the other of his successor, never come to a halt until they acquire a new meaning after the fall of the Berlin Wall.

Also in Johanna-Charlotte Horst's essay "Damaged Words and Closed Houses: Everyday and Memory Narratives in Georges Perec", the overlapping of memory and narration is evident. Perec, who follows a (Post-)Marxist aesthetic, also wrote autobiographical texts dealing with a phenomenon that is prominent in contemporary discourse: trauma, which, as Horst points out, is a "wound" and implies a fragmentation. It is this sudden and overwhelming rupture and conflict that generate new and ambitious forms of broken narrative, because trauma marks a border, therefore generating "impossible narrations" and "damaged words".

Next, Isabel Capeloa Gil's article leads the reader into the world of film. Analyzing films of Alexander Sokurov (*The Sun*, 2005) and Tom Hooper (*The King's Speech*, 2010), she expands on a phenomenon which she calls "broken voice". Sokurov's protagonist is Emperor Hirohito after the defeat of Japan, Hooper's is King George VI. In both cases, the articulation of their voice marks a rupture, a loss of power and legitimation. Thus, the rupture becomes part of the discursive level of the narration indicating the symbolic death of the ruler – who does not really understand what has happened?

Ana Mijić's contribution discusses the postwar identities in Bosnia-Herzegovina as "specific socio-historical constellations" of a region after a gory conflict. Following Berger's and Luckmann's theory, Mijić understands identity as a social construction. This perspective is connected with a narrative one: self-victimization as a kind of storytelling is popular because it delivers moral justification and neutralizes the question of one's own guilt. Thus the International Tribunal for Ex-Yugoslavia in The Hague became a battlefield for symbolical self-protection and a positive self-image; on the other hand, this moral alchemy which is connected with collective identity-building has undermined the possibility of open discussion and reconciliation.

Clemens Ruthner's essay discusses four versions of *Mitteleuropa* (Palacký, Neumann, Bibó and Kundera). From the very beginning, the author demonstrates how 'Central Europe' is a narrative construct in many versions, entailing a discourse that consists of conflicting and controversial elements. Ruthner postulates the end of this discourse for two reasons, 1) the Yugoslav Succession Wars and 2) the enlargement of the European Union in 2004. The mix (or 'mêlée' in Jean-Luc Nancy's words) that was so characteristic for the region before (in all its versions and variations), no longer exists.

Last, but not least, Ansgar und Vera Nünning present a new global narrative that has been created by American president George W. Bush and his think tank: the 'War on Terror' including a new enemy, the "axis of the evil", and an "omniscient storyteller". In their comprehensive close reading of Bush's speeches, it soon becomes clear that narratives including metaphors and fictional images of the Other have had real consequences in history. They are thus – in a critical sense – "world-making". What makes them dangerous as political devices is a rhetoric that suggests to speak of reality by inventing a new one (and after the most recent presidential elections in the US, in an age of 'Postfactuality', these processes have gained an eerie topicality again).

Here, cultural analysis and theory can make an important contribution by demonstrating how the cultural dimension of symbolism is relevant also for the so-called reality of 'facts', because they are always formatted in symbolic forms. The narrative complex is enormously relevant, because its world-making power refers to central issues such as identity, memory, interpretation, or values. Like the professional politician, cultural theorists should be careful and responsible how they conceptualize narratives and how they make use of them.

What made our productive workshop and its subsequent publication fly, however, was not only our generous and patient contributors, but also the hosting institution, the *Trinity Long Room Hub*, to whose former Director, Professor Jürgen Barkhoff, and all his staff we are particularly grateful. Further thanks go to Becky McGinley (Dublin) and Christina Töpfer (*Camera Austria*, Graz) for their linguistic and editing assistance to this publication, and all the others helping us. Regardless of its sketchy nature, we hope the readership will enjoy this little book and obtain inspiration from it for further research into the cultural and social function of narrative.

Vienna and Dublin, August 2017

Works cited

Abbott, H. Porter (2008) *The Cambridge Introduction to Narrative* (Cambridge: Cambridge UP).

Bal, Mieke (2009) *Narratology: Introduction to the Theory of Narrative* (Toronto: U of T Press).

Erll, Astrid, and Ansgar Nünning (2008) *A Companion to Cultural Memory Studies* (Berlin and New York: De Gruyter).

Fiske, John (1990) *Understanding Popular Culture* (London and New York: Routledge).

Foucault, Michel (1980) *Power/Knowledge: Selected Interviews and Other Writings 1972–1977*, ed. Colin Gordon (New York: Pantheon Books).

Gramsci, Antonio (1978) *Selections from Political Writings 1921–1926*, transl. Quentin Hoare (New York: International Publishers).

Müller-Funk, Wolfgang (2008) *Die Kultur und ihre Narrative: Eine Einführung* (2nd edn. Vienna and New York: Springer).

Müller-Funk, Wolfgang (2012) *The Architecture of Modern Culture: Towards a Narrative Cultural Theory* (New York and Berlin: De Gruyter).

Nünning, Ansgar, and Vera Nünning (2016) "Conceptualizing 'Broken Narratives' from a Narratological Perspective: Domains, Concepts, Features, Functions, and Suggestions for Research", in *Broken Narratives: Theorien – Anwendungen*, ed. Wolfgang Müller-Funk et al. (Göttingen and Vienna: Vandenhoeck & Ruprecht / Vienna UP).

Rowner, Ilai (2015) *The Event: Literature and Theory* (Lincoln and London: Nebraska UP).

Ruthner, Clemens (2016) "KriegsErklärungen: The Notions of 'Event', 'Narrative' and 'Memory' as Critical Tools", in *'The Long Shots of Sarajevo', 1914: Ereignis – Narrativ – Gedächtnis*, ed. Vahidin Preljević and Clemens Ruthner (Tübingen: Francke).

White, Hayden (1987) *The Content of the Form: Narrative Discourse and Historical Representation* (Baltimore: Johns Hopkins UP).

White, Hayden (1973) *Metahistory: The Historical Imagination in Nineteenth Century Europe* (Baltimore, MD and London: Johns Hopkins UP).

Wolfgang Müller-Funk (University of Vienna)

Broken Narratives: Modernism and the Tradition of Rupture

I

> The very specific aspect of our comparative research project is that we understand rupture not only as a simple historical "fact", but as a form of a narrative emplotment.
> (Babka, Bidwell-Steiner & Müller-Funk 2016: 1)[1]

Within a cultural understanding of narrative, rupture is a concept that makes us view certain types of individual and collective experiences in terms of coherent sequences brought to a sudden end by violent disruption. Narrating is conceived as "a cultural technique" (Müller-Funk 2008: 20) providing humans with the possibility to give meaning to their experiences, to transmit them and to create new forms of belonging. In a narratological definition, "rupture" is then any cessation of a narrative sequence, which contrary to narrative closure does not arise out of a story's inherent causal logic. Narrative rupture is inherently dynamic: it is engendered by sequentiality and in turn triggers a new chain of events. For our Viennese research project (see footnote 1), we use the following typology of rupture: aesthetic ruptures, ruptures in history, and in our *Lebenswelt*. Comparing different aspects of rupture is one axis of our project; the other is based on a comparison between modern and pre-modern, European and non-European cultures (Babka, Bidwell-Steiner & Müller-Funk 2016).

In the following, I will discuss different meanings of terms such as *break*, *caesura*, and *rupture* that are equivalents to the German word *Bruch*. In a second step, I will interpret Octavio Paz's famous essay *Los Hijos del Limo* (*The Sons of the Mud*), which includes a central narrative of Modernism and modernity, namely the idea that rupture has become the central paradoxical "tradition" of classical Modernism (Paz 1974: 13–20). In a third step, I will come back to the idea of what broken narratives can mean from a perspective after and beyond classical Modernism.

---

1 This paper refers, on the one hand, to my book *The Architecture of Modern Culture* (Müller-Funk 2012) and, on the other hand, to the research platform *Broken Narratives* of the Faculty of Philology and Cultural Studies at the University of Vienna, established in the years of 2011 and 2012, from which the programmatic quote is taken. The concept of *emplotment* has been elaborated by Hayden White in several publications (see e.g. White 1987: 52–55).

https://doi.org/10.1515/9783110556858-002

II

If one reads the quotation from our programmatic manifesto on *Broken Narratives*[2] very carefully, then it becomes quite clear that such terms as *rupture* and *broken narratives* have a different, or even an opposite, connotation. Understanding depends on a operation that is central for the analysis of narratives: focus and focalization. When rupture is seen negatively, then it is told from the perspective of the victims, and when it is seen positively, it is narrated from the focus of the 'culprits'.

On all levels mentioned before, but especially in history and *Lebenswelt*, 'rupture' suggests a radical state of victimization ("trauma"), in which man and woman suffer from historical and biographical events such as individual or mass-murder, segregation (apartheid), rape, displacement, ethnic cleansing, or exile. Here, the position of the individual or a collective group is more or less passive. He, she, or it suffers from a kind of event that is experienced as a quasi-natural, political or cultural earthquake.

In all these cases, a massive element of destruction comes into play that implies a generally bad ending and an irreversible irritation of the symbolic 'household' of a culture. On the level of symbolic forms (Cassirer 1967; Müller-Funk 2010: 23–47), this means that the structure of classical great narratives has lost its legitimacy, the idea of linear progress on the one hand and the return to an innocent origin on the other. Moreover, this rupture is so dramatic that it seems to neutralize one central function of narratives: the production of meaning, giving the senseless a meaningful interpretation. Narratives are namely not, or at least not only, mimetic constructions and inventions of events *a posteriori.*[3] Because of their temporary logic they always entail a specific kind of interpretation of the events they refer to. 'Broken narratives' might thus also mean that a central function of narrativization is no longer working. With regard to Adorno, but also to authors of the Shoah such as Imre Kertész and Jorge Semprun, this creates resistance against the idea that narrating is a symbolic medicine, that story-telling is a moment of self-healing (Schelling 1985: VI, 456f–58). Absurdist theatre from Witold Gombrowicz and Federico García Lorca to French Existentialism is a good and paradoxical example of that kind of aesthetic and political resistance. As is the case in Gombrowicz's *Iwona. Księżniczka Burgunda* or in Lor-

2 See above..

3 Theodor Lessing writes: "Jene Wesensseiten, die sich im nachhinein aus den historischen Schicksalen eines Volks abstrahieren lassen, werden durch einen wunderlichen Paralogismus zuletzt als die 'Ursachen' des historischen Schicksals bezeichnet." (Lessing 1983: 60)

ca's *La Casa de Bernarda Alba*, the neutralization of the narrative function of producing meaning 'shows' *ex negativo* how narrative works. Usually storytelling eliminates contingency and gives every event a logical place; this is not the case in absurd emplotments.

In this respect, this kind of modernist storytelling (or non-storytelling) proves to be a rupture in literary narration. It has a paradoxical structure: by rejecting the traditional aesthetics of storytelling and its functions (creation of meaning, teleology, rational explication of the evens, deleting contingency), it reveals the narrative process as such. To that effect, Modernism can be seen as a principial rupture with literary common sense (Del Valle Lattanzio 2015).

But 'breaking', 'break'/'breach', and 'rupture' also have a radical contrary meaning in which the individual or a group plays an emphatic active role. Here destruction is seen as a positive act of breaking with the past, for example with the *ancien régime*, or with the traditional canon of the arts. Indeed Friedrich Wilhelm Joseph Schelling (in his *Philosophy of Mythology*) interpreted the Indian god Shiva in this ambivalent meaning as a power of destruction and rebuilding (cf. Müller-Funk 2012: chapter 3).[4] Here the rupture is close to all kinds of revolutions in politics, culture, and aesthetics. It is seen as an essential part of modern culture in which the destruction of the past is inscribed into nearly all fields. This destruction including the traditional narratives and myths is the precondition for the possibility of creating a new world that shall overcome the old one: *We've gotta get out of this place.*[5] The active break-up with the old times and their places also includes a break on the semantic and indeed on the structural level. Because of its critical self-understanding, it also undermines our traditional and positive understanding of narrative techniques that produce linearity in history and memory, creating a kind of identity that comes across as 'natural'.

---

4 Schelling asks what kind of destruction is meant with regard to Shiva:

> "Gemeinhin wird er unbestimmter als das *zerstörende* Prinzip erklärt. Dabei wird aber nicht bestimmt, worauf sich die zerstörende Wirkung beziehe. Man könnte nach diesem Begriff auch wohl Erdbeben, vulkanische Ausbrüche, die Länder und Städte verwüsten, oder Meerestluthen, die stets Land verschlingen, als Wirkungen des Schiwa ansehen. Aber davon ist die indische Vorstellung weit entfernt [...] Gewöhnlich sucht man Schiwa als göttliche Potenz dadurch zu erklären, daß man sagt: in der Natur sey ein steter Wechsel von Entstehen und Vergehen, indem die eine untergeht, entsteht eine andere; Schiwa sey also der zerstörende und dadurch immer neues schaffende Gott."

In this interpretation, destruction becomes a creative act not only in nature, but also in culture and politics.

5 Song by Barry Mann and Cynthia Weil, performed by Eric Burdon & The Animals in 1965: "We've gotta get out of this place, if it's the last thing we ever do." (www.metrolyrics.com, downloaded on 12.01.2014)

How can one piece together these two contrasting understandings of "broken narratives"? The reference to the first passive aspect is really important because it is a central aspect of modern times. Broken narratives as a logo of Modernity and Modernism have a presupposition, a hidden narrative aspect: ambivalence. Or, in other words, the first and the second type of broken narratives do not neutralize each other. They are not able to delegitimize the positive and active aspect of breaking narratives with reference to the dramatic sufferings of broken narratives in the twentieth century. Since World War II it has become a challenge to deal with all sorts of destructions on all human levels. That is the very reason why Shoa literature is no longer a special kind of writing, but has become the invisible center of post-war-Modernism, a Modernism without any illusion and without naïve hope in linear *progress* in the future.

There exists another challenge to our project, for the German word *Bruch*, which is translated into English as 'rupture', 'caesura', or 'break'/'breach', also has different, if not opposite denotations and connotations. There are perhaps even more meanings of the German term *Bruch* (such as the rupture of genres, subjects, and media), but I will concentrate on four that seem most important for our topic.

The first aspect of *Bruch* is 'splitting into pieces' as is the case with broken glass or a broken mirror, which also symbolizes the disintegration of modern human identity: *I am another.* It has a Romantic origin and dates back to the concept of the fragment in early German Romanticism, in Novalis and Friedrich Schlegel. As Schlegel argues, many works of the ancients have become fragments, whereas many works in modern time are fragments from the beginning.[6] The fragment is seen as a part of a lost whole that cannot be restored by assembling all of the broken elements. The fragment only makes totality visible in poetry and in essayistic forms. This is possible because of the synthetic power of poetry. Walter Benjamin makes use of this figure in his essay on the translator to describe the relations between single languages:

> Fragments of a vessel in order to be articulated together must follow one another in the smallest details although they need not be *like* one another. – In the same way a translation, instead of making itself similar to the meaning of the original, must lovingly and in detail form itself according to the manner of meaning of the original, to make them both recognizable as the broken fragments of the greater language, just as fragments are the broken parts of a vessel. (Benjamin 1972: IV, 18)[7]

6 "Viele Werke der Alten sind Fragmente geworden. Viele Werke der Neuern sind es gleich bei der Entstehung." (Schlegel 1972: 27)

7 English transl. by Timothy Bahti and Andrew Benjamin, qtd. after Bhabha 1994: 170.

Benjamin's figure, which has been adapted by Homi Bhabha's post-colonial cultural theory, is based not only on Romanticism but also on Jewish Gnosis, the Kabbalah of Isaac Luria (a Platonic narrative), in which the breaking of the vessels, the *Shebirah*, is seen as the dramatic issue of a cosmogonist event embedded in a story which starts with the concentration and self-reduction of God to build a unity (*Zimzum*), followed by the destruction of the unity (*Shebirah*); it finally ends with the restoration of the broken elements (*Tikkun*). With regard to our topic, there are two important moments, firstly, the act of *Shebirah* can be interpreted as characteristic and constitutive of modern art, its acting and its performance especially in modernist and avant-garde groups (Scholem 1973: 146–158). But also the other two aspects, self-reduction and -construction, plus the longing for creating a new unity can be seen as central for classical Modernism from Novalis to the twentieth century. Already in early German Romanticism, there is some sort of productive resignation, namely the idea that the restoration of the whole, the collection and recollecting of the broken elements is only possible in poetry which is a counter-world to the prosaic world of modernity. Modernism can be interpreted as the stage of the broken vessels without an absolute beginning and an absolute ending, *Shebirah* without *Zimzum* and *Tikkun*. What has been called Romantic irony is part of that kind of symbolic stage (Bloom 1975: chapter 6).

The second aspect of the German word *Bruch* refers to the end of a relation. Here, breaking means terminating a relationship or a friendship or leaving of symbolic place, for example the places of the past. This kind of breaking (up) goes hand in hand with high estimation of the new and contempt for the previous generation. This is what Octavio Paz has called the *tradition of rupture*, which I will discuss later.

The third aspect of the German term opens a new door. Discontinuity has become, ironically speaking, a reliable phenomenon in cultural and political life. All narratives including discontinuity focalize phenomena as interruption, surprise, caesura or incision. Whereas in traditional and patriarchal communities caesura or incision is strictly organized and ritualized, for example, for male adolescents becoming adults (Victor Turner's concept of liminality), in modern times such kinds of caesura no longer have a strong and stabilizing meaning, but are the unexpected turning point of a broken existence (Turner 1964).

The fourth and last meaning of *Bruch* in our context means the crossing of such symbolic limits that have been understood as absolute before. This *kind* of breaking taboos is totally ambivalent, it suggests the gesture of liberation and emancipation but also – as in the case of the Shoah – the horrible idea of being in the heart of the darkness, the technical collective overkill and mass-murder: the rupture of civilization and traditional humanism.

I hope it has become clear that all these four different connotations of broken narratives have an ambivalent meaning with regard to suffering and the traumatic aspects of rupture, and with reference to the modern idea of emancipating from the burdens of lasting past, which seems to be responsible for all human evils. In his *The Eighteenth Brumaire of Louis Napoleon*, Marx writes about the drama of Modernism: modern (wo)man will break free from the past, but will be caught by its nightmares/traditions (Marx 1966). So a key question might be to what extent all these active breaks lead to a strong and paradoxical dependence on the past they reject. Breaking could also mean remaining in a paradoxical relationship with whomever or whatever one has broken up with. Thus the concept of "broken narratives" is implemented in the idea of a culture that is in a permanent conflict not only with its past, but also with its present and its future.

III

Octavio Paz's Harvard lectures *Los Hijos del Limo* are remarkable for many reasons. They have a double vision, the perspective of a poet and writer who is part of the modern literature and culture he describes, but also the focus of a theorist who develops a concept of Postmodernism some years before the French philosopher Jean-François Lyotard (1979). His book also includes a grand narrative on Modernism and Globalization *avant la letter*, written from a post-colonial perspective, because this literary work is based on the experiment of a Non-European colonial background: Latin America.

Paz starts his lecture with a question, which may appear old-fashioned at first glance: What is the specific moment(um) in and of poetry?[8] In contrast to all other non-poetic forms of speaking, it is characterized by a certain contradiction, or more precisely, by an inconsistency with regard to history and to the narrative process. The poem is, as Paz points out, a machine that produces anti-history, even if the poet does not have this in mind.[9] Poetic narratives are structurally different from prosaic ones; the poetic procedure is based on the inversion

8 "En un libro publicado hace más de quince años, El arco y la lira (México, 1956), intenté responder a tres preguntas sobre la poesía: el decir poético, el poema ¿es irreductible a todo otro decir? ¿Qué dicen los poemas? ¿Cómo se comunican los poemas? (Paz 1974: 1).

9 Ibid.: "El poema es una máquina que produce, incluso sin que el poeta se lo proponga, antihistoria."

and the transformation of the stream of time. Poetry does not stop time, it contradicts and transforms it. This conflict is already true and characteristic of premodern forms of poetry such as the sonnet, the popular epic, or the fable.

In modern times, this conflict becomes productive and striking. The modernist poetry of the Occident, which Paz considers a globalizing cultural unit, includes a double move: it is in conflict with the past, but also with the present. Modernism is not only a representation of modern society and culture, but also a counter-world to the disenchanted and prosaic cultural, technical, and political modernity. From the very beginning, Paz writes, modernist poetry was a reaction to and a reaction against modernity; modernity here means Enlightenment, rationalism, liberalism, and scientism (Paz 1974: 8).

There is a certain structural analogy between the modern political revolutionary and the avant-garde modernist who tries to establish and develop a new aesthetic system – the Shiva-moment of destroying and rebuilding. Modern poetry has, as Paz declares pathetically, a revolutionary passion embracing a strong desire for radical change.[10] The program of a violent break with the system, especially with modern capitalism, for example, can be seen as the fragile foundation of the temporary cohabitation between Trotsky and Breton. But after a while, the break-up with those movements – in the twentieth century for example with Socialism and Communism – becomes inevitable.[11]

Modern poetry establishes its own, autonomous world, the world of languages as a double of and against the world. Thus, it is a central part of Freud's discontent in civilization (Müller-Funk 2010: 23–47). On the one hand, German and English Romantics, and the French Symbolists build a new world which is characterized by analogy, but on the other hand, this counter-world is subverted by irony, i.e., by the consciousness of Modernism and its criticism of traditional religious narratives, for example of Christianity. Ultimately, this kind of irony is directed back to Modernism itself.

Thus the 'tradition' of modern poetry is based on criticism and crisis. This dialogue between analogy and irony entails a more or less aggressive dispute with traditional religiosity, but also with modern ideology. It opens the dialogue

10 Paz 1974: 21: "La edad moderna se concibe a sí misma como revolucionaria. Lo es de varias maneras. La primera y más obvia es de orden semántico: la modernidad comienza por cambiar el sentido de la palabra revolución. A la significación original – giro de los mundos y de los astros – se yuxtapuso otra, que es ahora la más frecuente; ruptura violenta del orden antiguo y establecimiento de un orden social más justo y racional."

11 Paz 1974: 30: "La poesía moderna ha sido y es una pasión revolucionaria, pero esa pasión ha sido desdichada. Afinidad y ruptura: no han sido los filósofos, sino los revolucionarios, los que han expulsado a los poetas de su república." Also see von Beyme 2005: 536.

between various linguistic and cultural traditions, between the center and the periphery. This is the most important heritage of classical Modernism.

However, with regard to our own recent past, to the prosaic reality of modern society, but also with regard to all our Modernist forebears, this proves to be a polemical and aggressive tradition. This is the dynamic moment Paz calls the tradition of rupture. It is a form of tradition that consists of interruptions, a form of transmission, in which every rupture is seen as a new beginning. This tradition is extremely paradoxical and fragile: the tradition of rupture does not imply the negation of tradition, but also in an act of self-destruction, the negation of rupture itself.

If tradition is defined by continuity and transmission, to what extent can one understand Modernism as a form of tradition? As Paz points out, Modernism is a new form, which consists of two elements, the emphasis on novelty, and the idea of heterogeneity. It is not contingent that – to mention Bakhtin – one new genre of Modernism is called the novel (Bakhtin 1979). Modernism in Paz's eyes is neither the continuance of the past in the present, nor is today a child of yesterday. Modernism breaks with the past, today negates yesterday. Modernism is, as Paz states, self-sufficient. Whenever it appears, Modernism creates its own tradition (Paz 1974: 13).

The cult of absolute novelty substitutes the aesthetic ideal of imitation, but is not automatically identical with rupture. What is striking is the fact that the new entails a programmatic rupture, a criticism of the immediate past and the interruption of identity. Modern art is not only the product of a critical age, but also a criticism of it, too (Paz 1974: 14). It is – at least in the self-image of modernist art – the result of a creative act of self-destruction and the longing to be completely different from anything that existed before. It functions within a binary structure, in which the negation of the past suggests the affirmation of something. Paz's text mentions and analyzes nearly all aspects of the German word *Bruch*, especially 'ending' and 'interruption', but to some extent also 'fragmentation' (heterogeneity) and, less so, 'overcoming' and 'crossing lines and limits', opening the doors; or, to quote a famous song of the American group The Doors: *Break on through to the other Side.*[12]

But in Paz there is nearly no reflection as to what extent the de-legitimization of classical Modernism and the narratives of modern times are not only the result of the self-critical tradition of rupture, but also the consequence of radical social, cultural and political failure, the World Wars of the twentieth century,

12 Song by The Doors (1967), cf. www.azlyrics.com/doors/breakonthroughtotheotherside, downloaded on 14.01.2014.

the temporary triumph of modern totalitarianism, which was to some extent a part of the project of modernity, too, and the implosion and collapse of Socialism.[13]

At this point, I'd like to come back to the dynamic process of Modernism. The very old, the archaic can also be integrated into Modernism, insofar as it is interpreted as a negation of all traditional traditions. These archaic elements that are re-contextualized can be understood as masks used and put on by Modernism in its fight against pre-modern traditions. Because of its structure, Modernism as the tradition of rupture makes a large contribution to acceleration and to a phenomenon Paz calls the "premature". What seems to be new at the moment becomes old very soon. But as Paz analyzes in the following chapter, this acceleration shows that the contrast of the denied is not the present, but the future. Nearly all modernist movements have a vector towards the future, and the present is only a sneak preview of the radical form that will happen.

It is evident that Paz tells his story about the dynamic process of Modernism from a perspective *a posteriori*, from a world that is already characterized by the effect of the tradition of rupture. Postmodernism can be understood here as a world which is not in contrast to Modernism, but is its logical result, because the tradition of revolutionary break ultimately negates its own highly fragile 'tradition'. It is in a state similar to revolutionary children living off the heritage of their rich parents.

When Paz claims the discovery of the present instead of traditional past and modernist future, one of his definitions of poetry from the very beginning of the book comes into play again, namely the idea that poetry is structurally organized against history. Therefore it could work as an aesthetic instrument of negating pre-modern traditions and its symbolic allies, myths, and other types of closed narratives; it was also successful in subverting the grand linear narratives of modernity since the age of Enlightenment. Paz does not see this Postmodernist concentration on the present as negative, as an attack by the present on all other forms of time. On the contrary, he believes that this kind of concentration here and now means liberation from historical constraints. With reference to our topic, narratives, this means that the time of storytelling dominates the time of the events, which are told by a narrator who from time to time – in Postmod-

13 "En circunstancias históricas distintas, el fenómeno se manifiesta una y otra vez, primero a lo largo del siglo XIX y después, con mayor intensidad, en lo que va del que corre. Apenas si vale la pena recordar los casos de Esenin, Mandelstam, Pasternak y tantos otros poetas, artistas y escritores rusos; las polémicas de los surrealistas con la Tercera Internacional; la amargura de César Vallejo, dividido entre su fidelidad a la poesía y su fidelidad al Partido Comunista; las querellas en torno al 'realismo socialista' y todo lo que ha seguido después." (Paz 1974: 30)

ernism – becomes visible again as the instance that integrates and contextualizes different modes of the past and possible futures into the present.

IV

The new tradition, i.e. the horizon of Paz's narrative of classical Modernism, is no longer based on the tradition of rupture. It follows a completely new logic. In contrast to all various modernisms, there is no longer any principal hostility towards the past including the past of classical Modernism and its movements. On the contrary, the rhetorical idea of burning down the monuments of the past, the academies, libraries and museums, the fantasy of blank pages, and of a new beginning has been substituted by a new understanding of an archive in movement. One can compare it with a central ecological idea: recycling. Postmodernist literature and art is a form of symbolic recycling that works similarly to advertising and fashion. Its dynamic does not result from the energy of fighting for the past being forgotten; the new proves to be the forgotten old.

It is quite evident that Modernism was not only based on narratives of rupture and friction, but it created and presented new narrative forms: montage, self-reference, the subversion of beginning and ending, the denial of consistency, techniques of disillusion, etc. All these new forms of narrative construction – which are, as Michel Butor (1965) has shown, principally inherent to the cultural technique of storytelling – do exist in postmodernist writing, too. But in contrast to classical Modernism, these broken forms of narrative have lost their pathos-laden and programmatic meaning.

The other new narrative figure is dialogue. I think deconstruction is a very good example of this kind of a *braking* instead of breaking, i.e. deceleration rather than rupture. It denies the logic of binary opposition by creating third spaces and in-between-places of communication with all sorts of past. To borrow from Freud's terminology, it can be seen as sublimation of all those aggressive energies that made Modernism so fruitful and at the same time so problematic. The author, philosopher, or poet is in permanent dialogue with his or her predecessors. Hyper- or Postmodern literature is obsessed with an intertextual technique the Croatian literary theorist Dubravka Oraić-Tolić (1995) has called "Zitatenhaftigkeit": the mannerist cult of quotation.

Thus, the author of a text follows the spaces of the text of the predecessor very carefully; but ultimately, s/he has left his or her own way. This holds true for Derrida's concept which also understands narrative as an intermediate phenomenon. He suggests reading the text of the predecessor in contrast to itself. What he has in mind is not a revolutionary split, a rupture or a radical farewell from the past; what he is about is finding the 'breaks', that is the inconsistencies in the texts or works of art of the predecessors. This is the very reason why deconstruction creates broken narratives, arguing that all narratives are broken somehow. So the phenomenon of rupture has radically changed its place, and the philosopher or literary author of our times is not in consistent and principal opposition to the modernist and revolutionary past of the nineteenth and twentieth centuries. He or she is also the heir of Modernism. This heritage is not slight and shabby. It includes the sense of irony, the affirmation of heterogeneity, and the conviction that there is no way back to traditional forms of tradition. But in contrast to the modernist forebears, there is no melancholy that the paradise is lost, and there is no longer a march into a foreseeable future.

My last point leads me to another theory of poetry, to Harold Bloom's essay on the "Anxiety of Influence" (1973). Linking it with my reading of Paz, it can be read as a book that describes the energies behind the struggle between the ancients and the moderns making use of the Freudian narrative of Oedipus who will substitute the father with himself (Blumenberg 1979). One can interpret Bloom's description of the battle between the literary sons and fathers in Paz's version as a narrative of programmatic rupture with the intention of murdering the father. Or with Jim Morrison's obscene formula in his song *The End:* kill your father, fuck your mother.[14]

But step by step the revision of the text of the mighty forebear undergoes a process of sublimation. Bloom's six versions of revision, which he demonstrates in *The Anxiety of Influence,* are in a fragile balance between accepting the influence of the mighty other and establishing one's own way of writing. All six ways of describing the text made of past texts include the 'breaking' element of *clinamen*, which is seen as a poetic of misreading, *tessera*, which combines completion with anti-thesis in order to restore the vessel of the poem and, moreover, *kenosis*, self-emptying, as a form of discussion that has the goal of banning the Freudian force of repetition, *demonism,* which generalizes the meaning of the lit-

14 Song by The Doors, composed and lyrics by Jim Morrison (1967). The relevant passage is:
"The killer awoke before dawn, he put his boots on
He took a face from the ancient gallery
And he walked on down the hall
He went into the room where his sister lived, and...then he
Paid a visit to his brother, and then he
He walked on down the hall, and
And he came to a door...and he looked inside
Father, yes son, I want to kill you
Mother...I want to...WAAAAAA"
(www.lyricfreaks.com/d/doors/the+end_20042686.html, downloaded on 14.01.2014)

erary father, *askesis* as a form of self-incision which makes use of the aesthetic equipment of the predecessor, and – this is the last state of the process – *apophrades*, the return of the dead poet at a certain date; this figure suggests that it is the later poet who theoretically could have written the characteristic work of his precursor (Bloom 1973).

Interesting is the fact that all of these forms of literary revisionism include elements of break, rupture and discontinuity, but feature at the same time a moment of integration. After the absolute modernist revolt, the power and the influence of the past is apparently not broken. As the figure of *apophrades* makes clear, the dead demons from the past temporarily return to have a dialogue with us. But the rules of this dialogue that creates continuity in discontinuity are in the hands of the sons and daughters, who create the way of breaking narratives with regard to an always-new cultural context (Bloom 1973: introduction).

With regard to the general topic, a narrative cultural theory, it has been said quite often (e. g. recently by Koschorke 2012) that narrating and narratives have a universal, perhaps anthropological base. However, it is evident that cultures differ in their methods of storytelling, in their topics, in their modes of organizing time(s) and space(s), in their complexity. But also the focus of this essay, rupture and breaking, forms of discontinuity, is rooted in a universal shift that happens at least twice in every narrative: between the time of the past and the time of its narrative construction in the present either of the author or of the reader.

Works cited

Babka, Anna, Marlen Bidwell-Steiner, and Wolfgang Müller-Funk (2016) *Broken Narratives/Narrative im Bruch: Theoretische Positionen und Anwendungen* (Göttingen and Vienna: Vandenhoeck & Ruprecht/Vienna UP).

Babka, Anna, Daniela Finzi, and Clemens Ruthner (eds.) (2012) *Die Lust an der Kultur/theorie: Transdisziplinäre Interventionen. Für Wolfgang Müller-Funk* (Vienna: Turia + Kant).

Bachtin, Michail (1979) *Die Ästhetik des Wortes*, ed. Rainer Grübel (Frankfurt/M.: Suhrkamp).

Beyme, Klaus von (2005) *Das Zeitalter der Avantgarden: Kunst und Gesellschaft 1905–1955* (Munich: C.H. Beck).

Benjamin, Walter (1972) *Gesammelte Schriften*, Vol. IV, ed. Theodor W. Adorno, Gershom Scholem, Rolf Tiedemann, and Hermann Schweppenhäuser (Frankfurt/M.: Suhrkamp).

Bhabha, Homi K. (1994) *The Location of Culture* (London: Routledge).

Bloom, Harold (1973) *The Anxiety of Influence* (Oxford: Oxford UP).

Blumenberg, Hans (1979) *Die Arbeit am Mythos* (Frankfurt/M.: Suhrkamp).

Butor, Michel (1965) *Probleme des Romans,* transl. Helmut Scheffel (Munich: C.H. Beck).

Cassirer, Ernst (1967) *Philosophie der symbolischen Formen* (Wiesbaden: WBG).

Del Valle Lattanzio, Camillo (2015) *Unterwegs zur Quelle der Sprache: Zur Theorie des Schreibens in der Poetik Octavio Paz'* (University of Vienna: Master thesis [unpubl.]).

Koschorke, Albrecht (2012) *Wahrheit und Erfindung: Grundzüge einer allgemeinen Erzähltheorie* (Frankfurt/M.: Fischer).
Lessing, Theodor (1983) *Geschichte als Sinngebung des Sinnlosen* [1919] (Munich: Matthes & Seitz).
Lyotard, Jean-François (1979) *La condition postmoderne* (Paris: Editions de Minuit).
Marx, Karl (1966) "Der achtzehnte Brumaire des Louis Napoleon" [1852], in *Schriften*, ed. Iring Fetscher (Frankfurt/M.: Fischer), IV: 34–121.
Müller-Funk, Wolfgang (2008) *Die Kultur und ihre Narrative: Eine Einführung* (2nd edn. Vienna and New York: Springer).
Müller-Funk, Wolfgang (2010) *Kulturtheorie: Einführung in Schlüsseltexte der Kulturwissenschaften* (2nd edn. Tübingen: Francke/UTB).
Müller-Funk, Wolfgang (2012) *The Architecture of Modern Culture: Towards a Narrative Cultural Theory* (New York and Berlin: De Gruyter).
Oraić-Tolić, Dubravka (1995) *Das Zitat in Literatur und Kunst: Versuch einer Theorie* (Vienna and Cologne: Böhlau).
Paz, Octavio (1974) *Los Hijos del Limo: Dal romanticismo a la vanguardia* (Barcelona: Editorial Seix Barral).
Schelling, Friedrich W. J. (1985) *Schriften*, ed. Manfred Frank (Frankfurt/M. Suhrkamp).
Schlegel, Friedrich (1972) *Athenäumsfragmente: Schriften zur Literatur*, ed. Wolfdietrich Rasch (Munich: dtv).
Scholem, Gershom (1973) *Die Kabbala und ihre Symbolik* (Frankfurt/M.: Suhrkamp).
Turner, Victor (1964) "Betwixt and Between: The Liminal Period in Rites de Passage", in *Symposium on New Approaches to the Study of Religion*, ed. Melford E. Spiro (Seattle: American Ethnological Society), 46–55.
White, Hayden (1987) *The Content of the Form: Narrative Discourse and Historical Representation* (Baltimore: Johns Hopkins UP).

Andrea Seidler (University of Vienna)

Discourses on the Ottomans in Old Hungarian Literature: Observations on a Volatile Image

From the Middle Ages on, the Ottomans had filled South Eastern Europe with terror – their vast gains in power and their goal of pressing towards Europe meant that as early as in the fourteenth century, the Hungarian perspective in chronicles, sermons, pamphlets, and letters expressed grave concerns for an uncertain future. Whereas the dynasty of the Hunyadis had managed to keep the Ottomans at bay through a combination of diplomacy and canny negotiation throughout their reign, their successors to the Hungarian Kingdom were faced with a disjointed country caught up in disagreement over the degree of loyalty owed to foreign monarchs. During the time of Matthias Corvinus, János Thuróczi wrote in his *Chronica Hungarorum* of Sultan Mohammed II (1432–1481), the Conqueror of Constantinople:

> King Ladislaus was staying at the castle in Buda when word spread that the Turkish Emperor, Mohammed, was about to attack Hungary and take the fortress of Belgrade as soon as possible. This news caused great concern not only to the Hungarian people, but all the neighbouring areas, indeed to Christianity in its entirety, and set them thinking. The savage defeat of the city of Constantinople was uppermost in the minds of all Christians. And this aroused no little fear in everyone. For since his victory over the Greeks, the Turkish Emperor had become a different person – in his lust for power and his even greater arrogance he thought he embodied the return of the old Macedonian Alexander the Great and his glorious epoch. He is said to have proclaimed, 'Only one god reigns in Heaven, hence only one ruler should reign on earth.' [no pagination, translation mine, A.S]

The distant arch-enemy thus drew ever closer. Weakened through its internal politics, with the Battle of Mohács in 1526 the Kingdom of Hungary suffered not only a defeat, but the loss of its king no less: Ludwig died in the battle, drowning in a river. The death of a king, especially in battle, cripples a pre-modern society and takes away its political confidence and strength. This was also the case for Hungary, its military reserves being exhausted and without hope of assistance from the rest of Europe.

The two centuries of Turkish occupation of Hungary left the country divided into three parts. The Turks themselves had driven a wedge through the country – Transylvania was ruled by the local prince, the western part by the Habsburgs. Buda became the base of the Ottomans, and the Hungarian capital was moved

https://doi.org/10.1515/9783110556858-003

to Pressburg (Pozsony), where it remained until 1783. But what did the protagonists of the literary scene, the writers, the preachers, have to say on the matter?

- The image of the *Querela Hungariae*. The Ottoman conquest of Hungary was expressed in literary texts almost immediately after the defeat at Mohács. Hungary considered itself a victim of history, attacked, pillaged, and abandoned by its allies. One of the topoi that has survived to this day in Hungarian literature and cultural history is the 'Lamentation of Hungary'. Examples can be found not only in texts from Hungary, but throughout Europe, whereby the perspective sometimes shifts.
- The 'Bastion of Hungary'. A further topos is Hungary as a bullwark, a shield from the threat of Islam spreading across Christian Europe. This too reflects concerns for the political role Hungary's geographical location forced it to play vis-à-vis the Turks. The country is sometimes portrayed in heroic terms, sometimes as an abandoned victim. In both cases, Hungary is considered the great loser in the struggle to force back the Ottomans.
- *Fertilitas Hungariae*. This image is based on the lamentation of the once so rich and enviable country that had been ravaged and defiled by the Turks.
- The 'Punishment of Hungary'. Hungary had only been dealt such a terrible fate because God had forsaken the country to punish it for earlier misdemeanors (see Tarnai 1969 and Mihály 1995).

It is not my intention to examine the early phase of literary production in the Kingdom of Hungary or in Europe as a whole.[1] The topoi mentioned above, however, are important milestones which are still evident in the literary and political life of Hungary to this day, and hence I feel it is important to touch on their roots.

What I am primarily interested in is the period of consolidation, the phase in the confrontation with the Ottoman culture, in which the spectrum of protagonists from the cultural scene had already undergone a complete shift. The figure of the author and the reader had changed together with the book market: a continent could no longer be scared by religion, particularly not against the backdrop of increasing secularization. Experience had shown that in recent centuries the Turks were not in the slightest concerned with enforcing religious conversion – and long since, the Ottomans had been in political decline in Central Europe. The centuries-old myth of their supremacy had already taken plenty of knocks in the seventeenth century. The arch-enemies of Europe, depicted as bloodthirsty and the "cruellest of the cruel", had lost much of their power, and their invinci-

1 For this purpose, I recommend the work of Brigitta Pesti (2014), who has intensively studied the varied reception of the Ottomans in both Southeastern and Western Europe.

bility had long been called into question by modern military commanders who were united in the Turkish question.

The defeat of the Turks at Vienna in 1683, the victory of Prince Eugene, the "noble knight", at Zenta in 1697, the subsequent Treaties of Karlowitz in 1699 and Passarowitz in 1718 brought an end to the almost two-hundred-year occupation of Hungary, and with it the core of the Habsburg Empire. The partition of the Magyar Kingdom was undone, and political affairs were back in the hands of the Habsburg Emperor Charles VI. A sigh of relief could be breathed, then, by part of the monarchy, but certainly not by all the actors in this political sphere.

While the Ottomans' fall from power took several decades, its course was unstoppable. All that was left to them after Passarowitz was mainly the treaties stating that Turkish subjects on Habsburg territory were to be granted freedom of trade. They had almost lost the country entirely. Granted, the political and military tug of war was not over for good, since the southern regions of the Habsburg Empire were still subjected to Ottoman presence and aggression, and the sympathies of the Transylvanian princes still lay more firmly with the Sultan than with the Kaiser. But for the Kingdom of Hungary and the hereditary lands – and indeed, for the whole of Western Europe – the terror was over. (At least for the time being; in the late 1780s new frictions occurred under Joseph II.)

The image of the Turks in the parts of Europe far away from the occupied lands had long since undergone a change or become more nuanced. They had learnt to differentiate: on the one hand, they saw the Turks as an army of merciless warriors, destroying everything in their path, and on the other hand, they were enchanted by what one might call fascination with the exotic. This wave of enthusiastic reception of Turkish customs and fashions, music and architecture was to go down in the history of European culture as "la turquerie" (see e.g. Friehs 2013). Certainly by the time of the visit of the Turkish emissary Soliman Musta-Ferraga to Versailles in 1669, society had become widely interested in Turkish splendor, pomp, and ostentation. It was not only everything Turkish, but everything Oriental that became the desirable model of a completely new attitude towards life.[2] In this context, I would like to point to the opulent entry made by the Moroccan emissary to Vienna in 1783, whose disarming pomposity had a lasting, favorable influence on contemporary thought concerning all what was Oriental and foreign. This imitation of Turkish fashion, detailed art and architecture was joined by a curiosity regarding "the Turk" as a bearer of cultural values and symbols. The analysis of the eroticism of the Other went hand in

2 For example: the fine arts, or music "alla turca", primarily characterized by percussion instruments; in Turkish military music intended to intimidate the enemy.

hand with the idea that the Ottomans were an extremely lascivious people. The very institution of the Serail seemed to point to an attitude vastly different from the Christian traditions' restrained culture of shame.

In 1773, for example, Christian Wilhelm Kindleben composed two volumes with the title *Galanterieen der Türken* (Turkish Gallantries), describing not only the society, the officials and dignitaries, the treasures of the Sultan and means of raising money, but, most intensely, Turkish sexual practices. Along with a description of his idea of a serail, in some chapters Kindleben went into rather speculative detail, presenting his thoughts with regard to differences in the culture of head and body hair between Europeans and Muslims, and explaining them in terms of the unbridled lust of men from the Bosphorus (Ch. 12).

The Other, then, took on a certain capacity to excite; it was shrouded in secrecy, and had become, in certain respects, something to emulate. The former arch-enemy – now physically distant – became a kind of subject of observation or exhibit, similar to the Africans and Polynesians imported from the colonies, a historical and ethnological subject of research, and ultimately the favorite subject of European literature and the educated press. Academies were founded which were to further the study of Oriental languages and provide insight into the lifestyle of the Turks / the Orient – predominantly attended, presumably, by aspiring diplomats, for in the new political circumstances it had become desirable to negotiate independently, without interpreters, and to be able to represent one's own interests. As Julia Friehs states,

> [t]he long-lived Turkish fashion was fuelled from a broad spectrum of images ranging from the barbaric foe of the West and the brave warrior to the cultivated, even erotic exotic figure. Writers and philosophers used the Orient as a screen onto which they could project critiques of their own societies and designs for better ones. (Friehs 2013)

In the course of the nineteenth century, financial considerations led the Habsburg monarchy to courting the Ottoman Empire. It is said that Emperor Franz Joseph I personally met Sultan Abdulaziz off the train when he first visited Vienna in 1864 and accompanied him to Schönbrunn. The Kingdom of Hungary placed high symbolic value on the return of a considerable collection of plundered works from the Bibliotheca Corviniana to mark the completion of the Suez Canal in 1869. In 1877, Sultan Abdul Hamid II returned a further 35 codices to the Hungarians as a token of thanks for their political support, all of which had been part of the Topkapi Museum's collection since the sixteenth century. Also Joseph von Hammer-Purgstall's (1774–1856) activities show a growing interest in the world of the Orient and an academic, albeit Eurocentric approach both to the subject and to a world which, liberated for over a century from Turkish rule, seemed to have been officially rehabilitated by the political powers.

But neither practical political ties nor scholarly discourse could prevent the prevalence of the image of the bloodthirsty Turk, an image that was fostered not least by literature. A prime example is the children's book *Hatschi Bratschis Luftballon* (first ed. 1904) by Franz Karl Ginzkey. Published in the early twentieth century, the work portrays the Turks as evil, bloodthirsty child snatchers: "He speaks and threatens with his hand: You're off with me to the Turkish land" (Ginzkey 1922: 9).

So the theme flourished in European literature and was particularly cultivated by travellers, some of whom had actually spent time in the Ottoman Empire. A key protagonist in this regard is Lady Mary Montagu, who accompanied her husband to Istanbul in 1716 in his capacity as an English diplomat. The family stayed in the country for two years. During this time, Lady Mary wrote famous letters about the "Orient", although they also describe plenty of other European countries. They appeared in print in 1763, a year after the author's death, but they had already circulated in handwritten form among intellectuals interested in the subject.

The Turks, or, rather, life in the Ottoman Empire, were also the subject of the first Hungarian novel, *Törökországi levelek* [Letters from Turkey] by Kelemen Mikes (1690 – 1761). The actual title of the work was *Konstantinapolyban groff P...E... Irot levelei M...K....* Published in 1794, thirty years after the death of the author, by István Kultsár in Szombathely (Steinamanger), the text contained a number of alterations to the original manuscript. The letters were initially read as a historical document, their fictionality being doubted.

In this work revolving around the story of Prince Francis II Rákóczi's life in Turkish exile and his death in Tekirdağ (Rodostó in Hungarian) by the Marmara Sea, we read for the most part of the life of Hungarian political refugees, their contact with the local population and their encounters with a new, foreign culture into which they cannot assimilate. Francis II Rákóczi had fled in 1711 after the Treaty of Szatmár, first to Poland, then to Paris, and finally took up an invitation to live in the Ottoman Empire as the guest of the Sultan. He stayed there for the rest of his life. The reason for his emigration was his objection to the Habsburgs remaining the kings of Hungary and refusing to recognize him as a sovereign prince of Transylvania.

The former enemy, through his support of exiles now a political ally, is certainly reappraised in the letters, but the ethnic and religious prejudices built up over centuries are not entirely absent. From many perspectives and in a variety of scenarios, Mikes describes the roughness of the Ottomans, their bellicose nature, the religious differences between Islam and Christianity, and the inability of the author of the letters to accept the societal position of women. He suffers in particular from his inadequate knowledge of the Turkish language, which increasingly forces the exile into isolation. We no longer feel fear of the Turks, but a kind of disenchantment, a sober examination of a world with which none of the protagonists had, nor wanted to have, anything in common.

The work comprises 207 letters to a Countess P.E. (addressed as "my dearest aunt"). This presumably fictitious relative has an emotional, almost erotic affinity with her nephew. The text is reminiscent of the tradition of writing fictitious letters and the epistolary novel (such as Montesquieu's *Lettres persanes*), but also of the first authentic travel reports in European literature (for instance, Lady Montagu). It is also possible to see a further connection to the *missilis* tradition.

The text is somehow a rarity, for the novel did not become established in Hungarian literature before the nineteenth century; it was simply not on the agenda for writers. Mikes's epistolary novel – insofar as it may be considered one – is, along with the fictional diary *Fanni Hagyományai*, the only noteworthy work of prose in eighteenth-century Hungarian literature. Both writers and readers were convinced that the renewal and establishment of the Hungarian language could only be achieved by poetry (and literary translation).

Mikes's hotchpotch is certainly not structured as a novel, rather it is a collection of unconnected (fictional) letters. They are not conceived as a series, and the correspondence is not brought to an end; the first letter is dated October 1717, the last December 1758. Incidentally, this work notwithstanding, the author did not leave a considerable corpus of correspondence. What does remain, however, are letters, some of them composed in his official capacity as secretary to Prince Rákóczi II, in which he refers to his Turkish exile.

Whereas Lady Montagu's letters are characterized by admiration for and recognition of the foreign culture in which she immersed herself and in which she partook as much as possible – albeit as the wife of a diplomat bolstered by the power of the English crown – Mikes leaves a different impression. Despite spending some fifty years in Turkey, Mikes displays an irreconcilable attitude, marked on the one hand by gratitude for the protection provided by the Sultan, but on the other by his grief about isolation, suffering, being at the mercy of others, and the inability to accept the Other (even after several decades).

The only manuscript of the M.K. letters was to be found, incidentally, in the library in Eger / Erlau (the Archepiscopal Library) and is a copy in the author's own hand. The letters were, as mentioned earlier, first published in 1794 in Szombathely. A contemporary journal, *Hadi és más Nevezetes Történetek*, relates in its edition of 27 November 1789, how the letters got to Hungary. According to this report, a merchant took the work from the Ottoman Empire to Hungary, having received it from a former servant of Prince Rákóczi II, who had died in 1735.[3]

Of course there are also several eighteenth-century Hungarian journals in which we can read of Ottoman hegemony in Southeastern Europe, of the history of the Ottomans and their origins, often in the form of anecdotes, but mostly in so-called scholarly contributions. Historical documents and analyses dominate this discourse which appears emotionless and detached. Then follow didactic pieces on the "manners, customs and religion" of the Turks. The history of coffee, matrimonial customs, the interaction of the sexes, disapproval of the religious oppression of women and gender issues are the usual fayre with which the reader is entertained and educated. A cursory search for the term "Turks" in the *Hungarus Digitalis* database, which contains only the German-language periodicals that appeared in the Kingdom of Hungary in the eighteenth century, shows 118 relevant pieces. Most of them have, as mentioned above, a historical focus. The anecdotes reveal the beginnings of something that comes to dominate in the novel of the nineteenth century: the birth of genuinely Hungarian virtues through the examination of the enemy, a permanent state of self-development *through* the enemy.

It was only through centuries of oppression that the Hungarians could become a self-determining people that would ultimately find emancipation in the struggle for an autonomous position within the Habsburg Empire – that is the image that is conveyed. Only through the struggle for survival in the heart of Europe, into which they had advanced almost a thousand years earlier, they would develop virtues on which the entire nation could build: fearlessness, courage, adherence to their own values – central pillars of the prevailing self-image in the Hungarian political culture of the nineteenth century.

Works cited

Database of the Hungarian National Library Széchenyi, http://mek.oszk.hu/07800/07840/index.phtml#

Friehs, Julia Teresa (2013) "Turquerie – Turquerie: The Reception of the Orient in Europe", in *Die Welt der Habsburger*, online http://www.habsburger.net/de/kapitel/turquerie-die-europaeische-orient-rezeption

Ginzkey, Franz Karl (1922) *Hatschi Bratschis Luftballon: Eine Dichtung für Kinder mit vielen Bildern* von Erwin Tintner (Vienna: Rikola).

3 See the database of the Hungarian National Library.

Kindleben, Christian Wilhelm: *Galanterieen der Türken*. 2 vols. Frankfurt/M. and Leipzig: anonym. 1783. Online under https://books.google.de/

Mihály, Imre (1995) *Magyarország panasza – A Querela Hungariae toposz a XVI–XVII. század irodalmában* (Debrecen: Kossuth)

Pesti, Brigitta (2014) "Zwischen Wittenberg und der Hohen Pforte: Konstruktionen von Fremd- und Selbstbildern in der ungarischen Literatur der Frühen Neuzeit", in *Osmanischer Orient und Ostmitteleuropa*, ed. Robert Born and Andreas Puth (Stuttgart: F. Steiner), 107–131.

Tarnai, Andor (1969) *Extra Hungariam non est vita: Egy szállóige történetéhez* (Budapest: Akadémiai kiadó). Online: http://mek.niif.hu/05400/05453/05453.htm

Thuróczi, János (1488) *Chronica Hungarorum*. Augsburg: Th. Feger and E. Ratdolt 1488. Online: http://www.kincstar.oszk.hu/ukhtml/books/chronicahungarorum_uk.htm

Treaty of Passarowitz (1718), online http://www.ieg-friedensvertraege.de/de/vertraege

Davor Dukić (University of Zagreb)

Ivan Mažuranić's *The Death of Smail-aga Čengić* (1846): The Controversial Reception of an Epic Poem

1 The epic poem and its historical material

Ismail-aga Čengić, a local Ottoman commander in Eastern Herzegovina, was killed in October 1840 in a night attack on his camp. It was an act of revenge by Petar II Petrović Njegoš, Prince-Bishop of Montenegro, for the defeat of his army at the Battle of Grahovo (in Northwestern Montenegro) in 1836. In the battle, Njegoš's brother and, according to some sources, seven other men from his house had been killed by Ismail-aga Čengić himself (Živančević 1988: 203). According to modern historiography as well as to the testimonies of his contemporaries, the victor of Grahovo and several other battles against Christian troops was not only a brave Ottoman army general, but also an honest and righteous man, especially towards his tax-paying Christian subjects (Barac 1945: 142–143).

Six years after the death of the historical Ismail-aga, Ivan Mažuranić (1814–1890), one of the leading Croatian poets of the Illyrian Movement, which is regarded as the first step in the formation of modern Croatian literature, published his epic poem *The Death of Smail-aga Čengić*. Mažuranić never saw the setting of his poem, he never even visited Montenegro (Barac 1945: 232); he probably read about Ismail-aga's death in local newspaper articles only. One of them, although extremely biased, was also published in the Croatian newspaper *Ilirske narodne novine* on 17 November 1840 (Živančević 1988: 205–206).[1] However, Mažuranić's epic poem soon became a canonical text in Croatian literature and has kept that status until today. For the purpose of this essay and for a better understanding of my discussion, I will briefly describe the poem. It consists of 1134 verses of eight or ten syllables and is divided into five cantos.

The action of the first canto, "The Aga's Rule" ("Agovanje", 113 verses), is set in Smail-aga's fortress of Stolac in Herzegovina. Smail-aga orders the execution of the Montenegrins who were captured by the river of Morača for some unmentioned reason. He has also sentenced to death the old Muslim Durak who advised him to let the Montenegrins go home, which would prevent any kind of re-

1 For more on the sources of Mažuranić's knowledge about Montenegro (newspaper articles, travel books, oral sources), see Barac (1945: 137, 148–149) and Živančević (1988: 217–220).

https://doi.org/10.1515/9783110556858-004

venge. Novica, the son of Durak and Smail-aga's bodyguard, begs his master for mercy – in vain.

In the second canto, "The Night Person" ("Noćnik", 80 verses), Novica runs from Stolac to Cetinje in Montenegro at night. In the third canto, "The Troop" ("Četa", 284 verses), about hundred armed Montenegrins under the command of a man called Mirko move toward the river of Morača, where an old priest encounters them and starts his sermon. He is giving them communion when Novica comes and asks the priest to baptize him.

The fourth canto, "Tribute" ("Harač), is the longest one (623 verses). Smail-aga's men forcibly collect taxes from the poor Christians in the field of Gacko in Herzegovina. Smail-aga tries to hit one Christian with the javelin out of sheer arrogance, but, missing him, hits his own soldier instead and knocks out his eye. The angered Smail-aga then orders his servants to prepare torture for the Christians (to hoist them up a tree by their feet and set a fire underneath). At night, while the old Muslim Bauk is singing a song about a Muslim hero in Smail-aga's tent, a troop of Montenegrins suddenly attacks his camp. Smail-aga is shot, probably by Mirko, while trying to escape, and almost all his men are killed. Novica is also mortally wounded in the fight with his former comrades.

The last and shortest canto, "Fate" ("Kob", only 34 verses), describes a puppet in a small house on a field near the mountain of Lovćen. The puppet dressed in Smail-aga's clothes bows to the cross.

2 Intrinsic meaning and evaluation

The analysis of the intrinsic meaning of the poem reveals an extremely negative evaluation of Smail-aga and his comrades. Although the narrator gives Smail-aga the attribute of a "hero" exactly six times, it happens three times in the fourth canto within some kind of refrain, which emphasizes the opposite meaning – the shame of Smail-aga:

> Shame it were on such a hero,
> to gather taxes, yet to get no tax;
> to aim a javelin, yet not strike the mark.
> More shame to blind a Turk instead of a raya,
> and yet more shame that Christian dogs should mock!
> (Mažuranić 1925: 39, 47)[2]

2 "Sramota je takome junaku / kupit harač, ne skupit harača, / džilitnut se, ne pogodit cilja, /

Therefore, Smail-aga's other unambiguously negative attributes such as "furious" ("bijesan"), "angry" ("ljutit"), and "ugly monster" ("ružna neman") seem more appropriate because everything he does is only a cruel, sadistic torment to the powerless Christians (Barac 1945: 369; Živančević 1988: 281; Dukić 1998: 136–156). Mažuranić avoids a pure axiological division grounded in confession: the old Muslim Durak is an archetypical figure of the "wise old man" who pays with his life for his reasonable advice to Smail-aga to let the Montenegrins go, which leads his son Novica to betrayal and revenge. This axiological hybridization is actually an invention of the poet, i.e. a deviation from history: the historical Novica Cerović was Christian and his father an orthodox priest. The other poetic invention that is also crucial for the intrinsic axiology of the poem is its last scene: the puppet of Smail-aga bows to the cross. This allegorical ending could be interpreted only as the ultimate defeat of Islam (at least) in the South Slavic space.[3]

These insights, deriving from a close reading of the denotative meanings of the poem and its transparent allegory, are not controversial in themselves. What becomes and remains controversial are the attempts to justify the author's manipulation of historical facts, which causes some discomfort for the interpretation of the poem.

3 Traditional explanations

Besides the – at least from the point of view of modern literature – ever-applicable poetic axiom of the 'aesthetic suspension of the ethical', which enables the appearance of various ideological peculiarities and 'political incorrectness' in works of art, the critics have always tried to bridge the gap between the historical Ismail-aga and his literary counterpart. The long tradition of editing the poem and the immense literature on the topic enable us to distinguish three typical ex-

---

kamol' slijepit mješte raje Turke, / kamol' da mu zlorad krst se smije." (Mažuranić 1979: 88, 94, 99)

3 Milorad Živančević lists five points where the epic deviates from the historical events:

> "1. The Aga's Rule. In reality there was no capture and torture of the Montenegrins in connection with this event. Durak is not mentioned. 2. Mirko [the historical local commander Mirko Aleksić Damjanović] was neither a troop leader nor the murderer of Smail-aga. 3. Novica was neither a Turk nor a *poturica* [a Muslim convert]. He was the son of the priest Milutin Cerović who was killed by Mehmed-paša Selmanović and not by Smail-aga. 4. The 'Tribute' ['Harač'] as such does not exist in the given circumstances. 5. The cause for this whole event." (Živančević 1988: 203–204; translation mine).

planations for the demonization of Smail-aga and his men. These explanations can be analytically separated, but in historiographical practice they are usually combined as they complement each other in the flow of argument construction:

a. The poetical explanation. The demonization of Smail-aga, just as a strict evaluative polarization between the Montenegrins and Smail-aga's troops, is only an example of the hyperbolic characterization, which is a typical Romantic device. This explanation, usually termed as M Byronism, has become a commonplace in the literary historiography dealing with the Romantic features of the Illyrian Movement (Barac 1945: 373; Tomasović 1988: 88–89, 2009), and has even been included in high school textbooks (*Čitanka* 2008: 37–38; Dujmović-Markusi and Rosseti Bazdan 2011: 51, 54).
b. The allegorical explanations. They also ignore the historical background of the poem, but keep its meaning, i.e. transform its denotative level into some higher sense. Smail-aga is admittedly a Muslim from Herzegovina and only one cog in the Ottoman bureaucratic machine, but he symbolizes inhumanity as such and every unjust and brutal power (Marković 1875: 822; Živančević 1988: 208; Rosandić 2005: 25; *Čitanka* 2008: 33; Dujmović-Markusi and Rosseti Bazdan 2011: 53; Ristanović et al. 2012: 168). The understanding of the poem as a condemnation of legal tyranny and the approval of collective violence in the name of natural right is only one version of that allegorical interpretation which has been around in literary criticism from 1945 (Barac 1945: 182–185, Fališevac 2003: 180–186, Protrka 2012).[4]
c. The historical-typological explanation according to which Smail-aga symbolizes the oppression of the Christian South Slavs under Ottoman rule. The fact that the historical Ismail-aga was not an unjust tyrant seems to be irrelevant compared to the supposedly true historical generalization. This historical-typological explanation is also a commonplace in literary criticism, especially in the older one (Marković 1875: 836, 852–853; Barac 1945: 130–131, 157–162, 179–182), and it seems to be the most important justification of the historical incorrectness of the epic poem.

The argument for this assumption can be supported by the status of the poem in high school programs, as already indicated. *The Death of Smail-aga Čengić* was, of course, included in the school reading curriculum in both Yugoslavias. Therefore, the topic of the poem and many of its anthological verses are well-known to

4 Based on the same semantic framework, it is possible to offer a historically more specific, but less convincing interpretation of Smail-aga as an allegory of contemporary political tensions between the Croats and the Hungarians that would culminate soon in the War of 1848.

every average, educated, middle-aged or older person in the former Yugoslavia, who regards the language of *The Death of Smail-aga Čengić* as his/her mother tongue. In spite of the recent tendency of a national closure of the literary canon in ex-Yugoslav countries, the poem remains a part of the required school reading list not only in Croatia, but also in Serbia, Montenegro, Republika Srpska and in some cantons in the Federation of Bosnia and Herzegovina.[5] But how to explain the resistance of Mažuranić's epic poem to the turbulent political and aesthetic changes since the 1850s? The sluggishness of the educational system could be an acceptable explanation, but only for some shorter periods. For example, the actual Croatian curriculum for the Croatian language course was introduced in the early 1990s without major changes. The aforementioned poetical justification for the demonization of Smail-aga can serve as an explanation of the long-lasting canonical status of the epic poem: *The Death of Smail-aga Čengić* is a work of verbal art, the best example of the Croatian Romantic narrative poetry, which received the prefix of a classic long time ago. The analysis of the poem in high school textbooks remains within the limits of poetics and stylistics and avoids the awkward questions about the relationship between the historical event and its literary treatment. It is usually only mentioned that the poem has a historical background or, at best, that the epic presentation deviates from the historical event, but without any further explanation (Nikolić and Milić 2004: 126; Rosandić 2005: 21; *Čitanka* 2008: 32; Dujmović-Markusi and Rosseti Bazdan 2011: 50; Ristanović et al. 2012: 168).

4 The Anti-Turkish historical narrative

The indifference to historical accuracy in high school textbooks is not self-evident. It is possible to imagine many historical events which would be unacceptable in the curriculum: for example, the victory of Smail-aga's troops in the battle of Grahovo in 1836. Therefore, we should start from the assumption that there is something that, in the ideological sense, still connects the Romantic period (Illyrian Movement) and our time. And that "something" I will call here simply the *historical narrative*. Under this term I imply a collectively accepted model, filled with a narratively structured historical content, which fulfils two functions: it

5 For information about the status of *The Death of Smail-aga Čengić* in the curricula of other ex-Yugoslav countries, I thank my colleagues Tihomir Brajović (University of Belgrade), Sanjin Kodrić (University of Sarajevo) and Goran Milašin (University of Banja Luka).

summarizes some essential chain of events in the history of the concerned group and provides explanations for its fate.

A concrete historical narrative should be named according to the represented historical events. *The Death of Smail-aga Čengić* belongs to the South-Slavic anti-Ottoman/anti-Turkish narrative, which was developing during the early modern period and reached its final form in the nineteenth century. According to that historical narrative, the Ottomans were cruel invaders and religious enemies; their rule over the Balkans caused the backwardness of the South Slavic Christians in relation to Western Europe.[6]

A historical narrative does not exist in a fixed form, but rather in a multitude of variations that repeat and vary its meanings, i. e., it is a part of the historical discourse. In that sense, *The Death of Smail-aga Čengić* and many other literary and non-literary contemporary and early modern Croatian and South-Slavic texts, as well as many texts of the recent historiography are variants of the same historical narrative.

The first domain of historical narratives is the written culture, but they exist also in oral communication, as a ready-made, everyday key for explanation, derived from ordinary historical knowledge. The essential cognitive differences between oral and written culture identified by Alexander Romanovich Luria, Eric A. Havelock, and Walter J. Ong are to be confirmed in the case of Smail-aga as well. The assassination of Ismail-aga was a topic of many epic narratives, but all oral versions are, according to their principle of focusing on the factuality of real life, much closer to the historical facts than Mažuranić's poem (Živančević 1988: 211–217).

The knowledge which is provided by the historical narrative has the character of a stereotypical explanation, and therefore it could be termed a historical stereotype, myth or cliché. Paradoxically, historical narratives originate in historiography, but they are also undermined by historiography: for instance, criticism of essential points of the anti-Turkish historical narrative, i. e. the main attributes of the Christian pre-modern and modern image of the Turks, such as cruelty against non-Islamic populations, cultural, technological and economic backwardness, poverty, etc. can be found in recent historiography (see e. g. Fleet, Suraiya and Kasaba 2006–12).

6 For reconstruction of the Croatian anti-Turkish narrative and description of the key sources, see Dukić 2013.

5 Interrelated narratives: I. Mažuranić vs. A. Starčević

Historical narratives circulate in a specific culture, but not as an isolated entity. They are interrelated, sometimes even contradictory. *The Death of Smail-aga Čengić* and its author provide a good example: Ivan Mažuranić is not only the writer of the most popular Croatian modern epic poem, but in the national cultural memory he is also remembered as the first Croatian Ban (governor) from 1873 till 1880 who descended from common people. His political activities were based on pragmatic collaboration with the Viennese Court and focused on the liberalization and secularization, i.e., on the modernization of the Croatian society. Among other things, the modern secular educational system and the modern University of Zagreb were established during his mandate.

The main opponent of Mažuranić's pragmatic and liberal politics was Ante Starčević (1823–1896), the founder and longtime leader of the Party of Rights (*Stranka hrvatskog državnog prava*), the first political party which strived for a Croatian independent State. In national memory Starčević is remembered as the "Father of the Fatherland". As the first advocate of modern Croatian statehood, he has always been positively evaluated in all discourses that accepted the idea of Croatian political independence. On the other hand, his unambiguously chauvinist (although in a cultural and not biological sense), anti-Serb and even anti-Semitic statements have provoked ideological controversies and are today seen as the dark side of his thought and temperament.[7]

Mažuranić and Starčević seem to be two metonymies for two completely different policies, ideologies, worldviews. However, it is not surprising that there is a place for both of them in the great national historical master narrative, reproduced in serious and less serious historiography, and in school textbooks.[8] It is maybe more surprising that they also find a place in the modern history of Croatian liberalism (Cipek and Vrandečić 2004), which, of course, could not be regarded as a historical narrative in the sense defined here. But what about their place in the great anti-Turkish narrative? As we have seen, the epic poem of the later pragmatic and liberal politician is the climax of Croatian Islamophobia. On the other hand, Ante Kovačić, a writer who comes from Starčević's political party, published a travesty *The Death of Grandma Čengić* (*Smrt babe Čengićkinje*)

7 Gross 1973: 134–135, 148, 202–206, 268.

8 Seemingly banal, national banknotes can also offer an interesting insight into the difference in value between these two historical figures: the portrait of Ivan Mažuranić is depicted on the banknote of 100 kuna and the portrait of Ante Starčević on the banknote of 1000 kuna.

in 1880. It was not only a parody of Mažuranić's epic poem, but of his entire political program (Nemec 1991). It was also part of the Islamophile narrative which was established in Croatian culture exactly by Ante Starčević who regarded the Bosnian Muslims as the most purist part of the Croatian nation (Gross 1973: 33, 164–165). This is, therefore, the other brighter side of his racial thought, as it were.

The epic poem *The Death of Smail-aga Čengić* is located at the intersection of several historical narratives that carry various seemingly mutually exclusive ideological contents (liberal, nationalistic, even racist). Mažuranić's Islamophobia can be studied in historical discourse, but as a part of cultural imagery it still represents some kind of an uneasy historical controversy. Historians are reluctant to study historical narratives, i. e., the stereotypical narrativization of historical insights, maybe because this kind of research includes a critical analysis not only of so-called factual sources and historiography, but also of fictional texts. Some branches of contemporary literary studies, especially (poststructuralist) narratology, are less hesitant in dealing with such matters. The results of such investigations, in spite of their seemingly arbitrary methodological procedures, may be useful, at least as further research hypotheses, for participants of the analyzed culture (cultural insiders) as confrontation with historical interpretations/ manipulations, for domestic and foreign experts (cultural outsiders) as historical meta-knowledge and deep generalizations, and finally for theory as case-study material for revealing cultural tendencies.

Works cited

Barac, Antun (1945) *Mažuranić* (Zagreb: Matica hrvatska).

Cipek, Tihomir, and Josip Vrandečić (eds.) (2004) *Hrestomatija liberalnih ideja u Hrvatskoj* (Zagreb: Disput).

Čitanka (2008) (Group of authors) *Čitanka za 3. razred gimnazije* (Zagreb: Školska knjiga).

Dujmović-Markus, Dragica, and Sandra Rosetti-Bazdan (2011) *Književni vremeplov 3: čitanka iz hrvatskog jezika za treći razred gimnazije* (Zagreb: Profil).

Dukić, Davor (1998) *Figura protivnika u hrvatskoj povijesnoj epici* (Zagreb: Hrvatska sveučilišna naklada).

Dukić, Davor (2013) "Das Türkenbild in der kroatischen literarischen Kultur vom 15. bis zur Mitte des 19. Jahrhunderts", in *Osmanen und Islam in Südosteuropa*, ed. Reinhard Lauer and Hans Georg Majer (Berlin and Boston: De Gruyter), 157–191.

Fališevac, Dunja (2003) "Romantički žanrovi i moderne ideologije naracije u stihu u doba preporoda", in *Kaliopin vrt II: studije o poetičkim i ideološkim aspektima hrvatske epike* (Split: Književni krug), 173–86.

Fleet, Kate, Suraiya N. Faroqhi, and Reşat Kasaba (eds.) (2006 – 2012) *The Cambridge History of Turkey*, vol. I – IV (Cambridge, New York: Cambridge UP).
Gross, Mirjana (1973) *Povijest pravaške ideologije* (Zagreb Sveučilište u Zagrebu – Institut za hrvatsku povijest).
Mažuranić, Ivan (1925) *The Death of Smail-Aga*, transl. James Wiles (London: Allen & Unwin).
Mažuranić, Ivan (1979) *Smrt Smail-age Čengića*, ed. Ivo Frangeš and Milorad Živančević (Zagreb: Sveučilišna naklada Liber, Nakladni zavod Matice hrvatske).
Marković, Franjo (1875) "O Čengijić-agi Ivana Mažuranića", *Vienac*, 821 – 822, 835 – 836, 849 – 853.
Nikolić, Ljiljana, and Bosiljka Milić (2004) *Čitanka sa književnoteorijskim pojmovima za II razred srednje škole* (Beograd: Zavod za udžbenike i nastavna sredstva).
Nemec, Krešimir (1991) "Književnost kao ideologija – ideologija kao književnost (Travestija *Smrt babe Čengićkinje* Ante Kovačića)", *Forum*, 569 – 579.
Protrka, Marina (2012) "Pravda iznad osvete i strasti: ideja povijesti u *Smrti Smail-age Čengića* Ivana Mažuranića", in *Perivoj od slave: zbornik Dunje Fališevac*, ed. Tomislav Bogdan, Ivana Brković, Davor Dukić and Lahorka Plejić Poje (Zagreb: FF Press), 443 – 451.
Rosandić, Dragutin (2005) *Književnost 3* (Zagreb: Profil).
Ristanović, Cvijetin, Branko Savić, and Vuk Milatović (2012) *Čitanka za drugi razred gimnazije i stručnih škola* (Istočno Sarajevo: Zavod za udžbenike i nastavna sredstva).
Tomasović, Mirko (1988) "Romantičarska obilježja u hrvatskoj preporodnoj književnosti", in *Tradicija i kontekst: komparatističko-kroatističke teme* (Zagreb: August Cesarec), 75 – 92.
Tomasović, Mirko (2009) "Hrvatski književni romantizam – velika stečevina ilirizma (1835 – 2005)", in *Domaća tradicija i europski obzor* (Split: Književni krug), 246 – 279.
Živančević, Milorad (1988) *Ivan Mažuranić* (Novi Sad: Matica srpska; Zagreb: Globus).

Rüdiger Görner (Queen Mary University of London)

Conflicting Narratives: Notes on the Compositional Nature of Poems in Prose

I

In the assumed "autumn of occidental culture" the protagonist in Arthur Rimbaud's lyrical composition *Une Saison en Enfer* (1873) reports that he has to bury his dreams and recollections. In the section *Adieu* he mocks the "belle gloire d'artiste et de conteur", which he had allegedly acquired (see Israel-Pelletier 2012: 53–58). Rimbaud's poetic tableaux *Une Saison en Enfer* represents a *mixtum compositum* like all his other *poèmes en prose*. It includes memoirs, poems, declarations and the utterances in the first person singular of a subject which refers to itself as an "opéra fabuleux", an operatic display, or embodiment, of fables, stories, and tales without fairies. This lyrical subject regards himself as a "conteur", a narrator who amalgamates in his narrative all possible forms of poetic expression.

Arguably, a poem in prose represents a potential opposition between the lyrical and the prosaic. Verbal beauty opposes – as in Rimbaud's œuvre – an often gruesome plot where alleged beauty can be the outcome of verbal hallucinations. For this is Rimbaud's most significant give-away: an admission that words themselves can hallucinate. Therefore, words should be referred to as the 'real' protagonists in poetic texts, notably in prose poems, in which the lyrical encounters, and confronts, the prosaic and *vice versa*.

In poetological terms, one needs to differentiate between prose poems and so-called long poems, even though both contain a strong narrative element. The need to differentiate, quite apart from the issue of their distinct traditions, derives from the way in which both deal with this very conflict between the sublime and the ordinary, the lyrical and the profane. Whilst the long poem is more closely related to the ballad, the poem in prose contains, at times, poetological elements in that it suggests self-reflection tinged with sensual immediacy. Its intellectual and sensual qualities are, however, rarely at ease and more often at odds with each other. The long poem in a modern sense of the word can be traced back to Walt Whitman (*Leaves of Grass*, first published in 1855) and, in its balladesque form, to Alfred Tennyson (1809–92). Its development is connected with names like William Carlos Williams (1883–1963), Charles Olson (1910–70), Allen Ginsberg (1926–97), W.G. Sebald (*After Nature*, 1986) and Pau-

https://doi.org/10.1515/9783110556858-005

lus Böhmer (in particular *Kaddish*, 2002).[1] The prose poem owes a great deal to the early symbolists, Charles Baudelaire (1821–67) in particular, but also – in a more realist vein – Ivan Turgenev (1818–83), before it gained exemplary significance in Rimbaud's contribution to the genre.

II

In his autobiographical writings, Franz Grillparzer (1791–1872) suggested that he emerged as a poet and dramatist from his early attempts in writing poetic prose (Pörnbacher 1970: 9). His teachers told him he had no ear for writing in metric structure and therefore he seemed to have fused his inner musical sense with prose. It appears that he perceived an aesthetic conflict between verse and prose and the need to redeem it. With Georg Trakl (1887–1914), the prose poem emerged from his writing of verses. His poems in prose, however, offer a specific form of narration portrayed as intrinsic conflicts that generated haunting metaphors. Yet in order to assess Trakl's prose poems as "conflicting narratives" within this genre, it might be helpful to examine, albeit briefly, how Turgenev's much overlooked approach to writing, or indeed composing, poems in prose can help illustrate their narrative and symbolic value.

The aesthetics of narration normally treats the prose poem as a grey area or, at best, an awkward appendix to discourses on either the abstraction from prose in poetry or the dissolution of prose in lyrical compositions. Turgenev provides a particular challenge or test case in that he shared with Grillparzer his concern for reconciling aesthetic objectives through producing poems in prose, which could include some striking, if not extravagant metaphors. But mainly known as a master of level-headed narrative prose of the most subtle kind, Turgenev is normally not considered in reflections on this specific hybrid in the theory of genres. A particularly telling example is his prose poem "The Skulls", written in April 1878:

---

1 See Kramer 2012; Höllerer 1965; Ryan 2007. The most comprehensive approach to the history of the genre within German literature and its European context is offered by Wolfgang Bunzel: his chapters on "Zur Lage der Forschung" and "Umrisse einer Theorie des Prosagedichts" (Bunzel 2005: 13–26 and 27–52) are of particular interest. Bunzel stresses the "Doppelcodierung der Textform" which, according to him, makes this genre contribute ideally to the aesthetics of ambiguity so characteristic for literary modernism (51).

> A sumptuous, brilliantly lighted hall; a number of ladies and gentlemen.
>
> All the faces are animated, the talk is lively... A noisy conversation is being carried on about a famous singer. They call her divine, immortal... O, how finely yesterday she rendered her last trill!
>
> And suddenly – as by the wave of an enchanter's wand – from every head and from every face, slipped off the delicate covering of skin, and instantaneously exposed the deadly whiteness of skulls, with here and there the leaden shimmer of bare jaws and gums.
>
> With horror I beheld the movements of those jaws and gums; the turning, the glistening in the light of the lamps and candles, of those lumpy bony balls, and the rolling in them of other smaller balls, the balls of the meaningless eyes.
>
> I dared not touch my own face, dared not glance at myself in the glass.
>
> And the skulls turned from side to side as before... And with their former noise, peeping like little red rags out of the grinning teeth, rapid tongues lisped how marvelously, how inimitably the immortal... yes, immortal... singer had rendered that last trill! (Turgenev 1982: 78).

What is characteristic about this text is that it tells a story by implication. It gives no reason for the strange occurrences, other than the talk about a voice, or rather a form of singing, the trill. During this conversation the faces drop like masks. No actual plot unfolds. The poet witnesses the disintegration of worshippers of beauty, not in the face, but in the echo of the singer's trill. The conflict here is between beauty and horror. It takes the "last" trill literally and depicts in a few strokes of the verbal brush the backdrop to an endgame that remains, however, unplayed.

In another prose poem, "The Realm of Azure", also written in spring 1878, Turgenev solely concentrates on the rendering of atmospheric moments:

> O realm of azure! O realm of light and colour, of youth and happiness! I have beheld thee in dream. We were together, a few, in a beautiful little boat, gaily decked out. Like a swan's breast the white sail swelled below the streamers frolicking in the wind.
>
> [...] I beheld all round the boundless blue of the sea, dimpled with scales of gold, and overhead the same boundless sea of blue, and in it, triumphant and mirthful, it seemed, moved the sun. (Turgenev 1982: 80)

Conflict of any sort seems absent, and yet it is inherent in the fact that this boundless bliss cannot be sustained. It is endangered by the very medium of expression, the prose, and therefore prosaic, element in the poetic atmosphere. Similarly, the prose poem "On the Sea", referring to a voyage from Hamburg to London with the poetic narrator and a female monkey as the only passengers on a small steamer, replaces any hint of a plot with the depiction of the atmospheric condition of this passage:

> There was a dead calm. The sea stretched on all sides like a motionless sheet of leaden colour. It seemed narrowed and small; a thick fog overhung it, hiding the very mast-tops in cloud, and dazing and wearying the eyes with its soft obscurity. The sun hung, a dull red blur in this obscurity; but before evening it glowed with strange, mysterious, lurid light. (Turgenev 1982: 87)

Turgenev's prose poems illustrate the attempt to absorb, if not conceal, conflict by blurring its rough edges and dissolving them by means of metaphorization. This is particularly evident in a text Turgenev wrote at the end of 1878, his year of the prose poem, called "The Gemini". In it, the first-person singular observer, or rather would-be narrator, watches two identical twin brothers fiercely arguing with each other. He then intervenes actively by dragging one of the brothers before a mirror, telling him: "Now argue in front of this mirror. For you it would not make any difference but I would be more at ease watching you." (Turgenev 1982: 92)

These prose poems offer the potential for an unfolding narrative. They appear to toy with the idea of telling a story and with the reader's expectations by merely alluding to a plot and its development. Turgenev's distinctly modern approach consists of depictions of exteriors, mostly seascapes, which suggest the conditions of the protagonist's inner life.

Similarly, even though more radically dispositioned than Turgenev, Rimbaud in some of his poems in prose was interested in showing how a protagonist could be constructed and what it would take for a narrative to capture the protagonist's extreme behaviour, meaning his refusal to conform to bourgeois values. This is his theme in the short preface to his poetic sequel *Les Déserts de l'Amour.* It claims that the first-person narrator of the poetic segments to come was a young man who merely imagined his love life. Nauseated by his environment and past, he feels driven towards death ("Mais, lui, si ennuyé et si troublé, qu'il ne fit que s'amener à la mort comme une pudeur terrible et fatale." [Rimbaud 1972: 159]). The following sequences confirm this impression: Rimbaud's protagonist is drifting from one episode to another tinted by memories that appear unconnected. Even when there is a hint of a narrative, the prose arrives at a somewhat disjointed conclusion: "[...] ému jusqu'à la mort par le murmure du lait du matin et de la nuit du siècle dernier" / "saddened to death by the trickling of morning milk and the night of the past century" [Rimbaud 1972: 160]).

The prose poem occupies the place between exterior and interior, plot and impression, narration and intuition. But the very in-betweenness of this genre epitomizes conflicting modes of narrative and poetic expression and was therefore the chosen genre of writers who felt themselves increasingly exposed to emotional extremes. In *Les Déserts de l'Amour* Rimbaud enacted what the prose poem

(*Délires II:* "Alchimie du Verbe") itself refers to as "l'hallucination des mots" (Rimbaud 1972: 108), the hallucination of words. In this case, narration is seen as dissolving in a stream of fantasies, or imagined states of being and non-being, which serves but one purpose – generating verbal images.

Thus the poem in prose should not be regarded as a mediator between two different figures of verbal expression. Rather, it owes its existence to extrapolations from both literary registers. This is also the impression one gets from Stephane Mallarmé's (1842–98) contribution to this hybrid genre, which undermines the authority of a narrated story and the peculiar sovereignty of a poem. In his prose poems, Mallarmé centres on diverse objects ranging from a pipe that triggers memories, to a clock of Meissen porcelain that chimes thirteen times and the twitching ("grelotter") of cobwebs. The narrator illustrates that it is the matter, or objects of narration, and to a far lesser extent the narrator himself, which are "unreliable". In terms of observation, there are no reliable data anymore. The aging of objects has disfigured them and even the blue feathers of the hummingbird appear to have become paler, as Mallarmé's prose poem *Frisson d'Hiver* (Quivering of Winter) claims.

With these lyrical prose compositions, the textual stage was set for Georg Trakl's exploration of this genre, which remained his only venture into the realm of prose. This fact distinguishes him from, say, Rainer Maria Rilke's (1875–1926) major contribution to this genre; his novel *The Notebook of Malte Laurids Brigge* (1910), it could be argued, consists of a whole series of poems in prose that generates a string of parallel narratives. Ulrich Fülleborn, in his study *Das deutsche Prosagedicht,* suggested that this genre owes its attraction to the tension between the non-metrical form and the sheer intensity, concentration and evocativeness of poetic language (1970: 12–15). This definition draws on Rilke's own approach to a theory of this quintessentially "modern" genre, presented in his reflections on *Moderne Lyrik* in 1898. In it, Rilke emphasized the rhythm of lyrical prose as its hallmark, and, to a lesser extent, its narrative qualities (Rilke 1996, IV: 82).

Apart from Baudelaire's prose poems, Rilke regarded the works of the Norwegian symbolist poet Sigbjørn Obstfelder (1866–1900) as a model for his own lyrical compositions in prose. In an extensive appraisal of Obstfelder's legacy written in 1904, Rilke highlighted his prose poems in particular, with their "dance of atmospheres and voices" (Rilke IV: 564). According to Rilke, Obstfelder's poems in prose best reflected his extraordinary sensitivity, which allowed him – in Rilke's words – to hear the "snowdrops drop" or, in German, "die Schneeglöckchen läuten" (Rilke IV: 565). This does not make for reflections of conflict in poetic narratives, but may help to explain Rilke's own stance in respect of this genre.

He wrote the majority of his poems in prose in 1913–14, that is to say almost at the same time as Trakl. Rilke's preference was for the condensed rendering of particular scenes, for example a parade in front of the Dôme des Invalides in Paris, which speaks of a "thousand disparate noises unknown to each other [...] forming the background to the imminent sound" of the trumpet (Rilke 1996, II: 53; my translation). In another such poem, he reflects on the meaning of a black candle blessed by the spirit of a thunderstorm, which was sent to him by a befriended poetess from a place of pilgrimage in Bavaria. The image contains, rather than expresses, conflict, in this case between the spiritual and the blatantly threatening atmosphere of the time. These prose poems, mainly without titles, focus on specific contrasts, for instance between beggars on the stairs of a church in Paris and the richness of the organ sound from within the cathedral. Or they offer surprising openings like: "The thought was toying with its possibilities, resigning quietly" (Rilke 1996, II: 111, my transl.).

There is a strong sense of subjective authenticity in these compositions in poetic prose, but it was only in a prose poem written in October 1914 that Rilke exposed a genuine conflict as a trigger for a potential narrative (which nonetheless fails to unfold). Its opening phrase is sufficiently suggestive: "We have an apparition." (Rilke 1996, II: 122) It then transpires that "we" are dealing with a revenant who rises "from all graves" (122). The reader then realizes that the poem refers to the face of the war, hitherto unknown and as alien as was Amenophis IV until it was put up in the Egyptian Museum in Berlin. It is the face of the unimaginable, which humans should never be familiar with (122). At this point the poem almost turns into a pamphlet that calls for "starving this apparition" by accepting that it must not be known and therefore remain the most alien of aliens, even though it "is screaming through our walls" (122). The sight of this "face" stops all narrative elaboration. Its "screaming" ugliness silences the poet. The conflict between responsible action and the realization that "we" are paralysed by this horrific apparition cannot be resolved but remains a condition of being in times of war, or so Rilke's prose poem suggests.

III

So far, the question of temporality in prose poems has not been addressed. Intriguingly, the past tense as the traditional tempus of narration dominates the corpus of modern poems in prose. Its poetic immediacy therefore derives more from the effect their imagery has on the reader than the presence of the moment. With Georg Trakl's four major prose poems, "Transformation of Evil" (*Verwandlung des Bösen*), "Winter Night" (*Winternacht*), "Dream and Derangement" (*Traum *und Umnachtung*) and "Revelation and Perdition" (*Offenbarung und Untergang*), there is a difference in that half are written in the present tense, one in the past tense and the final one offers both temporal modes. Given Trakl's poetic practice, though, it is surprising to find past tense in his prose poems at all. But the really bewildering feature of these texts lies in their seemingly compact, if not seamless, structure. With the exception of "Winter Night" the sheer layout of these prose poems suggests coherent narratives in sizeable paragraphs. In the reader, Trakl creates the illusion of evenly narrated units that contain, however, dramatic conflict within the protagonist, partly present in the first person singular, partly as someone who is being addressed by an anonymous "other".

Again, and contrary to his usual poetic practice, Trakl reintroduces in his final prose poem ("Revelation and Perdition") the first person singular who internalizes all conflict with his social environment, represented by the parents, and – similar to Rimbaud – his own imaginations, or rather imaginings. Written in May 1914 in Innsbruck, this poem suggests immediately in its title a self-fulfilling prophecy; for what is being revealed in six stages is the decline of an entire culture. As it becomes apparent in the course of this poetic narration about a traumatized persona, the "conflict" in question is, at an individual level, that between being the father's "white son" and the realization of the "black Hell within my heart" (Trakl 2001: 127). At a more general cultural level, the conflict between the familiar and the alien, tradition and its disintegration drives the protagonist to insanity. The *Ich* of the prose poem keeps seeing itself as a stranger on familiar grounds. Nobody wants to communicate with him: "The huts of the villagers have closed mutely and the blue lament of the mountain stream in the black breathless calm is alarming." (129) The signals are unmistakable: this protagonist finds himself in a Kaspar Hauser situation, or that of Georg Büchner's Lenz (1835): The longing for human contact, conversation, exchange is overwhelming and, in fact, does overwhelm this *Ich*.

In "Revelation and Perdition" (Trakl 2001: 168), the author assembles virtually all of the main motifs which have hitherto distinguished his poetry, from the "woman-stranger", "purple lips", the figure of the "sister" and her "garden", the "putrefying blueness", the "silver soles" and "thorny steps". It is significant, though, that Trakl felt the need to reassemble them in the shape of poetic narration, through which he gave the indication that at least an idea of coherence could be achieved, if not "revealed".

There is a strong sense of motion in this text which is opposed to what is otherwise a mainly static environment where nothing really happens, other than the growing of nightmares. "Strange are the night-paths of Man" (Trakl 2001: 168) – this opening line indicates both the theme of alienation and penetration of spaces under post-Romantic conditions, of which the "night" is a reminder. It alludes to the elegiac mood and mode of Friedrich Hölderlin's (1770–1843) large-scale poems and could be referred to as the night version of the famous opening of "Elegy": "I venture out daily and always look for the Other, / All paths of the land I have long explored, questioningly" (Trakl 2001: 263). What follows in Hölderlin's poem is as mind-shattering as in Trakl's poetic prose, even though at the end Hölderlin's *Ich* finds its way back to life, hope and love. Not so with Trakl; his *Ich* remains trapped. Its perdition seems inevitable. This poetic prose does not offer any alternatives. Image after image appears to be utterly consequential. *Tertium non datur.* One impression follows from the other, even if conventional logic is mostly suspended. For how could a rational approach interpret the following sequences adequately?

> In silence I sat in a deserted inn under smoke-stained beams *and* alone with my wine; a radiant body inclined over a dark being *and* a dead lamb lay at my feet. Sister's pallid form emerged from putrefying blueness *and* so spoke her bleeding mouth: pierce black thorn. Oh my silver arms still resound with wild storms. (Trakl 2001: 129)

Like with his poems, Trakl seemed to have been at pains to make his lyrical prose resilient against interpretation. There is a sense of 'take it or leave it' in the way he constructed his texts. Little space is offered to the reader for hermeneutic negotiation over the content, but much for speculation. Speculative allusions are part of Trakl's rhetoric strategy, most famously in respect of the "sister" motif in his texts and the problem of "guilt". The pronounced use of the conjunction "and" is a relic of his earlier lyrical style turned narrative: Trakl preferred to string together impression after impression without use of subordinate clauses. He must be the poet with the lowest number of subordinate clauses in German-language poetry, meaning that for him all images and impressions were equal. There is no preferencing, no weighting, and little categorizing in his poetic œuvre. Again, one is reminded of Rimbaud's phrase "the hallucination of words"; for it seems that Trakl, too, had allowed his words to fantasize, arguably even more so in his prose poems, where verbal fantasy was unrestricted by the metre or, more importantly in his case, the rhyme structure.

The traces of the protagonist's inner conflict in Trakl's prose poems, particularly in "Revelation and Perdition", lead to the failure of homecoming. These texts are populated with prodigal sons who appear to be longing for reintegration into the bourgeois world, which they despise at the same time, and by which they are despised themselves. The interior this first-person lyric narrator encounters is void of bourgeois cosiness, of which it offers but a few relics: a "copper candlestick", a "little lamp" and a hyacinth flowering on the window sill (Trakl 2001: 127). It is a place where the sinister and the eerily beautiful meet: “Silent an unutterable countenance emerged from a chalky wall – a dying youth – the beauty of a homing generation.” (127) It may be “homing”, but in the knowledge that a home no longer exists but in one’s imagination.

More importantly perhaps, Trakl’s prose poems offer anticipations of conflict but also prophecies of its aftermath, painful trails that lead to antagonisms and others that led away from them. The texts allow specific senses to take over the lyrical narratives; in the case of “Revelation and Perdition” it is the taste of bitterness: “[...] crystalline tears fell from his eyelids, wept for the *bitter* world” (Trakl 2001: 129); “O bitter death” (ibid.); “it tasted bitterer than the poppy” (ibid.). The latter belongs to a prose segment that stands for the anticipation of conflict and reads as follows:

> And shimmering, a drop of blood fell into the lonesome man’s wine; and as I drank from it, it tasted bitterer than the poppy; and a blackish cloud enveloped my head, the crystalline tears of angels that are damned; and softly did my sister’s blood flow from its silver wound and fiery rain fell upon me. (129)

As the previous section indicated, it is a “dark voice” that speaks from within the protagonist who refers to himself as a “wild huntsman” putting up a “snowy quarry” (Trakl 2001: 129). The wide-ranging meaning of the English word “quarry” is helpful here, as it entails the location where slabs of stone are broken as well as the collective noun for deer, or prey. Trakl works exactly with both meanings: the “schneeige Wild” is followed by “steinerne Hölle” (128). Interestingly, though, when referring to the poetic narrative’s protagonist Trakl alternates often within one sentence between the first person singular and typological denominations: “man”, “huntsman”, “the lonesome man”.

The prose segment quoted above begins – like several other paragraphs of this text – with an unconnected “and” that is suggestive of coherence and a narrative stringency that does in fact not exist in this or other quasi narrative pieces by Trakl. The allusion to the Eucharist is as obvious as its main purpose, namely to show that any form of transfiguration can only create a bitter fore-, or aftertaste. Furthermore, the prose poem emphasizes the profane nature of this supposed Eucharist even more pronouncedly; for the “blood” is not Christ’s, but the “sister’s”. In scholarship, speculation as to the anatomic truth about her “silver wound” is rife. But the point is not to verify or falsify whether this is a covert or overt sexual allusion; rather, it is the fact that this cryptic narrative – to all intents and purposes – *wants* to generate speculation. It is an operational component of its rhetorical and compositional strategy.

Incidentally, the “silver arm” and the “silver wound” combined with frequent references to crystallizations of tears and meadows alike, provide examples for Trakl's interest in fusing, or merging the organic and inorganic. It exemplifies, too, his ambition to encompass in narrative and poetic terms the entirety of existence, no matter how condensed the textual results may seem.

Whether sacred or sexual, the blood in this segment triggers hallucinatory imagination of self-destruction expressed by the "fiery rain" falling upon the protagonist. Conceived and written in May 1914 it is – perhaps too – tempting to read signs of imminent catastrophe into this phrase. It can be said, however, that the 'signs on the wall' are a particular feature of this text – especially of the "dying youth" emerging "from a chalky wall".

The aftermath of the poetic protagonist's inner conflict is expressed by sustained speechlessness, the very state of mind and being in which the protagonist "lay under the ancient willows [...]; and as in my gazing I died by degrees, fear and the deepest of pains died within me [...]" (Trakl 2001: 131). The narrative itself attempts to generate a multi-perspectivism on this process of perdition. In doing so it is, or rather becomes, at odds with itself and its concern with the fate of the narrator's persona. This appears to be the reason why Trakl did not break off at this point, but added another prose segment explaining what happened to this *Ich* after its assumed death (which may only have been the result of self-deception): the very *Ich* who was dying by degrees now

> descended on silver soles the thorny steps and I entered the lime-washed chamber. A candlestick burned silently there, and in silence I buried my head in scarlet linen; and the earth gave up a childlike body, a moon-born shape that slowly emerged from my shadow, sank with broken arms down stony steeps, flaky snow. (Trakl 2001: 131)

The still-born or even, as Trakl's poem "Grodek" has it, the "unborn generations" (Trakl 2001: 127), the dead young man, or indeed child, condition these visions. They are emanations of a fundamentally rotten world Trakl's poetic persona had lost trust in. One important feature of his poems in prose is that their narrative refuses to generate a counter-world by means of narration. Instead, they explore the conflict between evil and beauty to the full. The segments quoted from "Revelation and Perdition" could easily be called after William Faulkner "As I Lay Dying" (1930), except the multi-perspectivism mentioned earlier had to wait until Faulkner's successful fusion of inner monologue and narrative depictions of the contextualizing outer worlds, which are themselves at conflict with each other.

Trakl's poems in prose are conditioned by numerous references to symbols of light – from the candle to the moon and white room – and indeed shade; again, "Revelation and Perdition" provides a prominent example. In fact, the narrated text itself can be seen as casting a shadow over the all-too-smooth surface of the reader's consciousness. The concluding image of "Revelation and Perdition" is that of the protagonist's shadow, who may or may not have reached the shadowlands himself by then, revealing by degrees the childlike corpse of this "moon-born" (non-)being. The original leaves it open whether, and to what extent, the protagonist's shadow was involved in the death of this actual or imagined moon-like shape and symbol of "perdition". But the emphasis on the shadow is characteristic of Trakl's use of the prose poem as an aesthetic form. In Trakl's handling of this genre prosaic narrative and lyrical expression overshadow each other. Even though he would not have gone as far as his exact contemporary, the Japanese writer Jun'ichirō Tanizaki (1886–1965), in his treatise *In Praise of Shadows*, Trakl evidently shared his East Asian contemporary's view that modern (i.e. Western) civilization entertained a fraud relationship with the meaning of the shadow and the contemplative effect of moon-viewing. According to Tanizaki (2001: 57), conflict-ridden modern civilization aimed to "dispel", if not "eradicate" every trace of shadow by full exposure of everything to glaring brightness.

Trakl, it can be said, offered in his prose poems the lyrical narrative of moonstruck protagonists trapped by the conflict between the equally oppressive demands of reality and nightmarish imagination as well as the dangers of deluding intoxication and dispiriting sobriety. He accomplished this with the choice of a genre that epitomizes the aesthetic conflict between two different registers of expression blended into one.

In his epitaph for Georg Trakl, written in 1919 in the shape of a poem and an explanatory narrative, the expressionist poet Albert Ehrenstein (1886–1950) suggested that in his "prophetic visions in prose", Trakl had demonstrated that he was capable of breaking through the "unsurpassable perfection of his poems" into another sphere of expression (Ehrenstein 2004: 81; my translation). This form of expression gave a hint of Trakl's potential as a modernist trying to find his space between narrative prose and pure poetry. But he had perished – a victim of the conflict between imagined realities and the real horrors of war – before he could tell a story about what was like to inhabit creatively this peculiar 'space' between poetic genres.

Works cited

Bunzel, Wolfgang (2005) *Das deutschsprachige Prosagedicht: Theorie und Geschichte einer literarischen Gattung der Moderne* (Tübingen: Niemeyer).

Ehrenstein, Albert (2004) *Werke*. Vol. 5: *Aufsätze und Essays*, ed. Hanni Mittelmann (Göttingen: Wallstein).

Fülleborn, Ulrich (1970) *Das deutsche Prosagedicht* (Munich: Fink).
Höllerer, Walter (1965) "Thesen zum langen Gedicht", *Akzente* 12, 128–130.
Israel-Pelletier, Aimée (2012) *Rimbaud's Impressionist Poetics: Vision and Visuality* (Cardiff: U of Wales Press).
Kramer, Andreas (2012) "'die Geschichte einer Vermehrung': Paulus Böhmer und die Tradition des langen Gedichts", *die horen* 247, 137–149.
Pörnbacher, Karl (ed.) (1970) *Franz Grillparzer: Dichter über ihre Dichtungen* (Munich: Heimeran).
Rilke, Rainer Maria (1996) *Werke: Kommentierte Ausgabe in vier Bänden*, ed. Manfred Engel, Ulrich Fülleborn, Horst Nalewski and August Stahl (Frankfurt/M. and Leipzig: Insel).
Rimbaud, Arthur (1972) *Œuvres complètes*, ed. Antoine Adam (Paris: Gallimard).
Ryan, Judith (2007) "The Long German Poem in the Long Twentieth Century", *German Life & Letters* 20, 348–364.
Tanizaki, Junichiro (2001) *In Praise of Shadows*, transl. Thomas J. Harper and Edward G. Seidensticker (London: Vintage Books).
Trakl, Georg (2001) *Poems & Prose*, transl. and ed. Alexander Stillmark (London: Libris).
Turgenjev, Ivan (1982) *Stories and Poems in Prose*, transl. David Borovsky (Moscow: Progress).

António Sousa Ribeiro (University of Coimbra)

Conflict, Narration, and Satirical Violence in Karl Kraus' *Die Fackel*

The proclaimed hostility towards the novel as a form stands out in *Die Fackel* as a recurrent strategy for the self-stylization of Karl Kraus (1874–1936) as a satirical persona. The main thread of the argument is based upon an understanding of the novel as being essentially the development of a plot for the sake of the reader's entertainment, with disregard of the demands of artistic composition and of the primacy of the art of language. "In the epic form there is something of a frozen superfluity", Kraus writes 1911 in an aphorism (*F* 315–316: 33).[1] And he repeatedly draws the sharp distinction to be found e. g. in the following passage: "It appears to me that the art of language is no other than the art of the sentence, while the novel does not begin with the sentence, but with the subject matter [Stoff]" (*F* 577–582: 48). Or, to provide one final example:

> Due to an in-born insufficiency I am not able to read a novel until the end, since, while I am capable of working for sixteen hours without interruption and without getting tired, I fall into a deep, dreamless sleep already at the slightest attempt to tell myself that Walter, entering the hallway, took a look at his watch, something that is of so little concern to me as everything that happened afterwards. (*F* 577–582: 47)

To be properly understood, such proclamations, of which several similar examples could be given, have to be carefully contextualized, not only in the framework of Kraus's satirical oeuvre, but more generally, which includes the consideration of the so-called crisis of the novel and the reconfigurations of narrative in the first decades of the twentieth century.[2] I am not going to engage here in the long-standing debate of narrativeness, i. e. the anthropological significance and the place of narrative in the order of knowledge. As is well-known, quite different traditions conflict on this issue, allowing to differentiate between what one could call a narrativist and an anti-narrativist trend in the history of Western

---

1 Quotations from *Die Fackel* are given throughout this article with the initial *F*, followed by the number of the issue and page. Unless otherwise indicated, translations are mine.

2 An obvious case in point, which presents striking similarities to Kraus's stance, would be Paul Valéry, whose contempt for the novel form goes hand in hand with the interest in and the practice of experimental forms of prose fiction. Valéry's famous mockery of the phrase "la marquise sortit à 5 h" ("the marchioness went out at 5 o'clock"), as a paradigmatic instance of the novel's arbitrariness, strikes the same chord as Kraus's example of "Walter, entering the hallway" quoted above. On Valéry and the novel, see Stimpson 1998.

https://doi.org/10.1515/9783110556858-006

thought (Morson 2003). In the present context, I am interested in singling out two main aspects of the way the problem of narrativeness presents itself in Karl Kraus. First, the question of how the refusal of narrative goes hand in hand with the insistent foregrounding of the fictional character of satire; and, second, how, paradoxically or not, narrative does indeed claim a place in Kraus's satiric discourse as a significant device for the projection of conflict and for the structuring of the violent gesture which is inherent to the very definition of satire.

Kraus's verdict does not stand alone. Consider for example the following quotation: "Nothing contributes more to the dangerous becoming silent of the inner person, nothing kills the spirit of narration so absolutely as the outrageous extent taken on by the reading of novels in the existence of us all." These are Walter Benjamin's words in his review of Alfred Döblin's *Berlin Alexanderplatz* (1929), "The Crisis of the Novel" (Benjamin 2000a: 231). Benjamin proceeds to quote approvingly a passage in Döblin's "The Construction of the Epic Work" ["Der Bau des epischen Werks"], where it is stated that the limits of the book form have a deleterious effect on language, since they lead to the disregarding of "the main constitutive forces of language." In fact, Döblin's own account of the crisis of the novel and his refusal of the traditional novel form amount, according to Benjamin, to a masterful defence of the restitution and reconfiguration of the epic, seen by him as an overwhelming feature of the age.

I recall these well-known references since they help to provide the more general framework that is needed for an understanding of the place of narration in Kraus's satiric discourse. My contention is that, contrary to deep-seated prejudices that still haunt the current image of the Viennese satirist, Kraus's literary strategies are as far as can be from being aesthetically conservative in nature. Quite the contrary, they are utterly modern – *Die Fackel* can indeed be seen and should be seen as a huge laboratory of experimental writing: for instance, when Döblin's groundbreaking use of the montage technique in *Berlin Alexanderplatz* runs parallel to quite similar strategies Kraus had been developing in his periodical since the first decade of the century. Above all the technique of the satiric gloss in its combination of the montage of quotations with commentary, often reduced to the simple title, is a case in point, which is very much akin to the use of the readymade or the *objet trouvé* by the European avant-garde.

In his central essay of 1928, Döblin's main advice to the authors engaged in the "epic work" is "to be decidedly lyric, dramatic, even reflective" (Döblin 1989a: 225). Such a questioning and blurring of the traditional identification of literary genres as well defined and self-contained territories is, of course, a central aspect of the explosion of the narrative mode in modernism. In this light, Kraus's satiric pieces cannot but be re-evaluated as being part of the revolution of literary discourse in aesthetic modernity, with the essential consequence that their strict definition in terms of genre has to give way to an understanding of their heterogeneous, polyphonic and multilayered character. When Kraus once defines *Die Fackel* as "a total work of art" (*F* 632–639: 88), the ironic quotation of Richard Wagner's formula has indeed a programmatic character, pointing at the protean nature of his understanding of satire.

If, following Benjamin in his essay on Karl Kraus, the satirist is but the civilized form of the cannibal (Benjamin 1980b: 355), the omnivorous character of Kraus's satire must have much in common with the re-conceptualization of the epic mode put forward by Döblin. Such an understanding, however, has an essential presupposition, namely the recognition of the fictional character of satire, a characteristic which brings satiric discourse to intersect the epic mode in several ways. Kraus once writes ironically about "people I have transformed in scenic figures and in the novel characters of the world of my glosses" and who, strangely, free themselves from the embrace of the sentence composition and return to real life as if they had not been liquidated once and for all by the satiric gaze ("Zweihundert Vorlesungen und das geistige Wien", *F* 676–678: 51–52).

For a long time, traditional theory has privileged the notion of satire's essentially mimetic and strictly referential character. True, in a sense satire is always local, in that it feeds on the intimate knowledge and close presentation of situations, stories and characters that may be identifiable within a given smaller or larger community. However, while the local reference remains a common component of satire, such an identification is by no means a necessary precondition for the unfolding of the meaning of a satirical text. Indeed, the definition of the genre is contingent upon the ability to project the referential link into a paradigmatic dimension, in other words, on the ability to fictionalize.

In a much forgotten text on the definition of satire written in 1932, Georg Lukács draws attention to the simple fact that in satire conflict is not simply the object of representation, but, rather, it determines the form of representation itself (Lukács 1971). It is a conflict governed by the affirmation of the satiric voice: unlike polemics, satire does not allow for the recognition of the other, the other being the object to be manipulated at will by the rhetorical apparatus set into motion by the satirist. To go back to Döblin's essay, "the truly productive author has to perform two steps: he must get very near to reality, to its matter-of-factness, its blood, its smell, and then he has to penetrate his object, that is his specific job" (Döblin 1989a: 219). Such a reflection aptly describes a process which is also inherent to Kraus's writing, where it takes the shape of a process of perpetual confrontation, since the satirist must again and again face the agonistic task of "giving form to that which prevents him from giving form", to paraphrase another aphorism (*F* 326–328: 39). In Kraus's – and Döblin's – case, getting very close to reality means in the first place to lend an attentive and seismographically sensitive ear to the multiplicity of discourses that populate the public space. In fact, the commonsensical conception of the genre of satire as being essentially monologic, governed by the authority of the single voice of a self-righteous and stern moralist, is totally mistaken. To be sure, such an authority has to be present, if the simultaneously aesthetic and ethic goals of satire are to be reached. But, if it is to be effective, that authority has to assert itself not in the terrain of abstract ideas and principles, but, instead, through a permanent confrontation on the concrete ground of the multiple utterances that compose the whole universe of public discourse of its time.

So in the tradition of Menippean satire, theorized by Mihail Bakhtin (1984), Kraus's satire is full of voices, i.e. intrinsically dialogic. This implies that the permanent use of documentary quotation does not simply fulfill the function of making available a set of references and of naming the exact source for Kraus's satiric indignation; more than that, it has a profoundly dramatic function, in that it provides his essays with a dynamic contrapuntal structure made of the clash of conflictual voices that has often more to do with the theatre or with the polyphonic novel than with the conventions of essayistic discourse. Kraus's approach to the scene of writing thus acquires a distinctly performative character, in that his use of language does not rest on the assumption of a pre-established meaning, but, instead, on the dialogic, polyphonic dynamics of a discursive space that is structured as an echo chamber where a multitude of conflicting voices keeps reverberating. Such a performativity transcends the limits of the book page, not just in the sense that it may be reenacted in direct oral performance, such as the public readings of which Kraus gave a total of seven hundred, but, in the first place, in the sense that it requires a textual understanding which is contingent upon a permanent putting into question of the apparently closed character of the text.

The fictional dimension of satire is something one finds recurrently not just practically performed, but also the object of poetological reflection in *Die Fackel*. A well-known aphorism reads:

> An understanding of my work is impeded by a knowledge of my material. People don't realize that what is there must first be invented, and that it is worth inventing. Nor do they see that a satirist for whom people exist as though he had invented them needs more strength than one who invents persons as though they existed. (Kraus 1986: 34)

Perhaps even more incisive is an epigram on Stefan Großmann (1873–1935), a journalist and writer who is almost forgotten today, but was of quite some prominence at the time. In this short poem, published in 1923, Kraus gave fitting expression to the utter disproportion between the empiric and the fictional object of satire:

> Großmann
> – the title alone
> is a novel chapter on its own. [...]
> Stefan Großmann? Ten lines at most!
> Großmann – At least a book! (*F* 622–631: 107)

Fictionalization is thus the essential strategy governing the anthropophagic gesture which incorporates the object of satire within a textual universe in the framework of which the apparent banality or irrelevance of the empiric reference is projected into a paradigmatic dimension. Of course, such a strategy does not necessarily employ the form of narrative. In important aspects, it has an essentially dramatic character. There are very good reasons for taking quite seriously Kraus's self-characterization as "the first case of a writer who experiences his own writing in the way of an actor" (*F* 389–390: 42). In fact, his art of quotation does not simply incorporate fragments of other people's voices in his own discourse, it appropriates those fragments as linguistic gestures, i.e. those voices become part of a dramatic universe where not only meaning, but also accent and intonation define an individual character. It is from this gestural conception of discourse defining a character that Elias Canetti (1905–94) would derive the concept of the "acoustic mask" he uses to qualify his technique of character composition not only in his plays, but also in his novel *Die Blendung* (*Auto-da-fé*, 1935). So, it is not just that Kraus's (and, for that matter, Canetti's) satiric universe is permeated by the topos of the *theatrum mundi;* not just that the theatre offers an apt metaphor for a textual universe in the framework of which the notion that all the world is a stage is literally an object of demonstration, since the business of satire is precisely to expose the multiple disguises under which the different social actors conceal their true selves. Not just that: the characters on the page become in a way dramatic characters, defined through techniques of composition that belong to a theatrical universe.

The point is, however, that, in my view, the theatrical universe of Kraus's satire is indissociable from other dimensions, among which, quite prominently, figures a narrative one. Let us look for a moment at *The Last Days of Mankind* (1919), a major case where documentary satire is presented in dramatic form and where characters often seem to hop out directly from the pages of the newspaper, as one can read in the preface:

> A document is a dramatis persona; newspaper reports come to life as personae; personae breathe their last as editorials; the feuilleton acquires a mouth that speaks itself in a monologue. (Kraus 1974: 3)

The role of narrative in this drama is yet insufficiently studied, but a quite salient dimension of the composition. As you may recall, Kraus's drama is framed by a preface ending with a quotation from the final scene of *Hamlet*, the words of Horatio promising to give a detailed account of the tragic action – "All this can I / Truly deliver." These words, which are repeated in the Grumbler's final monologue, set the scene for the whole of the drama in a quite ambivalent way, since, at the same time that they perform in *The Last Days of Mankind* the function of the initial monologue in Shakespearean drama, or in epic theatre, they promise not to show but to narrate, they constitute in themselves a gesture of narration. Accordingly, the dialogues between the Grumbler and the Optimist, which perform the function of providing a choric commentary on the action (i.e. the war), are closely intertwined with fragments of narration. The same is true of the Grumbler's last, apocalyptic monologue. One could say in general (this, of course, would require extensive analysis which I cannot provide here), that the plot of the tragedy is sustained by a narrative thread, which surfaces only fragmentarily as directly narrative discourse, but provides a fundamental element of textual cohesion in that it projects the action of the drama upon the underlying, implicit global narrative of the war years.

To return once again to Döblin's defense of montage as a device for a new way of epic composition where traditional genre distinctions are no longer operative, the point is no longer "to narrate, but to construct" ("man erzählt nicht, sondern baut"), as one can read in the author's "Berlin Program" (Döblin 1989b: 122). This is precisely also the point with Kraus's documentary satire, as a form of fictional prose where the narrative dimension is refunctionalized and reconfigured in several ways. One of these ways has to do with parody and pastiche as a strategy of deconstruction of current narrative patterns. If one follows up the many references to Stefan Großmann on the pages of *Die Fackel* (in the period from 1905 to 1934, the name is mentioned no less than 391 times, a handful of texts having Großmann as the direct subject), one can indeed witness the building of a fictional character through such a use of deconstructive devices. One of the first of several satiric essays focusing on this character, published in March 1914, is entitled "Eine gute Akquisition" ("A good acquisition"). The opening lines provide in condensed form a pastiche of the biographical synopsis common in traditional novel as the initial presentation of a character :

> Stefan Großmann is a good acquisition for the *Neue Freie Presse*. Originally destined to anarchism, he devoted himself later to social-democracy. He was a theatre director for a very short time and always a journalist. The good fortune of being able to attend the Hopf trial threw him at last, after so many delusions, into the arms of the *Neue Freie Presse*. (*F* 393–394: 25)

In the remaining part of this text, the satiric voice articulates itself as a commentary to several quotations from a newspaper article by Großmann, thus constructing a dialogic sequence which allows for the further presentation of the object of satire based in part on a reconstruction of the character's past trajectory in ways that could be viewed as fragmentary narrative. Another central piece of Kraus's long-lasting fascination with the Großmann character, simply entitled "Großmann", opens with the parodic imitation of a confession of love which could very well be a fragment of a letter inserted in a narrative, the beginning of a chapter in an epistolary novel, or the inner monologue of some novel character:

> I cannot help it. I feel more and more attracted. I will stick to him. I wish people would believe: it's the exhilaration of the longdesired, long imagined, predetermined embrace. One suddenly does not understand why it took so long; why we have denied it to ourselves, why we have waited for so long. And how much do we have to say to each other, to make up for! This is our honeymoon; let it be, this is nobody else's business. (*F* 622–631: 91)

Of course this could also be dramatic monologue, but the point is precisely, as I mentioned before, that throughout Kraus's satire the essayistic, the dramatic and the narrative are combined in ways that hardly allow for a disentanglement along the lines of traditional genre theory.

Another salient use of narrative in *Die Fackel* has to do with the insertion of stories or fragments of stories, normally taken from the pages of the press, which are projected by this extraction into a level of parabolic significance. Among the material Kraus selects there are often daily scenes on the street, which, as he once comments in his central essay on Nestroy, again with a reference to Shakespeare, allow the "flash-like illumination of a mental landscape"("Nestroy und die Nachwelt", *F* 349–350: 10). One such scene is the object of a satiric gloss written in 1916, "Ein Irrsinniger auf dem Einspännergaul" ("A madman on the carriage horse"): as narrated in a newspaper report quoted in full, in a central street in Vienna a man dressed in military uniform has taken hold of a carriage horse and forces it to ride with such speed that an accident seems inevitable and can only be avoided because a courageous policeman throws himself upon the horse and manages to make it stop. Kraus simply quotes the newspaper report and adds as an authorial comment: "When, when, when! When will he come, the policeman! When one is needed, of course there is none around." (*F* 418–422: 16).

For the reader or the listener, at a time when Austria-Hungary's situation in the world conflict was rapidly deteriorating, the allusion, whose elliptic character is also a way of avoiding censorship, would be quite evident: the madman stands for Germany, with which Austria-Hungary had entered a fateful alliance that will lead inevitably to disaster, if, in Kraus's eyes, a strong hand does not take control and put an end to the folly of war. It is a situation where, as Kraus had written in 1914, one cannot be sure if "crime and decadence are piling up before the eyes of a Hamlet or things are already ripe for the arm of a Fortinbras" ("In dieser großen Zeit", *F* 404: 4).

The logic of interruption which allows the extraction from the flux of things of an individual situation singled out as exemplary and paradigmatic, thus setting a process of critical reflection into motion, is clearly a distinctive mark of Kraus's technique. Such a use of scenic material which, once extracted from its original context, gives way to an explosion of meaning, literally an illumination, brings to mind Benjamin's notion of a "dialectics at a standstill", as the characterization of the gestural technique of Bertolt Brecht's epic theatre. But that material, in this and many other instances, is narrative material, and the performative reenactment by the satiric voice that transforms a newspaper report about a casual incident into a parable for the political situation in Central Europe, thus generating a new space of reflection, in no way cancels the narrative dimension; on the contrary, the performative gesture is framed as a gesture of interpretation of the hidden meaning of the story that is being retold.

To conclude my all too brief and fragmentary approach to a complex problem that is awaiting further research, I will touch upon yet another dimension of the satiric use of narrative patterns in *Die Fackel*. Let me quote a few lines of the great satire "The Entdeckung des Nordpols" ("The Discovery of the North Pole"), published in 1909. The text begins:

> The discovery – or, as it has also been called, the conquest – of the North Pole occurred in 1909. (Kraus 1984: 48)

Further ahead one can read:

> It was in the year 1909 that Christian civilization began to retreat from the East and to concentrate on the North. Yes, people counted on the Eskimos, for they considered the discovery of the North Pole not only as a way out of an embarrassing situation but also as the fulfilment of an old heart's desire. For centuries mankind had lacked a final something in order to be happy as it constantly marched forward and, despite the bunions of progress, did not take a rest. What could it have been? What was it that feverishly filled days and

> dreams? What kept in suspense a world whose pulse is counted by its records? What was the paradigm of all desire? The trump of ambition? The Ultima Thule of curiosity? The substitute for paradise lost? The big sausage on which science sicked all sled dogs at the earthly fair? [...] And in the nursery of mankind the question 'What would you like to be when you grow up?' always drew the resounding answer: 'The discoverer of the North Pole!' (Kraus 1984: 48–50)

The text was published in September 1909. The very creation of a fictitious historical distance – "the discovery [...] occurred in 1909" – and the use throughout of the simple past point at a text cast into the narrative mode. It is indeed a narrative voice we are hearing. But what is being narrated? To be sure, not the factual history of the discovery itself, in this case by the expedition of Robert Peary, who claimed to have reached the Pole on 6 April 1909. Throughout the text, that history is not told, but simply presupposed and the object of allusion. Instead, what we have is satiric commentary disguised as narrative. Since the reader cannot help noticing from the beginning the dominant ironic and parodistic tone, the deconstructive intention is immediately apparent. Indeed, the ferocious critique of progress – "The Discovery of the North Pole" cannot but be seen as a central piece in the archeology of the *Dialectics of Enlightenment* – operates through a logic of estrangement on two levels: first, of the current public narratives as reproduced stereotypically by the discourse of the press; second, on a deeper level, as a deconstruction of the master narrative of progress as the accepted common sense underlying that current discourse.

Following a pattern which is quite common in Kraus's satire, as the text progresses, the level of commentary keeps expanding and inscribing itself deeper and deeper into the narrative structure, signaling a marked increase in the potential of satiric violence. One final quote:

> Progress celebrates Pyrrhic victories over nature. Progress makes purses out of human skin. When people were travelling in mail coaches, the world got ahead better than it does now that salesmen fly through the air. What good is speed if the brain has oozed out on the way? (Kraus 1984: 56)

The use of the present tense here signals the transition from ironic narrative to satiric commentary. The fact that both levels distinctly overlap is a clear sign of the relevance of the deconstructive use of narration by Kraus as a central device for the framing of satiric conflict and the articulation of satiric violence. To go back to Benjamin's image, the cannibalization of narrative turns out to be one of the most salient and effective strategic devices in *Die Fackel*. One of Kraus's most incisive war-time aphorisms postulates that "the current state of affairs is the true Apocalypse: the stable Apocalypse" (*F* 445–453: 3). To put an end to such a stability by exposing the normal state of affairs as a state of exception is the thankless task of satire. The free experimentation with discursive structures and modes of discourse that are literally put out of orbit and ripped off conventional connections and boundaries, in other words, the violence of representation, is an essential precondition for the performance of that task.

Works cited

Bakhtin, Mihail M. (1984) *Problems of Dostoevsky's Poetics* (Minneapolis and London: U of Minnesota Press).

Benjamin, Walter (2000a) "Krisis des Romans: Zu Döblins *Berlin* 'Alexanderplatz'", in *Gesammelte Schriften*, vol. 8, ed. Hella Tiedemann-Bartels (Frankfurt/M.: Suhrkamp), 230–236.

Benjamin, Walter (2000b) "Karl Kraus", in *Gesammelte Schriften*, vol. 4, ed. Rolf Tiedemann and Hermann Schweppenhäuser (Frankfurt/M.: Suhrkamp), 334–367.

Döblin, Alfred (1989a), "Der Bau des epischen Werks", *Schriften zu Ästhetik, Poetik und Literatur*, ed. Erich Kleinschmidt (Olten and Freiburg/B.: Walter-Verlag), 215–245.

Döblin, Alfred (1989b), "An Romanautoren und ihre Kritiker: Berliner Programm", in *Schriften zu Ästhetik, Poetik und Literatur*, ed. Erich Kleinschmidt (Olten and Freiburg/B.: Walter-Verlag), 119–123.

Kraus, Karl (1974) *The Last Days of Mankind.* Abridged and ed. Frederick Ungar. Transl. Alexander Gode and Sue Ellen Wright (New York: Frederick Ungar).

Kraus, Karl (1984) *In These Great Times: A Karl Kraus Reader*, ed. Harry Zohn (Manchester and New York: Carcanet Press).

Kraus, Karl (1986) *Half-Truths and One-and-a-Half Truths: Selected Aphorisms*, ed. and transl. Harry Zohn (Manchester and New York: Carcanet Press).

Lukács, Georg (1971) "Zur Frage der Satire", in *Werke 4. Essays über Realismus* (Neuwied and Berlin: Luchterhand), 83–107.

Morson, Gary Saul (2003) "Narrativeness", *New Literary History* 34, 59–73.

Stimpson, Brian (1998) "Counter-fiction", in *Reading Paul Valéry: Universe in Mind*, ed. Paul Gifford and Brian Stimpson (Cambridge and New York: Cambridge UP), 138–154.

Nicola Creighton (Trinity College Dublin)

Peace Talks Between Image and Word: Carl Einstein's Struggle for a Non-Totalizing Ekphrasis

> How does Klee master his surfaces? At one point he sees darkness. A nightingale sings: pink infatuations open themselves incredibly tenderly and carefully. Melancholizing mauve resonates, and, de-blueing, dies off. Another song! Decidedly pink. The same mauve-bluish-reddish rapturousnesses twang yet again through the nightliness of the vision. Another, hastier song! Another nightingale? It came so brightly, that the gold-green spring branches visibly glowed – but only as much as if they had been exposed to the light of a June bug. It was the song of a nightingale! (Däubler 1918)[1]

This is a portion of art commentary by the Expressionist writer Theodor Däubler. Its prose will, for now, be left to twang through the nightliness of what follows, but it will, in its turn, receive commentary at a number of relevant junctures.

1 Whose art, whose art history?

Carl Einstein (1885 – 1940), a close friend of Georges Braque and of the art dealer and early champion of cubism, Daniel-Henry Kahnweiler, an acquaintance of many in the Parisian avant-garde circles and collaborator with the dissident surrealist Georges Bataille on the magazine *Documents*, was working, so to speak, at the coalface of experimental art during the first third of the twentieth century. As a historian, theorist and critic of art, Einstein's task was of course primarily to *write* about art. For him, however, this could never be a matter of course. Marcelin Pleynet, the art critic and long-time editor of the literary magazine *TelQuel*, stakes off the problem area: "The objective of the text of art criticism [...] is for me to place myself [...] before something that implies another discourse, a discourse that will not be in the text" (Pleynet 1984: v, quoted in Mitchell 1994:

1 The German reads as follows: "Wie beherrscht Klee seine Flächen? Einmal sieht er Finsternis. Da schlägt eine Nachtigall: rosa Verliebtheiten weiten sich unglaublich zart und behutsam. Melancholisierendes Lila tönt nach, stirbt entbläulichend ab. Wieder ein Schlag! Entschiedenrosa. Die gleichen lila-bläulichrötlichen Verzücktheiten schwirren abermals durch das Nachthafte des Gesichts. Noch ein rascheres Schlagen! Eine andere Nachtigall? Es kam so hell, daß die goldgrünen Frühlingszweige sichtbar glimmten – : nur so wenig, als ob sie ein Junikäfer belichtet hätte. Es war ein Nachtigallenschlag!" [All English translations are mine.]

https://doi.org/10.1515/9783110556858-007

157). Einstein, in the early twentieth century, sees a Copernican revolution taking place in the theory of knowledge and consciousness and in the arts, first and foremost in painting, specifically cubist painting.

A cubist painting will, within Western culture, tend to be read as differentiated from, or standing in opposition to, that which representationally it is not, and which came before it (namely a naturalistic, perspectival depiction of something), and later also as differentiated from that which has come after it. Similarly, Einstein's innovative approach to the writing of art history and criticism involuntarily conjures that which it is not, and performs, in this regard, a perhaps unintentional deictic gesture. A newcomer to his writings at the time when they appeared, in particular to his *Kunst des 20. Jahrhunderts* [The Art of the Twentieth Century], volume 16 of the prestigious *Propyläen Kunstgeschichte* encyclopedia,[2] with its forty plates and over 400 illustrations, would undoubtedly have been struck by the conspicuous absence of both a more traditional kind of description of paintings and an evocative or lyrical conjuring of the image typical of Expressionist critics, Theodor Däubler to the fore. Readers of his criticism nowadays, too, will be more or less aware of what the text is not doing. It is as if the text were pointing to itself or doubling back on itself and saying, 'Look what cannot be done by means of a text!' This is, however, a double deictic gesture, as the 'Look' exhortation is also the incentive to look to, and at, the painting itself. For Einstein, the point of departure was the issue of whether the experience of a work of art, or how the work impacts on the recipient, could be rendered in words.

The cubist revolution, with its obliteration of Renaissance perspective, was busy dethroning and decentring the subject. Einstein's understanding of subjectivity and of cubism meant that for him the art historian and critic's task could likewise not escape transformation. Painting seemed to him to be defying its own conventions and providing ever greater potential for cutting through reification to approach immediate experience.[3] What had become acutely questionable to Einstein, as to many of his generation, was the ability of words to defy reifi-

2 The art encyclopedia series remains pre-eminent in the German-speaking world. The current edition consists of volumes written by contemporary specialists. Einstein's contribution to the series was first published in 1926, with new editions in 1928 and 1931. The edition referred to in what follows is a reprint of that from 1931. It constitutes volume 5 of the Berlin edition of Einstein's *Werke*, and for convenience will be referred to as E5. The other volumes of Einstein's *Werke* will be referred to as E1, E2, E3 and E4, with E4 constituting the volume of posthumous publications.

3 This concept of immediate experience receives further commentary towards the end of the essay. My initial concern is with the mode of ekphrasis Einstein employs.

cation, or even register it. Einstein's answer is in one respect ambivalent, in another clear. First the ambivalence: at certain points in his writings, he seems to deny in principle the possibility of words providing the potential he finds in painting because words always already refer; elsewhere he seems to set comparable store by the word and demands that it reform itself in order to re-earn its status. Where Einstein is clear, however, is on the point of whether words can communicate what a work in the same or another medium does: the relationship here, he contends, is one of incommensurability. Hence, the 'Look' exhortation. That exhortation, implicit as it is, has, however, its flip-side. As with a cubist painting, which patently does something other than what a conventional perspectival work does, Einstein's text communicates also 'Look what can be done by means of a text'. The implications of this will be pursued in what follows.

Einstein's scholarly roots are in the German tradition of philosophical aesthetics.[4] In a Nietzschean vein, he strove to revolutionize art historiography, posing questions of power and interest, asking whose art, whose art history? Einstein is among the first aesthetic thinkers to take full consideration of the fact that every judgment (on art) is, but is not exclusively, historically and socially determined. While he advocates an end to mandarin aestheticism and a rehabilitation of *aisthesis* as the sensual that, to his mind, was systematically repressed in the Western tradition of aesthetics, he is far from advocating an 'anarchic' approach to art that would legitimize any and all responses to a work of art, and any and all ideas about what constitutes art. One strand of my investigation will pursue the question of how he legitimizes his judgments on art, a second considers his mode of ekphrastic writing in contrast to other such modes, and a final reflection questions the concept of the 'natural sign' in relation to his solution to the ekphrastic quandary of the art critic and historian.

1.1 Jetsam

In his quest to find a new mode of conducting art criticism and art history, and in the spirit of radical anti-traditionalism, which we know to have a story, a tradition of its own,[5] Einstein cheerfully discards a range of things he finds extraneous to his task. The history of art was no longer to be a series of awe-laden stories

4 Cf. Schulte-Sasse 1989: 36–39. On Einstein's early scholarly roots in humanism and his break from these, see Kiefer 1987: 60.

5 The narrative or tradition of revolution bears witness to the continuity of discontinuity, i.e. serial rupture. [On this topic, also see W. Müller-Funk's contribution to this volume.]

about paintings or painters, nor of ever more elaborate categorizations of style. Comparison, recognition and similarity (photographic realism and its representation of space) fared no better, as did genius aesthetics, rational critique, psychological argumentation, the philosophy of consciousness with its reified categories of subject and object and univalent notion of truth and reality, and the nineteenth-century paradigm of history as continuous and teleological.[6]

Take just one of those pieces of jetsam: conventional realism, or similarity to something 'given'. This was no longer to be considered a tenet of art. Cubism brought the progressive destruction of the figure or motif and thus of the conventionally representational function of art. In its analytical phase, the object was broken down and spatially so thoroughly reconfigured (keyword: "simultané") as to be barely recognizable to the eye approaching it with the criteria of a Renaissance model of spatial representation. In the collages and constructions of Georges Braque and Pablo Picasso approximately from 1910 to 1915, and in cubism's synthetic phase, traditional naturalist representation had been playfully subverted and drastically defied, and new a-mimetic objects emerged. Einstein saw Surrealist painting pushing yet farther towards liberating the imagination in the production of its own objects: production, not reproduction was the name of the game; the "Gestalt" or "Psychogramm" (Einstein's terms) was to be hurled out onto paper or canvas with little to no input from the rational, ordering mind.

Einstein has a quintessentially modernist fixation on 'the new', which he links with the principle of revolt and the valorized concept of catastrophe. His revision of art historiography and his critical aesthetics are predicated on the notion of 'bilden' or 'gestalten', to form or give form to, as opposed to 'abbilden', to represent or copy. Einstein propounds an a-mimetic idea of the work of art, a-mimetic as non-representational or opposed to traditional ideas of mimesis, which he understands as beholden to an aesthetic of resemblance, repetition and re-cognition. "Repetition" versus "the new", Klaus Kiefer aptly calls Einstein's Hamlet-question (1994: 470; the German terms are "Wiederholung" and "Neues"). If the work of art were to brook comparison and re-present, in the sense of make present again something already extant, it would, in Einstein's critical lexis, be nothing but tautology, precisely nothing new and therefore not art.

6 Such considerations are parsed throughout his writings, but a key text in which most of them appear together is in the first five chapters of his (anti-)monograph *Georges Braque* (E3: 252–371).

However, defiance of comparison and similarity is not only a crucial principle in Einstein's evaluation of the work of art. In other words, it is not just important at a thematic level, or even the main theme in his discourse on art. The principle of subversion of comparability is also a structuring principle of his writing on art. While he pleads for an end to snobbish aestheticism and to the mystifications of genius aesthetics, art criticism, according to Einstein, must emphatically not be a matter of combining words and sentences in a text of art criticism or art historiography to make a work of visual art recognizable, or comparable to something else. The critic, too, must divest him- or herself of mimetic habits and cease the practice of rendering similar.

While in Einstein's concept of the work of art the category of originality persists, there is clearly resistance to the dominant epistemological imperative of capture/contain/frame as driving forces of art criticism and art historiography, and therefore also of ekphrasis. That imperative involves a *modus operandi* in which a network of images, concepts, mechanisms of predator and quarry predominate and proliferate, a semiotics of hunt and capture. The seeing, active subject appropriates the seen, passive object. It just depends on which theory or epoch of ekphrasis one has in mind whether the active part is is the word or the image, language/literature or painting; for the larger part of the tradition, it has of course been the word.[7] Einstein's epistemology, with its roots in Mach and Nietzsche, however, prevents him from reproducing the age-old pattern of (covertly or overtly gendered) domination: active, infinite, eloquent, masculine word appropriates silent, passive image, or, conversely, active, infinite, eloquent, image vanquishes hollow, self-referential, and thus non-creative, earthbound, and by implication feminine, word. It is clear, moreover, from his work on spatial theory and African sculpture that Einstein understands also the colonialist dimension of dominant Western knowledge, i.e. that the logic of colonialism inheres in an epistemology that produces subjects whose chief mode of knowing the world is to frame, capture, and contain.

1.2 New criteria

Given these points of departure, the question is: how does Einstein respond to the problem of how to legitimize his judgments on art and what form does

7 On the constitutive and persistent power of such oppositions for the discourse of representation and of relations between the arts, see Mitchell 1986.

this problem take, if any, in his work, in particular in his encyclopedia volume *Die Kunst des 20. Jahrhunderts?*

With Nietzsche and the proponents of *Lebensphilosophie*, Einstein sees art partaking of life in a most direct way. He sees all images reaching towards the flux of life, but also many being thwarted by various different factors. Writing his history of art of the twentieth century – the encyclopedia volume – somewhat precociously, when barely a quarter of that century had elapsed, he reserves in it places of priority for particular kinds of art. In other words, he assesses the art of his day according to certain criteria, and, if his work is to be authentic, he must transmit or attempt to transmit the judgments he reaches to the reader. But how are such judgments to be made and transmitted once the traditional criteria of aesthetic evaluation, and the grounds upon which such criteria rested, have been cast aside?

Since we now know about the jetsam, the question arises of what remains on board and how it is transformed. What art criticism can and must be, according to Einstein, is an evaluative analysis of artistic forms that understands itself – its analysis, its evaluations and their preconditions – as historically determined. These forms are not to be researched for their own sake and in order that they might be categorized in a kind of morphology of groups positioned differently in time ["[eine] Morphologie zeitlich verschieden gelagerter Gruppen" (E4: 367)]. When this happens, the original reason why one might wish to know anything about past forms, that is, the confrontation with current problems, gets lost, Einstein stresses, amid the categorizing activity:

> What is actually historical, the activities of mankind, why and for what reasons people painted or sculpted in this particular way, what meaning such activities had for them, this remains a mystery. In other words, the historical movement remains unknown, with the result that the history of art is rather a kind of geology [...].[8]

In line with Nietzsche's reassessment of the task of historiography and his insistence that it must surpass complacent philately,[9] Einstein suggests turning the morphology of objects into a history of their production and consumption. This would mean shifting the art-producing human being – the "human

8 "[D]as eigentliche geschichtliche, das Tun der Menschen, warum u aus welchen gruenden [sic] Menschen gerade so bildeten oder malten, welchen Sinn solches Tun für sie enthielt, dies bleibt verborgen. dh. die geschichtliche Bewegung bleibt unerkannt u so ist Kunstgeschichte eher eine art [sic] Geologie [...]. (E4: 367)

9 The key text here is "On the Uses and Disadvantages of History for Life" ("Vom Nutzen und Nachteil der Historie für das Leben", 1874) (Nietzsche 1993).

doing" – in its full complexity into the middle of the event that is art and transforming art history from a historical classification of objects into a history of human activity (E4: 367). The result would be a fusion of anthropology, ethnology and history of art, with considerable implications for the three domains as conceived independently of one another.

2 Excavating the image

2.1 Constructing form

What Einstein attempts is a kind of excavation of the image: he wants to clear an area around the painting, do away with all emotive or evocative musings, and allow the image rather to step forth 'in its own right'. It is easy to see how this fits into the particularist bent of the Expressionist-era thinkers, and the phenomenological project is in the vicinity. The text of Einstein's encyclopedia volume cannot, therefore, be *about* painting(s) in the traditional sense. He wants to avoid writing *over* the image, i.e. obliterating it, with language; the materiality of the painting, the brute sensuous data, are to appear only in the painting. The writing must steer clear of attempting to reproduce or conjure those. Typically for a formalist aesthetics, he rejects an effusive or expressive response to the work – Romantic or Expressionist approaches – as an invalid way to conduct criticism.

A point must be raised at this juncture that has implications for a later part of the discussion. It has just been noted that Einstein wants to avoid obliterating the image with language. There are two ways to understand this: either language is capable of writing over an image and can appropriate the effects of the brute sensuous data for itself, or it cannot accomplish that for the simple reason that it is not the same medium and a written text can never equate to a painted surface. Assuming the first case to hold means language is taken to have great power. Assuming the second case to hold means language is taken to have less power, in which case it seems unnecessary to impose a prohibition: if verbal (written) language is incapable of re-presenting the materiality of a painting and is therefore unable to offer the experience of a painting, then there is no danger. Language may try all it likes; it will never match painting. It would appear from this logic that Einstein, despite overt claims to the contrary, takes language to have great power indeed. (This matter will receive fuller attention towards the end of the essay.)

Einstein does not locate art and its significance in the intention of the artist, nor in what the work might represent, nor again in what it might express. Shifting the experience and judgment of art into the execution of the work, as if to respond aesthetically to a work one would have to remake it, he focuses instead on the formal relationship of the elements within the work. He determines art and art criticism as follows: "The subject matter of art is not objects, but configured vision. What counts is the imperative of seeing, not the objects that happen to be seen." (Einstein 2004: 118)[10] His aim is a stringent construction of form within the written text that is to convey the construction of form in the visual work: this is to convey how the work accomplishes what it does. It is emphatically not to attempt to accomplish the same as what the work does.

2.2 Ekphrasis: a brief introduction

All this sits uneasily with received notions of ekphrasis, as the following section will clarify. The reason ekphrasis is germane to the discussion is that it is a key concept in writing about art. I wish to probe how Einstein's use of ekphrasis departs from the uses we find in his contemporaries to reflect a change in the tasks of art criticism and art history as he conceives them.

Ekphrasis, from the the Greek for 'out' and 'speak' [*ek phrazein*], means to proclaim or call an inanimate object by its name. In ancient Greece, ekphrasis denoted an exercise for students of rhetoric, the challenge being to bring the experience of a person, place or object to an audience. Skill in the use of the figure was measured not simply by the detail provided in a description but by the ability to conjure and share the emotional dimensions of the experience with someone who had never encountered the person, place or object. The student of ekphrasis was encouraged to attend not only to the immediately perceptible qualities, but to make efforts to embody qualities beyond the physical aspects of what was encountered.

Over time, the term ekphrasis came to refer more to the texts employing the figure than to the figure itself, so that eventually ekphrasis denoted a body of texts that were predicated on the verbal rendering of an encounter with a work of (visual) art. That is how ekphrasis has been variously defined as a rhetorical figure, i.e. in terms of its effect on the listener, as a literary genre, an intertextual relation defined by its characteristic relationship to another text, or broadly as a mode of writing to be contrasted with 'description', 'argumentation',

10 The German original reads: "Gegenstand der Kunst sind nicht Objekte, sondern das gestaltete Sehen. In das notwendige Sehen, nicht in die zufälligen Objekte ist das Schwergewicht zu legen." (E1: 215)

and 'dialogue'. Each of these possibilities, and there are more, leads critics to emphasize different aspects or functions of ekphrasis.

James Heffernan, in his seminal book of 1993, *Museum of Words: The Poetics of Ekphrasis from Homer to Ashbery*, affirms that, traditionally defined, ekphrasis "turns the depicted moment [of visual art] into a story of what the painting represents" (1993: 183). Heffernan broadens and simultaneously refines this definition to "the verbal representation of visual representation" (1993: 3). This definition has, in its turn, been revised and expanded, for instance by Claus Clüver (1997: 26) and Siglind Bruhn, the latter going so far as to define ekphrasis as "the representation in one medium of a real or fictitious text composed in another medium" (2000: 8). According to Bruhn, therefore, the recreating medium need not be verbal and the source medium not visual. On account of the absence of consensus about what constitutes ekphrasis and how it can be distinguished from other similar phenomena, Bernhard Scholz suggests it is more fruitful to see it as a complex, multidimensional semiotic phenomenon, as a term with a "family of meanings, with each member of that family calling for a separate definition" (Scholz 1998: 73, quoted in Sager 2008: 11). What is clear is that we are dealing with a concept that is itself in a state of considerable conflict. Surveying words and concepts from the history of art and literature, it may be concluded that the story behind the word ekphrasis is one of unusually intense appropriation, contestation and resistance. If it were a state, it would be war-ravaged, with hotly contested boundaries.

2.3 Ekphrasis jettisoned?

Traditionally, to reiterate, ekphrasis turns the snap-shot we get on the canvas into a narrative about what the painting represents, and the traditionally ekphrastic impulse is obstetric: "to deliver in words the story signified by the pregnant moment of graphic art" (Heffernan 1993: 182). Leaving aside for the time being the markedly gendered term "pregnant", for Einstein that "pregnant moment" is, however, not accessible to language, nor does it signify any 'story': language can speak *about* it as long as it likes; it will never speak *it*. What Einstein targets here is the endless paraphrasing of the artwork and the accumulation of cliché and anecdote that he sees as constituting the bulk of contemporary academic writing about art. One critic, Uwe Fleckner, discussing along with Einstein's the art critical writing mode of Pierre Reverdy and Guillaume Apollinaire, concludes that Einstein does not simply demand a more careful description of the work of art but rather rejects all ekphrastic writing (Fleckner 1999: 523). Without recourse to the concepts of ekphrasis, pictorialism and iconicity, however, it is difficult to get any sense of how Einstein's way of writing about art differs from any other.

3 Ekphrasis transformed

3.1 Iconicity, pictorialism, ekphrasis

I contend, *pace* Fleckner, that rather than jettisoning ekphrasis as the basis of critical or historical writing about art, Einstein produces a body of work that retains, problematizes and transforms it. What needs further consideration is the concept of ekphrasis itself.

Ekphrasis may be defined in distinction from iconicity and pictorialism (see also Heffernan 1993: 3). Iconicity is any "natural or "motivated" similarity between words and what they signify (Heffernan 1993: 192, note 8). In other words, an icon is a sign that signifies by virtue of sharing a property or properties with what it represents, for example, the use of the shape of an aeroplane as an arrow to show the direction to an airport. Certain kinds of syntax can be iconic too, e. g. Caesar's "I came, I saw, I conquered." Here, the order of clauses corresponds to the chronological order of events they signify (Heffernan 1993: 192, note 8; the example is from Roman Jakobson's *Selected Writings*). Pictorialism conveys visual images in language. It uses language to attempt to generate images in the mind similar to those in the painted picture. Pictorialism and iconicity may remind us of graphic representation. As ways of mingling literature and the visual arts, however, they differ from ekphrasis.

Both pictorialism and iconicity aim chiefly to represent natural objects, human figures and artifacts, in other words some*thing* represented. Ekphrasis, on the other hand, if we recall the initial definition Heffernan offers, traditionally "turns the depicted moment into a story of what the painting represents". So it is clear that ekphrasis does not, or does not only, aim to describe what is in a painting. It aims rather to impart what a painting *is* in the fullest sense, what the significance of a painting is, where its power to move us lies. It does this not by telling us its power lies here or there; it is not a judgment or an assessment of a painting. Instead, it evokes that power with the power of words. Traditionally, ekphrasis wants to get at the essence of a work. The terms 'hunt' and 'capture', used earlier in relation to the epistemology underpinning this concept, are perilously close by.

Modernism must, however, deem this an inapt quest because of its bugbear, language skepticism. For Einstein, the modernist, language will never get at what we can visually experience at all, so we find in his œuvre remarks such as the following: "[W]e can vaguely describe styles and works of art; insofar as the visual can be grasped in words; and our describing will evince all the advantages and disadvantages of the craftiness of our metaphors."[11] Language, as Einstein understands it, will not give access to (visual) experience. It will only send us sliding on the icy surface of truth-as-metaphor, as Nietzsche had cautioned in his 1873 essay "On Truth and the Lie in an Extra-moral Sense".[12]

In literary and visual modernism, a reflexive turn in thought and practice narrowed the focus onto the medium employed: language and the two-dimensional surface of the canvas; the quiddity, or 'this-ness', of colour, texture, space, ground and figure. Modern ekphrastic writing contends with self-reflexive language as it confronts self-reflexive visual art. Modern and postmodern ekphrasis tackles works of art that contemplate their own medium. In other words, modern ekphrasis engages with the issue of representation itself and accepts the self-reflexive challenge involved. It is with this self-reflexive challenge in mind that Heffernan, revising the traditional conception of ekphrasis, arrives at his now seminal definition "the verbal representation of visual representation" (Heffernan 1993: 3–4).

3.2 Fernand Léger's fugues

Taking an example now from Einstein, it will become apparent that his transformed mode of writing coincides with this self-reflexive concept of ekphrasis, and that the extreme conclusion that he dispenses with all ekphrasis can only be reached with a suitably narrow definition in mind. By way of addressing the difference between literary and critical ekphrastic writing, it may be noted that if we are dealing with "the verbal representation of visual representation", a definition many writers on the subject now seem to accept, the first part of that phrase can only mean all writing or verbal commentary on images (poems, art historical accounts, critical assessments). All such writing is essentially ekphrastic: the difference between literary and critical versions is one of degree, not of mode or kind (Wagner 1996: 14).

---

11 "[W]ir koennen stile und kunstwerke vag beschreiben; soweit visuelles sich in worte fassen laesst; und unser beschreiben wird alle die vorteile und nachteile unserer metaforischen gerissenheit weisen." (E4: 229)

12 For a text of Einstein's that takes as its theme and its form the slippage of language, see 'Rossignol' ['Nightingale'], first published in *Documents* (No. 2, 1929), the magazine Einstein co-edited with Georges Bataille from 1929 to 1932, in the series 'Dictionnaire critique' ['Critical dictionary']. The text is reprinted in *Werke* (E3: 221–222).

The example is from the chapter on Fernand Léger in the encyclopedia volume, *Die Kunst des 20. Jahrhunderts.* Einstein mentions three paintings by Léger, two of which are reproduced in the illustration section of the work. He does not, however, proceed to write about any particular one. He gives instead the following:

> Colour is not used descriptively. Léger arranges it into stark contrasts. To increase the movement within the image, he sets geometrizing [sic] plastic bodies, a fugue of swaying volumes, against the surfaces. [...][13]

In the first sentence, as if to draw attention to the innovative ekphrastic solution, Einstein rejects a more traditional kind of description. He is referring now not to description in the language of the critic, but to description in painting: colour in Léger's painting is not used in the traditional mode of adding precision and verisimilitude to the illusion of a plastic form that constitutes the painting's theme or subject matter. Instead, colour is ordered into stark contrasts, Einstein writes. The writing simply says how the painting represents. It does not say what it represents, i.e. what is depicted or what the forms refer to, nor does it attempt to say what the affective impact of the painting is. The reader is not invited to imagine what colours are contrasted: none is mentioned. Nor is any sense of an emotive effect of colour contrast suggested. Against the flat surfaces, geometric, plastic figures are painted. "Geometrisierend" is a coinage of Einstein's. Rather than just 'geometric', it means 'geometrizing', approaching the geometrical. Again here, with the reference to how the sense of movement or dynamism is increased by setting the figures off against the flat surfaces, the words tell how the painting represents, without, however, making any broader or any narrower, more specific claims. With "eine Fuge schwingender Volumina", Einstein combines ekphrasis with the language of musical composition: the swinging or oscillating voluminous forms are seen to constitute the interwoven themes of a fugue. "Volumina" represents the visual representation of volume or plastic forms; "schwingend" can be taken to convey the visual dynamism of smaller and larger forms, perhaps on different planes in the space of the painting.

13 "Die Farbe wird nicht beschreibend verwandt; Léger ordnet diese in heftigen Kontrasten; um die Bewegtheit des Bildes zu erhöhen, setzt er gegen die Flächen geometrisierende, plastische Körper, eine Fuge schwingender Volumina. [...]" (E5: 148)

This is just one example of many in the work. It shows how Einstein recasts ekphrastic writing to align it with his own ideas about painterly form and how to write about such form.[14]

3.3 Peace talks

It is precisely at this point that the leverage of Einstein's transformed mode of ekphrastic writing can be detected. The controlling force of language as that which strives to contain the image is being challenged. If the relation between literature and the visual arts is "essentially *paragonal*, a struggle for dominance between the image and the word" (Heffernan 1993: 1, in reference to Mitchell's *Iconology*), then Einstein is seeking an entente in which they could acknowledge their heterogeneity and cease rivalry. He finds traditional ekphrasis inadequate. He rejects the understanding of it as "telling in full", which is the root meaning of the word and has clear totalizing implications, i.e. that words could indeed fully grasp the image. Einstein understands the totalizing ekphrastic mode as an attempt to bind the painted image, pin it down, in a narrative that would cancel its indeterminacy or that which makes it liable to "fix, excite, amaze, entrance, disturb or intimidate the viewer" (Heffernan 1993: 7). That, in his view, is an approach to art that has little to do with art and much to do with politics, a politics of appropriation and oppression.

The ekphrastic mode he employs has relinquished any totalizing impulse. It may evoke the power of the painting, but it foregoes any attempt to create the illusion of re-presenting – making present – the painting itself. This interpretive position, rooted in the understanding of word and image as ultimately incommensurable, is demonstrated by the text of *Die Kunst des 20. Jahrhunderts*. The text says this about text and image, but performatively, in other words, more by what it does than by what it says.

What Einstein succeeds in doing is creating a language with which to confront modern painting without having recourse to narrating the figures. To Einstein, all talk of 'deformation' is inadequate to modern painting, as it tacitly continues to measure with the redundant yardstick of naturalist realism. Within his theory of spatial and aesthetic form, Einstein develops a flexible repertoire of

14 It may be noted in passing, and this is a point to which I will return towards the end of the essay, that the example discussed can be understood to betray an affinity with Burke, Nietzsche and Pater, who, as Murray Krieger contends, feature on a trajectory on which we can "trace the movement toward the radical universal claim that 'all art constantly aspires towards the condition of music'" (1992: 104, quoting Pater [1935: 124]).

concepts with which to approach modern art without stifling its willful resistance to concepts and categories, i.e. its indeterminacy. He invites us to engage in the challenge of seeing what, by force of habit, we may not see. He transforms some older concepts and renders others obsolete. With this approach, he attempts to refrain from supplying narratives with which to displace or replace art in the name of only describing or naming it. Etymologically, 'ekphrasis', it will be recalled, derives from 'speaking out', calling a mute object by its name. Yet naming, as Einstein is aware, is no innocent operation. The moves from naming to attribution, from attribution to appropriation, and from appropriation to dis- or replacement are all too familiar in the history of Western civilization, in thought and in practice. Einstein calls attention to such moves, inviting resistance to hegemony.

3.4 Shoe talk

From the standpoint of ekphrasis, a comparison can be drawn with Jacques Derrida's dialogical text "Restitutions of the truth in pointing [*pointure*]" from *The Truth in Painting*, and how it approaches a painting of shoes by Vincent van Gogh (see Derrida 1987: 255–382).[15] The entire text is an elaborate ekphrastic meditation that samples and rejects countless ekphrastic moves, parsing their significance for a discourse of "truth in painting". Its chief target is Martin Heidegger's reading of a painting of boots by Van Gogh in "The Origin of the Work of Art" from 1935/36.

Ascribing the boots to a peasant woman who toils daily in the fields is already too much determinacy, and the image is stifled, appropriated as a result. The boots are poeticized and in the process, as Derrida shows, covertly politicized. Heidegger's discourse sets up propositions it cannot fulfill. Derrida unpicks the claims that underpin each interpretive move made by Heidegger (and after him Kurt Goldstein and Meyer Schapiro), tracing the manœuvres of

15 Most of Van Gogh's paintings of footwear look more like what we would, in contemporary English, call boots than shoes, but they remain 'Schuhe' (shoes) in Heidegger's German as they are not tall enough to be 'Stiefel' (boots). Here already, we fall foul of the vagaries of language as it moves from one linguistic system to another. Even basic agreement on the subject matter of the painting runs aground. 'Boots' and 'shoes' call forth different prototypes in the mind depending on which language system and indeed which era we are in, and cast us straight into a naming dilemma before any more elaborate interpretation can get underway. Contemporary fashion offers us 'shoots', a fusion of shoes and boots, but the prototype is not altogether in the vicinity of Van Gogh's clompers.

naming, attribution, appropriation and displacement. The text of "The Origin of the Work of Art", according to Derrida, belies Heidegger's claims about penetrating to the essence of the painting's significance, and further problematizes, rather than accessing, the notion of truth. We do not even know exactly which painting Heidegger had in mind: Van Gogh liked to paint shoes and boots often, over several years, and when two boots feature together in a painting, they do not necessarily even look like a pair. Heidegger's initiate ekphrastic commentary on the Van Gogh painting displaces it with a poetic meditation on a peasant woman. Notions of soil/earth and belonging replace the radical indeterminacy of the painted image, regarding which Derrida will vouch for no more than the bald statement "There are shoes". The text pursues each serpentine cul-de-sac, vis-à-vis the discourse of truth, of countless further textual elaborations on the image.

While the thrust of Derrida's text and broader project differs from Einstein's, the interrogation of the ekphrastic connection between naming, attribution, and dis- or replacement draws them into proximity with one another.

3.5 Encoding, decoding

Displacement or replacement of a work of art or of art in its entirety are on Russian art critic and media theorist Boris Groys' mind when he contends, plausibly, that the historical avant-gardes were intent on disempowering the recipient by producing incomprehensible works and offering only initiate critique (see Groys 2003: 38 and 2005). This point forms part of a broader sociological argument about the precariousness of the art-producing and art-administering classes in the early twentieth century. In such a context, certain aspects of the significance of ekphrasis become easily apparent. Persisting with an ekphrastic mode that casts painting in the role of silent, spatial (feminine) beauty in need of eloquent, temporal (masculine) expression in order to render it accessible involves vesting the critic with considerable power – and simultaneously divesting the work of art of its power to accomplish anything without that critic. The critic gains power as he/she is vested with it: this is a two-way street, Einstein is at pains to caution.[16] A direct encounter between artwork and recipient, the likelihood of which is decreased in a society that sets so much store by the critic, might well accomplish something that relates specifically to the dynamic of si-

16 The text of his fragmentary work "The Fabrication of Fictions: A Defence of the Real" [Die Fabrikation der Fiktionen: Eine Verteidigung des Wirklichen], which remained unpublished in his lifetime, attests this point.

lence and voice, space and time, seeing and being seen,[17] reading, encoding, agency and power.

My contention is that Einstein, with his creative recasting of the language of modern(ist) art criticism, was actively and carefully countering the mystifications of initiate critique. He was doing this already at the time when that art was emerging, so long before Derrida, Groys and others. His concern was to keep people in touch with art, not to repackage or pre-digest art for them. He welcomed the complexities of art but shunned the mystifications of those who wished to maintain it as a bulwark for the grasping ego of mainstream Western epistemology, which he saw reflected in the mesh of aesthetics, didactics, politics, economics and the military at work in society. One key dimension of his approach was to acknowledge that all speaking or writing about a work of art is partial – in both senses of the word: incomplete, and biased, not disinterested. His challenge to art and art history, it will be recalled, took the form of "whose art, whose art history?" In 1906, he had written "All speaking or writing about a work of art at some point assumes a lack" (E4: 267–268). With this consciousness of a lack or flaw, we have an inkling of a concept of aesthetic knowledge and ekphrasis that has begun to resist totalizing demands. Not to capitulate before this insight, but to write in and with the lack, is the challenge Einstein sees for any historically valid writing on art.

While the peace talks between image and word are productive and both can cease rivalry, a tension remains. Quite apart from that tension, which bears witness to the significance of the indeterminacy or autonomy of the work of art, Einstein's entire ekphrastic endeavour, even if I am calling it "peace talks", is anchored in an aesthetics that is predicated on struggle, resistance and the privileging of discontinuity, something which places him squarely in the Avant-garde camp. The indeterminacy of the work of art is at stake. Einstein seeks to defend it against the onslaughts of predatory critics who, via unreconstructed modes of ekphrastic writing, foist their own concerns onto artworks and, in doing so, re-inscribe particular networks of power and production into those works.

17 "[D]enn da ist keine Stelle, / die dich nicht sieht", as Rilke's "Archaïscher Torso Apollos" [Torso of an Archaic Apollo] admonishes (loosely: for here there is no place / that does not see you).

4 Return of the "natural sign?"

The image of the author I have presented so far is, translated into Deleuzian terms, the deterritorializing Einstein, who pushes against the networks of what for him are no longer legitimate forms of power and production in the name of lines of flight and discontinuity, attempts to salvage for desire the function of *aisthesis*. His ekphrastic mode must have appeared bizarre to contemporary readers of his text who were unfamiliar with his epistemological convictions. His efforts to safeguard the indeterminacy and autonomy of the work of art are undertaken in the name of a liberation of territorialized senses and sense perception. Yet, more is at stake in the view of language that underpins his ekphrastic mode.

4.1 Tectonics as origin

Although Einstein advocates a particular approach to literature, he seems to become progressively less interested in the prospect of words (as literature) bearing the fruit of such an approach. Given the constraints of space and topic, his approach cannot be elaborated here, except to summarize: he calls for a literature based in *aisthesis* that would shun conventional mimesis and the tyrannies of conventional spatial and temporal organization. From around the time he writes his radical treatise on African sculpture, *Negerplastik* (published in 1915), Einstein begins to move ever farther into the realm of the visual arts. In *Negerplastik* he had developed an aesthetic theory, based around a category, "das Plastische", the plastic. It is this category, which, with minor adjustments, comes to be replaced by "the tectonic" in the cubism section of *Die Kunst des 20. Jahrhunderts*. And it is in the concept of the tectonic that he finds, initially anyway, a viable alternative to what he regards as the deadlock of the word. This is key to the discussion of ekphrasis because likely since E. H. Gombrich and certainly since Murray Krieger, no discussion of ekphrasis can get by without consideration of the "natural sign". The "natural sign" denotes a sign that is not arbitrary but has somehow a more 'inherent', 'plausible', 'motivated', or 'natural' relationship with the thing it signifies than an arbitrary, or conventional, sign. The latter has only the convention to maintain the link between signifier and signified; the "natural sign" is deemed to have a stronger glue holding the two together.

In Einstein's *Georges Braque* text, the geometric forms of cubism are accorded the status of being more primal, more original than anything figurative or non-figurative painting can produce. They are taken to represent elements of the human body and the natural environment in which it is placed, and, as such, are understood by Einstein to be capable of apprehension by the human being in a more direct and primal way than the supposedly natural images of conventional 'realist' figurative representation. Those latter are, in his view, on a par with the dead concepts of traditional linguistic representation: figures, just like concepts, give us 'things', finished objects, objects which have had space and time imposed on them retrospectively in a bid to order the experience that took place between subject and object as more or less undifferentiated force fields. Space and time, Einstein holds, are not forms of perception but forms of the perceived.[18] The ordering is a deadening.

Einstein understands tectonic symbols to have an archaic, collective basis. The notion of collective underpinning is crucial for him from the time of inception of his concept of the tectonic until the late 1920s, when that concept gets curiously fraught. His interpretation of tectonics is important here because it provides him with a phenomenon whereby the communication of an experience can take place on a level other than the language of words, which cannot but refer. With words there is, generally speaking, always a more or less definite referent beyond the signifier-signified relationship. Einstein sees the potential for a more unprejudiced, original way of communicating an experience in the use of the – originally architectural but since cubism – painterly language of tectonics, which is, he maintains, uninhibited by the referent problem. Certainly, with this quest for a more primal expression of experience, the concept of ultimate origin, the "Ursprung" [origin, source], so ubiquitous in the cellar of many a Weimar text, haunts this work, too. What is of interest here is the form or guise the hunt for "Ursprung" takes.

Were one to attempt to use words for the task of communicating an experience more directly, one would constantly be faced with the contradiction that the words are 'always already there' and pointing to something already discretely extant, not emergent or new. Alternatively, one could simply make up words and defy the rules of grammar. But this would mean producing something that re-

18 Already early in his career, about 1904, Einstein had reconsidered Immanuel Kant's temporal and spatial apriorism through the eyes of *Lebensphilosophie* [the philosophy of life], concluding that time and space are forms of the perceived and not forms of perception ["Formen des Wahrgenommenen" and not "Formen der Wahrnehmung"] The notes date from the time Einstein spent studying in Berlin. "Kant said: time and space are forms of perception)(–no are forms of the perceived. perception: the process." ["Kant sagte: Zeit u Raum sind Formen der Wahrnehmung)(– nein sind Formen des Wahrgenommenen. das Wahrnehmen: der Prozeß."] (quoted in Oehm: 1976: 71). The round brackets used by Einstein in these notes are his own idiosyncratic note-taking marks.

mains in its own hermetic world, a problem Einstein saw in what he regarded as the nihilistic tendencies of Impressionism and Symbolism (see his critique of both in E5: 42–60). Einstein's conception of tectonics as collective allows him to step around this dilemma. Yet even once the concepts of "Dichtung" and "dichten"[19] emerge in the Braque book, and related as they are to the questionable solution of the tectonic, the move away from a distinctly pessimistic notion of language and towards a theory that encompasses image/figure *and* word as ultimately embedded in language is anything but clear-cut. Rather, Einstein holds to the idea of a figure that is pre-linguistically informed and all but conceals that fact in its expression.

The result is a state of affairs that bids us return to two of the keenest commentators on ekphrasis, Murray Krieger and W. J. T. Mitchell, who plead for caution with any signs that appear to exceed convention. Why the valorization, ultimately, of painting over literature in Einstein's work?

4.2 Valorization of painting

The answer, I believe, lies in the concept of the aesthetic particular to Einstein and inflected in his own peculiar fashion: the authenticity of representation he is pursuing (a hunt of another hue?) is that of the numinous in a particular guise, a pre-linguistic realm. Einstein does not believe language, in the (early twentieth century) state of decrepitude he diagnoses it to be in, is fit for the task. He does not rule out the possibility, but simply regards the likelihood as being, for the moment, very slim. Tectonics, however, in the manner in which he understands them as pre-linguistic signs, are more promising candidates. These signs, on his interpretation, are hurled from the unconscious, where they are deemed to have collective validity on account of their basis in collective archaic symbols. As such, they are Einstein's version of the "natural sign" that, as Mitchell demonstrates over and over in *Iconology* and Krieger investigates meticulously in *Ekphrasis: The Illusion of the Natural Sign*, "convert humanly created signs into an immediate surrogate for the objective natural truth" (see Mitchell 1986: 75–94 and Krieger 1992). The conviction that such signs are somehow more primal than the signs of language indicates two things. One is that we can understand Einstein to belong to a stream of thought one could designate, with David Pan, as primitivist (2001: 121–148; the chapter is entitled "Construc-

19 "Dichtung" is poetry; "dichten" usually means to write poetry but the more literal meaning is 'to condense'.

tion and Mimesis in Carl Einstein's Theory of Art"). The other is that, in one of two reterritorializing moves, it unwittingly reinscribes the nature-culture opposition at the base of many a theoretical endeavour in the Western tradition.

"What are we to make", asks Mitchell, "of this contest between the interests of verbal and pictorial representation?" (1986: 44). His answer is unequivocal: the point "is not to heal the split between words and images, but to see what interests and powers it serves" (1986: 44). Einstein indeed appears keen on healing the split. Once his partiality for painting becomes clear, however, his plea for a truce between image and word becomes understandable as a plea for language to quit its imperialist forays, its muscle-flexing and military sorties. It has been in the name-appropriate-displace business for too long. It must finally stand back and let painting be. Einstein's *Negerplastik* [Negro Sculpture] from 1915 is a fierce defence of an updated version of Lessing's doctrine of no mixing, but with the opposite valorization: in "Laocoon: An Essay upon the Limits of Poetry and Painting" (1766), Lessing is at pains not so much to separate and safeguard equality between the temporal and spatial arts but rather to ensure their apartheid, his assumption being that poetry (literature) has "the wider sphere".[20] Einstein is likewise of the conviction that language and painting, sculpture and painting must not contaminate one another. Sculpture ought not encroach on (period) painting by making a tableau of the sculpted figure(s), and painting ought reciprocate by avoiding the temptation to model. Painting and sculpture should in any event both abandon the tautology and anecdote of the tableau. In Einstein's art criticism, we find much to support the appeal 'Language (i.e. literature), leave painting alone!' and little to support the obverse, 'Painting, leave literature alone!' We do, however, find, 'Sculpture, leave painting alone', and when Einstein is in critical mode, for example tackling salon painters who in his view are appropriating cubism as a style without having understood cubist spatial form, 'Painting, leave literature alone, shun description and anecdote!' When faced with neo-classical tableaux still employing what to him is hopelessly outdated, intact Renaissance perspective, the implicit appeal is 'Painting, leave the past alone'.[21] The incursions, nonetheless, appear to go largely in one direction; it is painting that prompts Einstein's most ardent defence, except when he is discussing what he understands as poor quality painting. Einstein, it appears, is

---

20 "[I]f not every trait employed by the descriptive poet can produce an equally good effect on canvas or in marble, can every trait of the artist be equally effective in the work of the poet? Undoubtedly; for what pleases us in a work of art pleases not the eye, but the imagination through the eye." (Lessing 1969: 43; cf. Mitchell 1986: 107)

21 Zeidler (2005: in particular ch. 3) discusses at length Einstein's critique of the problems of painterly form intruding on sculpture and sculptural form invading painting.

emphatically against any hybridization and holds each art to have its proper domain and mode.

And yet, he takes painting, i.e. the kind of painting he champions in *Die Kunst des 20. Jahrhunderts*, to be the most primal. It approaches musicality in its absence of referent, yet with his theory of tectonics he can make claims for its collective reception and validity, its community-creating capacity. As such, and amid the apparent bid for an *entente cordiale*, rivalry between the arts persists – and ends: in a second reterritorializing move, a standard for the arts derived from one of them is, in fact, made to emerge. Just as Lessing, apparently promoting the mutual respect of borders between the temporal and spatial arts, grants the greater power to poetry, Einstein grants it to painting.

5 Conclusion

Returning to Mitchell's *Picture Theory*, the complication can be drawn to a conclusion:

> If ekphrastic hope involves what Francoise Meltzer has called a "reciprocity" or free exchange and transference between visual and verbal art [...], ekphrastic fear perceives this reciprocity as a dangerous promiscuity and tries to regulate the borders with firm distinctions between the senses, modes of representation, and the objects proper to each. (Mitchell 1994: 224 citing Meltzer 1987: 21)

As each realm is fenced off, rather than an *entente cordiale*, we have a *cordon sanitaire*, and the relation between literature (language) and the visual arts goes back to its age-old state of being "essentially *paragonal*, a struggle for dominance between the image and the word" (Heffernan 1993: 1).

In Einstein's work there is something akin to such "ekphrastic fear" Mitchell describes with a particular focus on Lessing. Einstein's fear is, however, born under a different sign and has substantively different grounds from that discussed by Mitchell. Einstein is concerned not to allow works of art to become objects of worship. He understands the development of art as an institution only too well, and grasps the disenchantment, the de-magification of the world (in the Weberian phrase "Entzauberung der Welt"). As his fragmentary work from the 1930s *Die Fabrikation der Fiktionen* [The Fabrication of Fictions] shows, he is concerned to protect art from its instrumentalization by groups with vested interests, initiates or experts who would speak (write) on its behalf, rendering its works as objects of worship rather than as opportunities for aisthetic encounter, development, and understanding.

Yet he is at pains to defend art, likewise, from rationalization, psychologization, and the depredations by philosophy whose approach to art was, in his view, colonizing or imperialistic: the aesthetic sphere was made to submit to the force of conceptualization and identitary logic. Einstein is keen not to have art taken out of the realm of understanding and into that of idolatry (objects of worship), yet he is as keen not to have it kept in the realms of particular forms of deadening understanding. Both, to him, end art's and therefore humans' life. In his bid to salvage art, he resorts to the illusion, or, as Mitchell designates it, the fetish of the "natural sign", in the idiosyncratic guise of tectonic forms. "The magic of the fetish", Mitchell writes, "depends on the projection of consciousness into the object and then a forgetting of that act of projection" (1986: 193). Einstein's primitivism is, certainly by the early 1930s, when he revises his encyclopedia volume for its third reprint and writes *Georges Braque*, very accomplished: he forgets very well, at least for some time, that he has projected into tectonics.

What emerges, ultimately, is a narrative in conflict with itself. Time and again, this holds for theories (narratives) of ekphrasis, or for accounts of the relationship between the arts. Such theories are narratives insofar as they contest and dispose of certain views with regard to the relations that obtain between the arts, and present other views as overwhelmingly more valid, Einstein, for instance, disposing of Däubler, among others, and, as Mitchell shows in *Iconology*, Lessing disposing of Winckelmann. When we interrogate the grounds for taking certain views to be disposable and others to be valorized, we come up against not a theory or an argument but a narrative, or, differently put, we reach the point where theory and narrative coincide: in this instance, in a story about the wrong and the right way to understand and steward the arts, a story based on a set of convictions that certainly has something to do with the arts themselves – that is, with modes and possibilities of creativity, imagination and aesthetic sense-making – but much more to do with the power of stewardship, which is ultimately political power in the broadest sense.

The text of Einstein's encyclopedia volume, with its struggle concerning the relationship between words and images, takes a stance on some of the issues in focus at the conference that gave rise to the present collection of essays: encounters between humans and textual objects, power, representation and mystification, conflict and contestation, story-making, struggle, strife-making and peace-making. Ekphrasis can, and in many instances has, become a way of staging such issues, giving us a locus in which to concentrate, reflect on and contest them, as it does in Einstein's fraught quest for a non-totalizing ekphrasis.

Works cited

Bruhn, Siglind (2000) *Musical Ekphrasis: Composers Responding to Poetry and Painting* (Hillsdale: Pendragon Press).

Clüver, Claus (1997) "Ekphrasis Reconsidered: On Verbal Representations of Non-Verbal Texts", in *Interart Poetics: Essay on the Interrelations of the Arts and Media, ed. Ulla-Britta Lagerroth, Hans Lund and Erik Hedling* (Amsterdam: Rodopi).

Däubler, Theodor (1918) *Neue Blätter für Kunst und Dichtung*, year 1, May edition.

Derrida, Jacques (1987) *The Truth in Painting*, transl. Geoff Bennington and Ian McLeod (Chicago: U of Chicago Press).

Einstein, Carl (1996) *Werke*, vol. 1 [= E1], 1907–1918, ed. Hermann Haarmann and Klaus Siebenhaar; vol. 3 [= E3], 1929–1940, ed. Hermann Haarmann, Klaus Siebenhaar, Katharina Langhammer; vol. 4 [= E4], *Texte aus dem Nachlaß I*, ed. Hermann Haarmann and Klaus Siebenhaar; vol. 5 [= E5], ed. Uwe Fleckner and Thomas Gaehtgens (Berlin: Fannei & Walz).

Einstein, Carl (2004) "Totality", transl. C. W. Haxthausen, in *October* 107 (Winter), 115–121.

Fleckner, Uwe (1999) "Das zerschlagene Wort: Kunstkritik des Kubismus und 'kubistische' Kunstkritik im Werk von Pierre Reverdy, Guillaume Apollinaire und Carl Einstein", in *"Prenez garde à la peinture!" Kunstkritik in Frankreich 1900–1945*, ed. Uwe Fleckner and Thomas W. Gaehtgens (Berlin: Akademie Verlag), 480–535.

Groys, Boris (2003) "Werbung für den Kommunismus", *Die Zeit*, 10, 27 February, 38.

Groys, Boris (2005) *Am Nullpunkt: Positionen der russischen Avantgarde* (Frankfurt/M.: Suhrkamp).

Heffernan, James A. W. (1993) *Museum of Words: The Poetics of Ekphrasis from Homer to Ashbery* (Chicago and London: U of Chicago Press).

Jakobson, Roman (1971) *Selected Writings* (The Hague: Mouton).

Kiefer, Klaus H. (1987) "'BEB II' – ein Phantombild", in *Text + Kritik* 95: Carl Einstein, 44–66.

Kiefer, Klaus H. (1994) *Diskurswandel im Werk Carl Einsteins: Ein Beitrag zur Theorie und Geschichte der europäischen Avantgarde* (Tübingen: Niemeyer).

Krieger, Murray (1992) *Ekphrasis: The Illusion of the Natural Sign* (Baltimore and London: The Johns Hopkins UP).

Lessing, Gotthold Ephraim (1969) *Laocoon: An Essay upon the Limits of Poetry and Painting*, transl. Ellen Frothingham (New York: Farrar, Straus and Giroux).

Meltzer, Françoise (1987) *Salome and the Dance of Writing: Portraits of Mimesis in Literature* (Chicago: U of Chicago Press).

Mitchell, W. J. T. (1986) *Iconology: Image, Text, Ideology* (Chicago: U of Chicago Press).

Mitchell, W. J. T. (1994) *Picture Theory: Essays on Verbal and Visual Representation* (Chicago: U of Chicago Press).

Nietzsche, Friedrich (1967) *Werke: Kritische Gesamtausgabe*, ed. Giorgio Colli and Mazzino Montinari (Berlin: De Gruyter).

Nietzsche, Friedrich (1993) "On the Uses and Disadvantages of History for Life", transl. R. J. Hollingdale, in *Untimely Meditations* (Cambridge and New York: Cambridge UP).

Oehm, Heidemarie (1976) *Die Kunsttheorie Carl Einsteins* (Munich: Fink).

Pan, David (2001) *Primitive Renaissance: Rethinking German Expressionism, Modern German Culture and Literature* (Lincoln and London: U of Nebraska Press).

Pater, Walter (1935) "The School of Giorgione" (1877), in *The Renaissance: Studies in Art and Poetry* (London: Macmillan).
Pleynet, Marcelin (1984) *Painting and System*, transl. Sima Godfrey (Chicago: U of Chicago Press).
Sager, Laura M. (2008) *Writing and Filming the Painting: Ekphrasis in Literature and Film* (Amsterdam and New York: Rodopi).
Scholz, Bernhard F. (1998) "'Sub Oculos Subiectio': Quintilian on Ekphrasis and Enargeia", in *Pictures into Words: Theoretical and Descriptive Approaches to Ekphrasis*, ed. Valerie Robillard and Els Jongeneel (Amsterdam: Vrije Universiteit Press).
Schulte-Sasse, Jochen (1989) "Carl Einstein; or, The Postmodern Transformation of Modernism", in *Modernity and the Text: Revisions of German Modernism*, ed. Andreas Huyssen and David Bathrick (New York: Columbia UP), 36–59.
Wagner, Peter (1996) "Introduction: Ekphrasis, Iconotexts and Intermediality – The State(s) of the Art(s)", in *Icons-Text-Iconotexts: Essays on Ekphrasis and Intermediality*, ed. Peter Wagner (Berlin and New York: De Gruyter), 1–42.
Zeidler, Sebastian (2005) *Defense of the Real: Carl Einstein's History and Theory of Art* (New York: Columbia UP).

Dorothea Depner (Trinity College Dublin)

The Importance of Conflict Elsewhere: Francis Stuart's and Hugo Hamilton's Literary Engagements with Germany and the Second World War

In "The Importance of Elsewhere", written after leaving his post at Queen's University Belfast and settling permanently in Hull, Philip Larkin (1922–85) famously sums up the advantage living "elsewhere" had afforded him: "Lonely in Ireland, since it was not home, / Strangeness made sense." Whereas his five years "abroad" had served as a reassuring confirmation of his sense of difference, proving him "separate, not unworkable", "[l]iving in England has no such excuse", for, he concludes, "[h]ere no elsewhere underwrites my existence" (1985 [1964]: 34). Irish-German writer Hugo Hamilton reiterated a similarly reflexive attitude to "elsewhere" in *Die redselige Insel* (2007), a work commissioned by his German publishers to celebrate the fiftieth anniversary of Heinrich Böll's *Irisches Tagebuch*. Quoting a line from Paul Durcan's poem "The Far Side of the Island" (2004), according to which the Irish are "globally sad" and "locally glad", Hamilton observes a common tendency to turn the exposure to 'elsewhere' into a self-affirming experience (Hamilton 2007: 136–137).

In her assessment of this peculiar relationship between home and abroad in contemporary Irish fiction, Roberta Gefter Wondrich suggests that the experience of living in a foreign place with its own troubled history more often than not serves the purpose of helping the disenchanted Irish "exile" understand the need "for a negotiating, less rigid attitude towards that complex, multiple site of allegiances which 'home' – their Irish 'home' – has become" (2000: 15). With this understanding, their every "return *becomes* homecoming" (Gefter Wondrich 2000: 15), as every immersion in a foreign country's past anchors them more firmly in their Irish environment in the present. Her conclusion supports Edith Hallberg's and Christoph Houswitschka's carefully voiced suspicion that "the infatuation with historical turning points on the Continent" (2005: 86), such as the Second World War or the Fall of the Berlin Wall, in the writings of, among others, Hugo Hamilton, affirms the stable outlines of the writer's sense of history and identity.

What remains insufficiently explored, however, in works by Irish writers which engage with conflict elsewhere are the implications they raise in relation to the way images of self and other are constructed, perpetuated, or questioned

https://doi.org/10.1515/9783110556858-008

in literature. Additionally, the ways in which the past is mediated needs to be considered, specifically, the intersections between foreign and domestic, self and other, past and present. In this essay, I propose to examine the engagements of Francis Stuart (1902–2000) and Hugo Hamilton with postwar Germany as an exciting testing ground for studying the dialogue between two different mnemonic communities outside the limiting frames of national memory.

The concept of cultural memory as a dynamic process that can define and redefine the way a community conceives of itself – developed by scholars like Aleida Assmann (1999, 2007), Ann Rigney (2005, 2012), Michael Rothberg (2009), and Astrid Erll (2006) – emphasizes the intercultural potential of memory mediated by the arts, and literature and film, in particular, to communicate beyond temporal and spatial boundaries and to foster "imagined communities" (Anderson 1991) far larger than the nation. Exciting as this prospect is, there is also an awareness that the sharing and recycling of mnemonic media, practices, and memories themselves, while offering the unique opportunity of building bridges among mnemonic groups previously unaware of, or indifferent to, each other's pasts, leaves it vulnerable to misuses by "specific people with specific agendas" (Erll 2011: 15). Therefore, even if the future for memory studies necessarily lies in a transcultural approach, as Erll points out, there is reason to be cautious of the processes memory undergoes as it "travels".[1]

By placing my reading of Stuart's *The Pillar of Cloud*[2] (1948) and Hamilton's *The Last Shot*[3] (1991) within the current discourses regarding the interpretation, representation, and transcultural/transgenerational translation of the Second World War, I will endeavour to show to what extent their works buttress a sense of alterity and provide a canvas to, in the words of Daniel Henri-Pageaux, "write, think, dream *differently*" (1988: 376, my translation). In the context of remembering and representing the Second World War, the challenge for Stuart and Hamilton lies in finding the right balance between critical and emotional recollection "as an antidote to complacency and temporal foreshortening" (Rigney 2012: 616). The vital significance of this concern is immediately apparent in Hamilton's introduction to the reissued edition of *The Pillar of Cloud* from 1994. In it, he recounts his first meeting with Stuart in autumn 1991 at an international literary festival organized by the *Literaturwerkstatt* Berlin. Sitting in a villa recently vacated by what Hamilton imagined were members of the GDR's political leader-

---

1 Erll's *caveat* is echoed in concerns expressed by historians like Pierre Nora (2002), Peter Burke (1989: 107) or R. F. Foster (2007: 176–177) about nationalist projects pursued by particular groups which seek to anchor their common identity in lost or hidden memories.

2 Hereafter cited as *POC*.

3 Hereafter cited as *LS*.

ship, the two Irish authors drew parallels between "the sweet air of victory" after 1945 and "the very same high-moral stance of the capitalist triumph over communism at the end of the Cold War" (*POC* 3). Noting Stuart's "mute satisfaction" (*POC* 1) that yet "another ideology had been wrong-footed and discredited" (*POC* 1), Hamilton – Stuart's junior by half a century – concludes his introduction by setting up the older writer as an example of intellectual leadership:

> If we can be as honest in our exposure of the new, totalitarian ideologies of fun and entertainment into the next century, if we can approach the blindspots of consumerism and the culture of exclusion, if we can be as much an intellectual "contra", then we have learned from Francis Stuart, his work and his life. (*POC* 4)

While this rather indiscriminate equation of the GDR, Third Reich and consumerism as equally totalitarian ideologies displays a blasé attitude on the part of Hamilton and Stuart, I would argue that it also foreshadows more serious issues which affect the two writers' literary engagement with twentieth-century German history.

1 Harvesting "the fruit of the great suffering of the war": Francis Stuart's *The Pillar of Cloud*

Francis Stuart's life has been documented in three biographies,[4] two of which were published in his lifetime and none of which escaped the myth Stuart created after the Second World War: that a lifelong "search for truth" (Elborn 1990: 8, also McCartney 2000: 1) and deep commitment to his writing compelled him to travel to Germany in January 1940 and live there for the duration of the war so that he would experience both the suffering of the war's victims and the end of the war on the side of the losers.[5] Quite apart from the fact that Stuart could not have anticipated the outcome of the war at the time of his departure, it seems more accurate to state marital and financial difficulties as compelling reasons to take up a post as guest lecturer in English at Berlin's Friedrich Wil-

4 By Jerry Natterstad (1974), Geoffrey Elborn (1990), and Kevin Kiely (2007), respectively.
5 This view has been expressed over the decades by, among others, W.J. McCormack (writing under his pseudonym Hugh Maxton 1970: 20), Elborn (1990: 190), David O'Donoghue (1998: 141–142), Anne McCartney (2000: 159), and even by Terry Eagleton (1998: 246), who is otherwise not sparing in his criticism of Stuart.

helm University.[6] Most importantly, however, contrary to his protestations of political naivety after the war, Stuart was cynical about Western democracies, deluded about the opposing ideologies, and politically calculating.[7] In a rare moment of straying from his script, Stuart once admitted that he had, in fact, hoped to blossom under the patronage of the Nazi dictator:

> Hitler because he was a fascist [...] had no more attraction for me than Stalin had. But I had a dream that some of these warlords had an interest in the writer that "professional" politicians never had. [...] I still cling on to the idea of an imaginative writer coming close to a revolutionary organisation which can't really achieve its very concrete social objectives without the insights of the imaginative artist. (Stuart in interview with Webb 1975: 10)

Indeed, his dream of a symbiosis worked out to his advantage: Stuart agreed to the approaches made to him by the German Foreign Office, which recruited him for propaganda broadcasting, and by the German Military Intelligence (the *Abwehr*);[8] in return, he enjoyed a period lasting from 1940 until the last few months

---

6 Stuart was leaving behind his wife, Iseult Gonne, daughter of Maud Gonne MacBride, and their two children. Although he had published eleven novels, an autobiographical work and a poetry collection by 1939, financial difficulties continued to plague him. In the first half of that year, he went on a lecture tour in Germany following an invitation from the German Academic Exchange Service (cf. Natterstad 1974: 53). He proceeded to make travel arrangements for a return to Germany after the outbreak of war and procured a visa for Switzerland on (feigned) medical grounds (cf. his letter to Irish Legation in Paris, 28 October 1939, DFA 10/A/72). As two Department of Foreign Affairs restricted-access files in the Irish National Archives show (DFA 10/A/72 and 10/A/72/A), he was not hindered in this by the Irish authorities, who suspected his real destination, as the position held by Joseph Walshe, Secretary of External Affairs, was to avoid the impression of partiality at a time when many Irish people were travelling to Britain in order to engage there in similarly "unneutral" activities, be it in the war industry or the army (cf. reply from Walsh [sic in DFA documents] to Liam Archer, G2 Branch [Irish Military Intelligence] from 8 November 1939, DFA 10/A/72).

7 Evidence of his knowing cynicism can be seen, for example, in Stuart's condemnation of appeals to help "suffering foreigners" in the aftermath of *Reichskristallnacht*, arguing that Ireland had better take care of its own poor and destitute before criticizing foreign governments and aiding foreign citizens (cf. Stuart's letters to the editor of *The Irish Times* from 13 and 19 December 1938). Almost a decade before Brendan Barrington made these letters public in his introduction to *The Wartime Broadcasts of Francis Stuart*, Natterstad revised his earlier sympathetic portrayal of Stuart, realizing that all his writing was marked by hostility towards modernity, pluralism and democracy. This ultimately seemed so irresponsible and thoughtless on Stuart's side that it beggared belief that his decision to go to Nazi Germany had not been motivated also by shared ideological beliefs (Natterstad 1991).

8 Stuart's broadcasting activities included not only weekly broadcasts for the *Irland Redaktion* in the Foreign Office's Cultural Policy Department – Radio Division (Kult-R) between March 1942 and spring 1944 (collected in Barrington 2000), but also broadcasts for Goebbels's *Reichsrund-*

of the war, which he celebrates over and over in his diaries as beneficial to his development as a writer, providing him with the time and financial security he needed to read, reflect and write as never before:

> What a blessing it is that these days in the midst of war I have so much time for my own life and its needs. There will never have been a better time for a writer than after this war – for a writer with a new way of life to reveal. I am glad that I got through the apprentice stage of my books before the war [...] [the following is crossed out:] – after will be the time when there will be a few people eager to read something about eternal truth. (diary entry on 15 May 1944)[9]

Shortly after writing these comments, Stuart once again demonstrated that realism rather than naivety guided his decisions when, following the Allied invasion of France, he made up his mind to leave the sinking ship and return with his precious gift of "eternal truth" to the safety of Ireland. Unfortunately for him, his suggestion of attempting another gun-smuggling mission to Ireland was of no interest whatsoever to his contacts in the German military at this stage.[10] This only left one option, that is, to try and return the way he had once entered Germany, via Switzerland. However, the fact that his involvement with the Nazis had be-

---

funkgesellschaft in 1940 and 1941 (cf. Keane 2004, Dickel 1983: 183, Roth 2001) and occasional contributions to the black propaganda stations of *Büro Concordia* (cf. Bergmeier and Lotz 1997: 208). In 1940, Stuart gave the German spy Hermann Görtz his wife's address in Laragh as a safe house. That year, Stuart also enlisted for a later abandoned plan of smuggling provisions for the IRA on board a fishing boat in order to pave the way for the arrival in Ireland of prominent IRA members Seán Russell and Frank Ryan (cf. O'Donoghue 1997: 51). He likewise assisted the *Abwehr* in its endeavour to recruit Irish prisoners for an Irish Brigade (cf. Carter 1977: 124–125). And while Frank Ryan was hospitalized in Charité Hospital in Berlin in January 1943, Stuart took it upon himself to act as Ryan's deputy, arranging to meet the German agent Haller in order to persuade German Intelligence to help the escaped Northern Irish IRA commander, Hugh McAteer, come to Germany (Stuart's diary note for 23 January 1943).

9 Stuart deposited seventeen diaries with the library of Ulster University, Coleraine. An additional notebook contains reflections on books Stuart was reading during the war and on his own work in progress at the time. The diaries cover the period from March 1942 until August 1977. The oldest extant notebook is missing several pages and it remains unclear why and when Stuart destroyed his diaries from 1940 and 1941. His claim after the war that he did so in the wake of hearing of the arrest of Libertas von Schulze-Boysen, whom he had once met at a party (Stuart 1976: 10), is likely untrue given that he noted, on 1 September 1947, his shock at having found out only the previous day that the Schulze-Boysens had been arrested and executed in autumn 1942 as leaders of a loose network the Gestapo labelled *Rote Kapelle*.

10 Although Stuart is cagey in his diary entry for 30 June 1944 about the nature of the plan he proposed to his contact man, fellow Irishman William Murphy, the latter stated to MI5 after his capture in early 1945 that Stuart had suggested participating in a smuggling mission to Ireland (Barrington 2000: 35).

come an embarrassment for the Irish government as the war went on meant that his successive applications for a passport renewal were all refused on the grounds that he had "forfeited any claim to [Irish] diplomatic protection by unneutral and disloyal activity" (telegram from Assistant Secretary Frederick Boland to Berlin Legation from 25 May 1944, DFA 10/A/72). Displaying foresight rather than a masochistic wish to share the lot of the losers, Stuart and his German lover, his former student Gertrude Meissner, fled to Munich, where he applied for a visa to the Swiss authorities in November 1944. His attempt in April 1945 to cross the Swiss border with Gertrude in tow using his expired Irish passport was unsuccessful, and after some weeks spent roaming around the area close to the border, the couple found a room in the Austrian town of Dornbirn. In August 1945, Stuart travelled to Paris on a repatriation programme for Displaced Persons, but, failing to obtain an Irish visa for Gertrude, he returned to her in the French-occupied zone in November. They were arrested by the French Allied authorities on 21 November on charges of having recruited agents for the *Abwehr* and broadcast propaganda for the Germans (cf. letter from French Foreign Ministry to Irish Legation in Paris from 18 July 1946, DFA 10/A/72).[11]

From the time of his imprisonment onwards, Stuart worked to change the perception of his political persona. In letters soliciting the help of a prewar admirer of his work, the British military historian Sir Basil Liddell-Hart, Stuart professed his opposition to the Nazis and downplayed the nature of his broadcasts:

> As you know that I was deeply opposed to Nazism and State tyranny, and my experiences during the war only deepened this opposition. It is not the hardship of detention here, but also the hold up in that work which I believe I could now do is hard to bear with patience... (quoted in Elborn 1990: 189)

---

11 At the behest of Iseult and of her brother, the later Foreign Minister Seán MacBride, External Affairs instructed the Irish Legation in Paris to make cautious enquiries with the French Foreign Office as to Stuart's whereabouts in May 1946. When they learned of his imprisonment, the Irish Envoy was instructed to offer the usual degree of diplomatic protection, legal and human aid (cf. telegram from 31 May 1946, DFA 10/A/72). The recent decision made by the British authorities not to prosecute another Irish citizen who had broadcast for the Germans, Charles Edward Bowlby, led Frederick Boland, Secretary of the Department of External Affairs, to believe that they would not prosecute Stuart either. He assumed that the French, therefore, had no reason to hold him any longer and that it was safe for Ireland to negotiate Stuart's release without risking any embarrassment (cf. his letter to Envoy Seán Murphy at the Paris Legation from 13 June 1946, DFA 10/A/72). Boland's assumption proved correct, for on 11 July the Envoy informed him that the French Foreign Office had indicated that, "unless the enquiries set on foot in the first week of June disclose[d] some grave charges, they [would] support the view that Stuart should be handed over to us." Two days later, Stuart and Gertrude were released.

What is striking about the novels Stuart wrote after his release from prison in the French-occupied zone – *The Pillar of Cloud*, *Redemption* and *The Flowering Cross*[12] – is that in all three he subordinates the assessment of the war to the celebration of a new way of life emerging from the rubble of a defeated Germany. Reflections on the causes of the disastrous events of the previous years are displaced, and the war is instead interpreted as foundational and inspirational for an "imagined community" that rarely extends beyond the constellation of a male and a female outsider, thinly disguised prototypes of the way Stuart and Gertrude portrayed themselves, and were portrayed, after the war: as "survivors" (O'Keeffe 1972: 7) and "victims" (O'Toole 1996: 77).[13]

A factor that must have helped them considerably to assert such claims was Gertrude's successful application for Polish Displaced Person status which, once certified by the Allied authorities, was tantamount to "an international recognition of victimization" (Cohen 2011: 37). By happy coincidence, non-Jewish Polish refugees were exempt from filling in UNRRA's rigorous eligibility questionnaires, as it was sufficient for them to raise "'valid objections' to returning to Communist Poland" (Cohen 2011: 37). Gertrude's birth in Danzig must have been considered sufficient to class her as Polish, despite the fact that her Kashubian parents had opted for German nationality after the First World War, a fact that would later allow their daughter, as a gifted student from a low-income family with several children, to avail of a state benefit for her university education at Berlin University between winter 1939 and spring 1944 (cf. M. Stuart 1984: 19).[14]

---

12 Stuart completed his first postwar novel, *The Pillar of Fire*, in 1946, but it was rejected by Victor Gollancz (see diary note for 29 June 1947) and several other British and American publishers. The manuscript appears to have been lost when Stuart moved from Paris to London in 1951.

13 Encouraged by the critical acclaim he received for *Black List, Section H*, Stuart even began to refer to himself as a "ghetto writer" (Stuart in interview with Eavan Boland 1973: 12). The kinship this language establishes is made explicit when Stuart – following the *pro forma* attempt to distinguish *his* use of the word ("It used to be a racial term, but we're not talking about that now") – then insinuates that he was imprisoned in "a camp" (E. Boland 1973: 12) after the war. In an ironic twist, Eavan Boland's article thus perpetuates her father's earlier wishful thinking, for on learning of Stuart's arrival at the Irish Legation in Paris, Secretary Boland had dared to hope that Stuart's unhindered travel might be proof that he had "rehabilitated himself" in the eyes of the Allies by having been interned towards the end of the war in a Nazi concentration camp (letter from F. Boland to Paris Legation from 16 August 1945, National Archives, DFA 10/A/72). His colleague in Paris disabused him of this idea, reporting back on 28 August that Stuart had stated he had not suffered imprisonment under the Germans.

14 The Meissners' complete acculturation is visible not only in the names of their daughters Traute, Gretel and Gertrude (a fourth daughter's name remains unmentioned in Gertrude's 1984 memoir, *Manna in the Morning*, which she published under her later name, Madeleine Stuart) but also in the German surname they adopted. Although Gertrude does not mention

Stuart's determination to position himself at the right end of the perpetrator-victim binary was a necessary precondition to shedding individual responsibility, regaining credibility with his audience abroad, and to eventually leaving occupied Germany behind. His nascent awareness of the kind of self-image he needed to promote was helped by outside prompting. His friend Ethel Mannin, for example, alerted him to the problem his "attitude during the war" might pose for British publishers, including his prewar publisher Victor Gollancz (diary entry 12 February 1947).[15] A day after receiving her letter, Stuart noted in his diary that he

> beg[a]n to see that the very difficulties that have arisen out of my attitude during the war have gone to help in my development as a writer. Not only were the war years in Germany necessary to me as a writer but the worse years of the aftermath too and the time of imprisonment. [...] It is not until last autumn in *The Pillar of Fire* that I began to write fairly surely in my own way and well. I shall never regress from that. (13 February 1947)

Taking its cue from an outline he had devised on 14 November 1944 in Munich, *The Pillar of Fire* was the account, in novel form, of his life during the war, illustrating his development, describing the civilian sufferings "in the place where these were worst", but mostly focusing on his personal struggle "without which", Stuart anticipated, "the end of the war would bring no peace" (cf. diary entry for 30 June 1947). However, his failure to find a publisher for the book indirectly showed him how much he still had to adjust his story of his time in Nazi Germany in order to make his narrative palatable. According to an unenthusiastic letter from the agent Curtis Brown, whom Mannin had charged with finding a publisher in the United States, the problem was that "the hero, although being in Germany during the war, [...] had little feeling about the

---

it, her father's name had been Niedzialkowski and her mother's maiden name Majewska (cf. letter and additional notes from 2 April 1947 from Fr. B. Kolenza to State Secretary Boland, DFA 10/A/72).

15 Stuart's supporters have often presented the fact that Victor Gollancz continued to publish Stuart's novels for a time after the war as implicit proof of the writer's integrity (e.g. McCormack 1982: vi; M. Stuart 1984: 85, Dermot Bolger in Donovan 1996: 12). Stuart himself liked to point out that the director in charge of the Southern Illinois University Press, which published *Black List* after it had been rejected by several English publishers, was also a Jew (cf. Stuart 1980: 14). This line of argument disregards, as Barrington points out, Gollancz's idiosyncratic views and business interests (cf. 2000: 55). It is also infected with the kind of "Jew-consciousness" (Piette 1995: 195) that has the effect of confirming the very racial prejudice of which it purports to be free. Besides, it is equally possible to use this kind of logic against Stuart, since the German-Jewish publicist and art critic Bruno Werner, a victim of the Nazis and father of sculptor Imogen Stuart, appears to have held the father-in-law of his daughter in very low esteem (cf. Scally 2009: B7).

war and being on the contrary concerned with his own personal life!" (quoted by Stuart in his entry for 7 October 1947). Although Stuart's reaction was defiant – "If that is the main fault they can find then I am really glad to know it. My God, what incredible people!" – his next books would avoid not only the setting of Germany during the war years, thus fending off questions about his characters' personal implication in the Nazis' policies, but also ensure that his concerns with inner growth were counterbalanced by a narrative incorporating strategic references to the suffering and victimization inflicted by the Nazis.

One such superficial marker of victimhood can be seen in Stuart's decision to change the name of his heroine in *The Pillar of Cloud* from the German "Klara" to the French "Céline" (diary note 26 June 1947), and then to the Polish "Halka Mayersky", a surname deceptively close to the maiden name of Gertrude's mother, Majewska (cf. Father Kolenza's letter, DFA 10/A/72). The hero of *The Pillar of Cloud*, "neutral" Irish poet Dominic Malone, while eager to be scapegoated on the general principle of suffering, insists he had never, "in any way, in thought or deed, sided with the captors against the captives, with the executioners against the victims" (*POC* 46). To bolster this claim, Stuart portrays Dominic's wartime visits to Irish prisoners-of-war as subversive acts rather than collaboration with the Nazis. Indeed, Dominic's contempt for the Nazis eventually earns him a month in a German concentration camp, although his alleged modesty about his own suffering prevents him from giving any details about this episode to the French authorities who suspect he may have been used merely as an *agent provocateur* (*POC* 44).

The expedient name change and new slant on his own actions during the war were not the only interventions Stuart made to set his hero and heroine as much as possible apart from their postwar German environment. He also resorts to national stereotypes in defining the various German, French, and Eastern European characters in the novel, portraying in particular the German ones in a more negative light than in any of his later texts:

> To Dominic Germans were still largely a mystery, although he had lived for years among them. They lacked any art of living. Not only now after their defeat, but they had always lacked it. They moved through life heavily, carefully, with the inexhaustible patience of beasts of burden plodding over stony paths. [...] The men were like little internal-combustion machines, grinding away, grinding away, and if you didn't look out, Dominic felt, you would be caught by them and ground out too. (*POC* 120)

Here, Stuart borrows and elaborates on the terms of literary antecedents who had shaped an image of Germans as inferior creatures. These terms, which can be found, for example, in mid nineteenth-century Irish travel accounts by Anglo-Irish writers such as Charles Lever (writing under the pseudonym Lorrequer) or Lady Wilde, were devised to create difference, flatter the onlooker's self-image, and ultimately justify their reluctance to admit commonalities with an other perceived as a graceless, cattle-like breed that "lacked any art of living".[16] Stuart's recourse to negative stereotypes, however, inadvertently undermines Dominic's claim of wanting to be on the side of the losers (cf. *POC* 46) as well as his proclaimed affinity with plain, simple people rather than with more sophisticated contemporaries he meets, such as the French anarchists Captain Renier and Dr. Varreau. The friction this causes is most apparent in the ambiguous portrayal of Frau Arnheim, a character modelled on *Mutti* ("Mummy"), a woman in whose kitchen Stuart experienced hospitality and generosity in the first half of 1947 and who gradually disappeared from his notebook's radar towards the end of that year. In the novel, Frau Arnheim evolves from motherly saviour in Dominic's time of need at the beginning of the story into an object of his scorn because of her reluctance to sanction the promiscuity of male-female relations after the war, which Dominic hails as the real liberation (cf. *POC* 195–196). All three characters, Halka, Dominic and Frau Arnheim, are indicative of Stuart's eagerness to establish a hierarchy of victimhood in his novel, but they remain examples of trading in clichés and half-truths, because Stuart remained incapable of writing them outside convenient tropes.

Stuart's failure to adequately respond to the other is most disappointing in his inability to create a female character in his postwar works that would live up to his avowed ambition of creating "the new woman". During his preparations for his last lecture at Berlin University on Shakespeare's vision of women like Miranda, Perdita and Marina in his Romance plays, Stuart resolved to attempt something similar in his next work (diary entry on, 2 August 1944). He took inspiration from John Middleton Murry's 1936 study of Shakespeare in which he proposed that the last plays, *Pericles*, *The Winter's Tale* and *The Tempest*, were marked by a "sensation",

> belong[ing] to a man to whom the re-birth of spring has become intolerably tender; a kind of sweet anguish and heart-break, a delicate and despaired-of miracle. "Daffodils that come before the swallow dares." What tenderness of hope is in that single phrase! [...] There is a connection, I am certain, between this ache of longing for spring, this exquisite celebration of the miracle of re-born Nature, which is uttered in so much of the loveliest verse of the latest plays, and the imagination of a re-born humanity, which takes substance in the

16 As Joachim Fischer explains, the revolution of 1848 and the creation of the second German Empire in 1871 sufficiently alarmed even former champions of a romantic image of Germany, such as Lever and Lady Wilde, to express views which made it clear that Germans were not considered in any way comparable or their equals (cf. Fischer 2000: 542).

> rare women, "tender as infancy and grace", who are the chief figures of their drama. (Murry 1954 [1936]: 385–386)

The plot Stuart began to develop as early as summer 1944 in light of these reflections and of his own "longing for spring" sketches out a formula he would use in *The Pillar of Cloud* and again in later novels. It can be summarized as follows: Irish poet Louis undergoes a process of contrition and spiritual growth in wartime Germany following the death of his fiancée, which he caused after learning of her unfaithfulness. He receives spiritual guidance from an older, wiser and mystically endowed woman (christened Dominica in a diary entry from May 1945). Dominica has reached her higher level of being through a suitably thorny path of her own which includes both extremes of brothel and convent. Although the two grow close, Dominica instructs the Irishman to prove his new sincerity by renouncing his own feelings for her and marrying instead a young pregnant girl, Lilo Freytag, in order to help her. Being simple, conventional and a little stupid, as Halka's consumptive younger sister Lisette would be in *The Pillar of Cloud*, Lilo holds no attraction for Louis, but Dominica declares his sacrifice a necessary step in his quest for truth. In a note added on 11 May 1945, however, Stuart decided against separating Louis and Dominica (which entailed killing off Lilo and later Lisette), making their "new love", rather than self-abnegation, the focus of his novel.

Stuart later supplemented his vision of Dominica with features of long-suffering inspired by Gaspara Stampa in Rilke's *Duino Elegies* (cf. diary entry on 13 February 1945) and by Sonia in Dostoyevsky's *Crime and Punishment* (cf. diary entry on 4 October 1945). Dominica was to be capable of similar endurance, cognisant of the depths of love and the human condition, and able to explain to man the mysteries of a "hidden God", of "love", of "inner life", and the consequences of man's disobedience (diary entry for Feast of the Holy Trinity in May 1945). Although this spells the promise of a strong female figure teaching the male protagonist how to live and love in ways that run counter to his inclinations and intuitions, Dominica's incarnation as Halka Mayersky in *The Pillar of Cloud* is troubling, not because she seems as vulnerable and defenceless as Miranda or Perdita, but because she equates "new woman" with the "abused woman" and creates a simplistic dichotomy between the natural, spiritual, foreign and the cold, rational, Irish or English female templates that populate the pages of Stuart's postwar novels. She is a fallen woman, violated by men and state institutions, physically marked, alone, suspicious of language to the point where she prefers to stay mute, inferior by such standards as her social background and lack of education, or, more insidiously, her Eastern European origin. Halka, who defied bourgeois conventions during the war and prostituted herself so she and her sister Lisette could survive after the death of both parents, risked hiding a Jew, for which she, somewhat incredibly, spent only a few months in a concentration camp. Despite these facts, her otherness is primarily conveyed through the superficial markers of her origin and sex, unwittingly confirming the racialist and gender tenets of the regime in whose shadow Stuart conceived of her. Halka makes the essential flaw in Stuart's conception of the "new woman" all the more apparent – that woman as the other has a limited value when she is subsumed under projections of male fantasies, blossoming when needed and withering when alone.[17]

In contrast to her, Dominic maintains his physical attractiveness and integrity throughout the war, although he is not immune to hunger, cold and skin diseases contracted in filthy prison cells. Like his creator, he confidently expresses himself through language and writing under the admiring gaze of his lover. He hails from a part of the Western world that, it is made clear, has been spared the depredation of continental Europe, and he retains a supportive social network at home, if only to repudiate it. His one lack or shortcoming by comparison to Halka is perhaps that of not having suffered as much during the war. Yet the spiritual ideal of "communion" towards which Stuart's characters strive is a state of oneness that at once redeems Dominic and fades out the specificities of history and victimhood in the glare of Halka's "unfathomable innocence that was on the earth to set over against the monstrous evil" (*POC* 223). With that, her courage and difference are absorbed by the protagonist and questions of causality and guilt become obstacles in the way of spiritual healing.

If historical experience is cancelled out by unreal aspirations to innocence, Shakespeare's ideal of "simple human love" (Murry 1954: 409) is transmuted in *The Pillar of Cloud* into a shield against the outside world by an egoistic couple. Instead of giving her an opportunity to work through her trauma, Stuart bestows on Halka the ability to forgive anything and to absolve from complicity or responsibility. Even when confronted with her former concentration camp warder in Dominic's prison cell, her response seems to conform to Dominic's needs rath-

17 McCartney points out the redemptive power Stuart places in the hands of his violated female characters, giving the victim the ability to forgive and thus to rise above the aggressor (cf. 2000: 146). However, the very fact that their degradation and exploitation is subordinated to the higher end of facilitating the transformation of the male character is symptomatic of their insignificance as other or as an individual in their own right in Stuart's novels. Since there is never any question of Stuart's "new woman" exercising the power McCartney believes she has been endowed with in a manner that does not serve the hero's development – for example, by going her separate way, as Stuart had originally envisioned for Dominica – it seems misleading to speak of her as "in control" (McCartney 2000: 146).

er than her own: her fear propels her into Dominic's arms, and while her erstwhile torturer huddles in one corner of the cell, fearful of his trial, Halka and Dominic make love for the first time in the opposite corner (*POC* 221). This act, Stuart would like the reader to believe, gives her strength to defy common expectation, forgive the Nazi, and refuse to incriminate him in front of the French authorities (*POC* 222). To Dominic, her behaviour confirms her innocence and purity of heart, but to the reader, it reveals a callous, eroticized engagement with the trauma suffered by the victims of the Nazis in concentration camps. It also shows the insidious competition Stuart establishes between Halka's near saintliness and Jewish claims of victimhood, as, prior to finding out that the witness summoned against the Nazi was Halka, Dominic had assumed that it was "just" a Jew. Hence, he had reassured the fellow prisoner that "[t]hey won't condemn you on the evidence of the Jew alone" (*POC* 214). While there is no question in Dominic's mind that Halka's testimony alone would have led to the warder's conviction – for him, the scars left by the Nazi's whip between her breasts are strategically placed stigmata that seek their rival – his attitude towards a potential Jewish witness is instinctively suspicious and pejorative.

It is in light of the above – Stuart's submission to stereotypes, his misrepresentation of the Second World War and misappropriation of the experience of its victims, resulting in his contrived valorization of suffering – that one can see that his proposed communion between self and other in *The Pillar of Cloud* serves to fill a void with the myth of a new beginning. It bears all the risks of distortion and conflation between personal experiences and those of the historical victims which scholars like Dominick LaCapra, Avishai Margalit, Aleida Assmann or Helmut Schmitz have so emphatically warned against in the context of writing in the force field of the Holocaust.[18] For all his aspirations to "truth", Stuart did not change his preconceptions during or after the war, making it impossible to conceive of a new image of the female, Jewish or German other. Tellingly, he considered the end of the war the time to harvest and incorporate "the fruit that [he] knew must grow out of the great suffering of the war", as Stuart wrote after translating a poem by Benjamin Fondane who perished in Auschwitz (cf. diary

18 See, for example, their respective responses to Binjamin Wilkomirski's *faux mémoire*, *Bruchstücke* (*Fragments*), published in German in 1995 and in English the following year (LaCapra 2001: 32–34, Margalit 2002: 173–174, Assmann 2007: 145–146). Schmitz's criticism specifically refers to a trend in contemporary German literature to represent the "immediacy" of traumatic war events experienced by individuals as a more "authentic" perspective, unimpaired by current values and knowledge (Schmitz 2007b: 198). Such representations, he argues, sacrifice critical insight to a sentimental, empathetic identification based on the realization of one's own ethical fallibility (cf. 2007b: 200).

note, 21 April 1947).[19] By de-particularizing Jewish suffering and replacing it with his own Christian code of suffering, Stuart deliberately obscured both the concrete historico-political context in which Halka and Dominic meet and the issue of individual responsibility. His levelling of distinctions resembles the reaction of German contemporaries,[20] but Stuart's instrumentalization of Holocaust memory as well as his misguided search for a foundation myth in the rubble of destroyed cities has escaped the same level of critical scrutiny. This ultimately allowed Stuart to overwrite his own record in successive works, culminating in *Black List, Section H* (1971) which convinced not only the publisher Timothy O'Keeffe, who had rejected an earlier version, that the narrative "ha[d] been progressively demythologised over the years so that it now reads much more like straightforward autobiography" (O'Keeffe 1972: 7). Ironically, in effacing the outlines of personal experience and blending it with the narrative models that had entered the frames of collective and cultural memory, Stuart created "autobiographical fiction" which itself spawned many hard-to-eradicate myths about his motivation to be in Nazi Germany and the extent of his collaboration.

2 Excavating the past, shaping the future: Hugo Hamilton's *The Last Shot*

Hamilton's affinity with Stuart appears to have been fuelled in part by a desire to recruit an ally against a mainstream Irish society he felt had arrogantly appropriated the high moral stance of the victors and had pigeonholed him in the "guil-

---

19 Stuart worked his translation of "Préface en prose" from *L'Exode* into *The Pillar of Cloud*, where the poem serves the Romanian refugee Petrov as proof that "all those who had suffered and died were martyrs from whose wounds and blood the seed of a new wisdom and love would be nourished" (*POC* 170). The passage is also quoted in Stuart's afterword to the 1994 edition of the novel where, despite Fondane's insistence in his poem that his suffering was not universal but specifically that of persecuted Jews, Stuart conflates their experience with his own. Showing his lifelong insensitivity to, and competition with, the victims of the Holocaust, Stuart adopts Fondane's words and experience as his own: "I have known disasters at dawn (in some moods I imagine I have seldom known anything else), and cattle trucks (or police cars) and the sight of humiliation" (*POC* 233).

20 See, for example, Hans-Joachim Hahn's contribution to *A Nation of Victims?*, an essay in which he discusses the postwar works of filmmaker Wolfgang Staudte (*Die Mörder sind unter uns*) and writer Wolfgang Weyrauch, both of whom leave the specifics of the Nazis' policy of extermination unmentioned in order to explore suffering without reference to the persecution of Jews or to other causes that led to the Germans' rude awakening after the war (2007: 51–70).

ty" category.[21] In the essay *Unschuldsgefühle* (2003), as well as in his best-selling memoirs, *The Speckled People* (2003) and *The Sailor in the Wardrobe* (2006), he relates how he suffered from being identified as "German" by his peers in 1950s and 1960s Dublin.[22] Struggling with a persistent feeling of being "tainted" through his German mother, and suffering under his domineering Irish father, Hamilton went to live in West Berlin in the mid-1970s. At first, he tried to blend in and even applied for German nationality in the hope that he might be eligible for a student grant which would have enabled him to enrol in university, an opportunity denied to him at home by his miserly father (see last chapter in *The Sailor in the Wardrobe* and National Library of Ireland MS48,124/6: "The Ruins of Identity"). However, soon after his application was rejected because his mother held no valid German passport at the time, Hamilton discovered that in Germany he could be, in his and everybody else's eyes, as typically Irish as he liked (McCann 2008: 18).

Free at last to pursue his own self-invention at will, he responded by speaking less fluent German than he was able to and by starting to play the tin whistle, much to his German flatmates' blue-eyed admiration and to his elderly German neighbour's annoyance (*The Sailor in the Wardrobe* 259–260, also MS 48,124/6: "The Ruins of Identity"). Playing up to a romantically distorted notion of Irishness accorded him social prestige with those of his German peers who, he instinctively recognized, envied him the refuge of an 'easy' Irish identity and who were aggressively trying to remake themselves in a new image by rejecting their parents and relocating to the victims' side.[23] Their example informs the views and lives of the German characters that people Hamilton's books and

---

21 Hamilton repeated his expression of admiration for Stuart's work in his contribution to the special Francis Stuart issue of *Writing Ulster*, published in 1996. In this piece, he recounts a recent negative experience with the producers of an Irish arts programme who had interviewed him about his collection of short stories, *Dublin where the Palm Trees Grow*, and had later fused his comments about having been called names like "Eichmann, Hitler, Goebbels" with images of a ranting *Führer*, "goose-stepping Germans and bulging Swastika banners" (Hamilton 1996: 74–75) in their broadcast. Understandably, he felt indignant about the ease with which the story of his personal victimization was subsumed under staple images of German aggression. Seeing in Stuart another innocent victim of Irish ignorance and arrogance, Hamilton later wrote an emotional letter to *The Irish Times* in December 1997 in which he accused critics of Stuart's appointment as *Saoi* of Aosdána, the affiliation of Irish artists, of "us[ing] the Holocaust like a moral board game in order to score points" (Hamilton 1997a).

22 *Birthmark*, the original title of *Unschuldsgefühle*, makes Hamilton's sense of being marked even more explicit.

23 See, for example, Hamilton's descriptions in *Unschuldsgefühle* of his German co-workers Boris and Norbert, both of whom resent their filial ties to the perpetrator generation (Hamilton 2003: 56–58).

proved inspirational for the author on a personal level: first, by rejecting his father's stamp and changing his first name from Seán to Hugo[24] and his surname from "Ó hUrmoltaigh" back to the anglicized name his grandfather had used. Most importantly, however, its effects can be traced in his writing, which unfailingly explores the individual's attempts to mine and to rewrite their given narrative, using all the cultural tools and discourses at their disposal to fashion their identity.

In his second novel, *The Last Shot*, Hamilton charts the attempt of an unnamed first-person narrator to research the forgotten story behind "the last shot" fired in the Second World War and, with that, the story of his own roots. Hamilton's motivation behind this excavation of the past is personal and slightly foreshadows a trend in German literature which, as Stuart Taberner explains, explores the imaginative return to lost or forgotten places in the former GDR and Eastern Europe in order to undertake the reappraisal of family histories (2009: 214). How personal the journey in *The Last Shot* is, can be deduced from the book's dedication, "*für* Irmgard", the author's German mother. Irmgard's own last diary notes provide the coordinates of Hamilton's novel. Her brief description of her retreat from the advancing Soviet army at the end of the war (see her "Curriculum Vitae" in MS 48, 168/6) is the foundation on which Hamilton builds Bertha Sommer's fictive return from the Czech front in the company of *Wehrmacht* officer Franz Kern in May 1945.[25] Franz Kern was in reality named Hans Kern and Irmgard's second name was Berta, after her own mother who had been a trained singer (MS 48, 168/6: 17 February 1979), as was the mother of the fictional character (*LS* 40).

Like Hamilton, the narrator happens upon his mother's diaries after her death and is eager to complete her own inconclusive attempts to account for herself towards the end of her life. Like Hamilton, the narrator carries out research into his mother's past in West Germany and the Czech Republic against the backdrop of the collapse of the Eastern Bloc. Returning from Prague in November 1989, Hamilton would ask in *The Irish Times* just one day after the German-German border fell, "what is this freedom the silent herds want so badly?" (1989: 6). Reactivating the same British-influenced nineteenth-century stereotype of Ger-

24 Hugo was his confirmation name (Bourke 2009: 180), in all likelihood chosen in honour of not just the saint, but also of Hugo Liedmann, the retired Dean of Neuss whom the family had met a month prior to his first communion on a visit to Germany in May 1960 and who subsequently wrote the occasional letter to the young boy (MS 48, 168/3: March 1961).

25 The six diaries of Irmgard Ó hUrmoltaigh, née Kaiser, are part of the Hugo Hamilton Papers at the National Library in Dublin. My translation of these diaries into English has been deposited with the original German notebooks.

mans as a cattle-like breed, which Stuart employed in *The Pillar of Cloud* with the same air of superiority, Hamilton's answer prefigures his critique of contemporary German society in *The Last Shot:* namely that the mythical term "freedom" boiled down to purely materialistic desires in most East Germans, in which they resembled their Western contemporaries.

The secret in Bertha's narrative – her rape – which her son seeks to discover is likewise inspired by Irmgard's life, for as Hamilton would disclose in his memoir *The Speckled People*, his mother had been abused by her boss during the war. However, in contrast to Irmgard, who was raped by a Nazi, Bertha's rape happens at the hands of two famished, vengeful Polish forced labourers she meets on the trek home. Yet even this plot twist is based on Irmgard's mention in her diary of having been forced to be careful on her journey in order to avoid "returning Poles" who "were relieving all Germans of their possessions: watches, wedding rings, cameras etc." (MS 48/168, 6). By reconfiguring this fragment from his mother's past differently in the novel, Hamilton gives Franz's killing of the two Poles a further level of meaning that reflects on crime and punishment and the long haunting of those who participated in the Second World War as well as of their descendants. Through fiction, Hamilton thus both gives form to his mother's memories and shapes them anew, recognizing the importance of a continuous engagement with history by bringing the past forth in a new interpretation that is pertinent to his understanding of the present.

The juxtaposition of past and present in *The Last Shot* emphasizes the repetition of history by mirroring events which occurred in Bertha's life in May 1945 in the life of her son decades later. Even the geographical frame of the novel enforces the vision of recurring, interconnected places and events, as the trajectories travelled by Bertha and Franz from Louny to Nuremberg run almost parallel to those repeatedly travelled by the narrator between Düsseldorf and Münster, where his lover Anke and her husband Jürgen, the narrator's best friend, live. His train journeys between all four coordinates, in turn, connect them to delineate the historical territory at the centre of Europe which the narrator feels compelled to excavate (*LS* 120).

The probes into the past are presented in a chronological narrative, steadily advancing in step with Bertha and Franz's slow, dogged progress towards a clearly defined goal: home, or, alternatively, "new homes [...] where they could find peace" (*LS* 96). In this respect, the narrative conforms to the pattern established in postwar writing like *The Pillar of Cloud*, yet it introduces a hidden, subjective dimension into the parameters of mediated memories through the "private, arcane names" (*LS* 13). Bertha assigns to the events she witnesses and the places she passes through on her return. "The morning of the end of the Reich" or "the hill of the last time looking back" (*LS* 13) are later supplemented with "the Timber-yard of silent breath" (*LS* 47), by which she remembers an execution, and "[t]he Breakfast of Lovers" (*LS* 100). Her rape puts a sudden end to Bertha's wish to recollect the events and places of the war. It is her conspicuous silence which prompts her son to become active, almost half a century later, in order to gather and arrange more "facts" from the local archives in Louny and the eye-witness account of Franz Kern. His efforts reveal the extent to which the smooth narrative of his mother's past is, really, a mediated artefact, built from various sources and subject to the narrator's interpretation. As a result, hindsight creeps into Bertha's story, both explicitly, in the use of knowing references to Theresienstadt and to the fate of the Sudeten Germans after the war, and implicitly, in the use of anachronistic language, such as the reference to a peaceful demonstration in Louny in 1945 as "a premature but unsuccessful attempt at the velvet approach" (*LS* 8).

The narrator's attempt to make sense of the present, by contrast, defies the deceptive stability he imposes on the past. Mobility, personal and historical, propels him forward and at the same time seems to arrest his judgement. His determination to grapple with "the nightmare of history", while television is showing "[t]he ecstasy of history" (*LS* 85), is founded on the belief that the connection to the past must be renewed in order for the present generation to comprehend where it is heading. By indicating how events that seem disconnected are part of a larger pattern, the narrator's message replicates a dynamic understanding of cultural memory. Accordingly, "[a] new era for Germany" (*LS* 127) should not begin by repeating the mistakes of the past, that is, by figuratively "burning" (*LS* 21) every trace of it, as Bertha was ordered to do before the German army started its retreat in 1945. Her five failed attempts to write down the traumatic memory of her rape (*LS* 157) are emblematic of both the taboos revolving around rape and, more generally, the alleged taboos surrounding German wartime suffering.[26] This latter set of taboos, it is implied, her son – an American[27] – can break by gathering witness accounts, testimonies, every scrap of documentation

26 As the title of Schmitz's introduction to *A Nation of Victims?* suggests, the growing body of works over the past two decades discussing German wartime suffering marks the return of a subject that had not really been a taboo after the war (Schmitz 2007a). Hamilton's mother Irmgard, for example, carefully listed in her diaries all the material losses and hardships she and her relatives experienced during the war and in its aftermath.

27 The nameless American narrator serves as an alter ego for Hamilton who knew that his mother had been offered work with the family of an American Colonel in Vermont just after the war. In *The Sailor in the Wardrobe*, he would vainly wonder "how different our lives would have been" (Hamilton 2006: 84) had she accepted.

that enables later generations to access the past and empathize with the experience of those who lived before.

The specific taboo of talking about rape is broken in the present by Anke, who confides in the narrator that her husband Jürgen raped her in a wish "to act like a complete stranger" (*LS* 147–148). This couple, like all German couples in Hamilton's works, are from educated, liberal backgrounds, have travelled the world, and, ironically, have learned how to "mourn" thanks to reading Heinrich Böll (*LS* 24), that eminent critic of a cold, self-involved bourgeoisie in postwar Germany. Yet for all their efforts to detach themselves from their roots, the narrator's outsider perspective on German society on the eve of unification suggests that taboos persist in the hostility towards foreigners, the reluctance to share with those who have less, and in an intolerant attitude towards the disabled, old and slow. Alex, the son of Jürgen and Anke who suffers from Down syndrome and leukaemia, is presented by his father, a gynaecologist, as a "refugee" of history, born after the Third Reich, where he would have been considered "unworthy of life" (*LS* 80), but before it became possible to detect his condition in the womb. His existence is prefigured in the novel by that of a Czech boy with Down syndrome mentioned in Bertha's story as a hopeful proof of "an overt act of revolution" (*LS* 7) in which life triumphed despite the Nazis' deadly policies. In the Federal Republic, by contrast, the attitude of Alex's parents shifts from feeling proud of having "saved his life" (*LS* 80) to contemplating a mercy killing for their terminally ill child. Although their decision is taken in the interest of sparing Alex further pain, it is also apparent that his disability and illness present a curtailment of their "personal freedom", the only "real" freedom worth having according to Jürgen (*LS* 71).

In this, they are no different to Halka and Dominic, except that in the case of the latter, the obstacle to their being together – Halka's consumptive sister Lisette – dies shortly after Dominic nobly marries her in order to be able to take her to Ireland for treatment. There is no such easy resolution in *The Last Shot*, where Jürgen actively administers euthanasia. Alex's death and the subsequent cremation are evoked in terms that conjure up memories of the Holocaust, of defenceless victims and of perpetrators acting with clinical precision. The representation of Alex's funeral as an event at the limit brings the narrative close to a halt, as the narrator feels paralysed in the face of "a set of images or symbols" (*LS* 168) which all signify one thing only: death. Vaguely realizing that his bereaved friends, Jürgen and Anke, are almost flirting with a formulaic iconography of catastrophe, the narrator concludes that the time has come for him to leave.

Were the novel to close like this, the message about German society's engagement with its history would be very bleak indeed. Instead, Hamilton chooses to dip back into the past in the final chapter to conclude on an uplifting note. Although Bertha's and Franz's budding love ends when they reach Nuremberg, where Franz returns to his wife, Bertha's sudden independence – "the sound of her own footsteps and the thought of her own home" (*LS* 175) – gives her a sense of freedom which Stuart denied his postwar heroine Halka. The German song she sings to entertain the GIs who offer her a lift encapsulates both the experience of departure from home and the hope of returning there. Her son's own return, decades later, allows him to review his mother's story in light of his position in the present at the intersection of different historical events, yet the conclusions he draws from the past – and those left for readers to draw by the author's juxtaposition of the two narratives – do not quite penetrate to the core. Instead of realizing the potential of this kind of memory fiction as a new dimension between historiography and commemoration, ideally enabling "a more nuanced remembering and thus a less suspect form of forgetting" (Taberner 2009: 217), Hamilton prefers to extrapolate from the narrator's individual act of excavation to present the empathetic recollection of the suffering experienced by dead ancestors as the necessary condition to cure the "unhappiness" assailing their descendants. That the final encounter between the narrator and Franz Kern, the father figure he so longed to meet, should culminate in the following diagnosis of German society's shortcomings seems completely anticlimactic, if not beside the point: "Today we take luck for granted, here in Germany, and we don't know what to do with it. I have never seen Germans so unhappy. This business with the Wall and German unity is not going to make them happier either." (*LS* 157)

Old Kern's indignant dismissal of contemporary events is reminiscent of Stuart's flattening of historical causality and distinctions for the sake of superimposing his own moral lessons. More pressing than a cultural critique lamenting the Germans' inability to be happy would be the recognition that the way out of aporia and melancholic self-involvement requires the kind of work the Mitscherlichs called for in *The Inability to Mourn* – a critical engagement with, and mourning of, the past in which Bertha and Franz had a stake, and not a romantic reconstruction of the circumstances behind "the last shot" as a site providing solace in the present or validating a critique of consumerist contemporary society.

Whereas Stuart's method of adjusting the conflict of the Second World War and his self-image to correspond to his need for a temporal and geographical 'elsewhere' never openly acknowledged his interventions, letting his audience believe instead – and coming to believe himself – in his fiction as fact, Hamilton self-consciously problematizes the issues involved in excavating and narrating the past in order to derive meaning in the present. He is firmly embedded in a dialogue which recognizes that the path into the future is not predicated on the retreat into an exclusive community of outsiders, as Stuart postulated. However, although Hamilton's narratives acknowledge the importance of an open, ongoing and individual engagement with elsewhere, its people and history, they sometimes also fall prey to limiting identity constructions and interpretations of the past. As such, it is interesting to note that Hamilton adopted the same critical perspective he had applied to the conflicts in postwar German society in *The Last Shot* in his later articles decrying the cultural and spiritual decline in Celtic Tiger Ireland (see his introduction to *The Pillar of Cloud* as well as Hamilton 1997b, 1998a and 1998b). Addressing the deficiencies in his native home gradually resulted in a re-purposing of Germany as elsewhere: in articles such as "I'm a Kraut, and I'm Proud" (an article from 2004, first published in German and later in English as "The Loneliness of Being German"), "After a 60-Year Guilt Trip You Can Mention the War" (2005), and "Rescuing Germans from their Past" (2005), Hamilton now liked to present Germany as a model for its engagement with the past, for its pluralism, and for its openness to other cultures and countries. These new appropriations of 'elsewhere' themselves need to be examined as part of memory's travels from Ireland to Germany and back.

Works cited

Anderson, Benedict (1991) *Imagined Communities. Reflections on the Origin and Spread of Nationalism* (London et al.: Verso).

Assmann, Aleida (2007 [2006]) *Der lange Schatten der Vergangenheit: Erinnerungskultur und Geschichtspolitik* (Bonn: Bundeszentrale für politische Bildung).

Assmann, Aleida (1999) *Erinnerungsräume: Formen und Wandlungen des kulturellen Gedächtnisses* (Munich: C.H. Beck).

Barrington, Brendan (ed.) (2000) *The Wartime Broadcasts of Francis Stuart: 1942–1944* (Dublin: Lilliput Press).

Bergmeier, Horst J. P., and Rainer E. Lotz (1997) *Hitler's Airwaves: The Inside Story of Nazi Radio Broadcasting and Propaganda Swing* (New Haven, CT and London: Yale UP).

Boland, Eavan (1973) "Francis Stuart: The Ghetto Novelist", *The Irish Times*, 30 March, 12.

Bourke, Eoin (2009) "The Birthmark of Germanness: Hugo Hamilton and the Question of Belonging", in *Creative Influences: Selected Irish-German Biographies*, ed. Joachim Fischer and Gisela Holfter (Trier: Wissenschaftlicher Verlag), 179–193.

Burke, Peter (1989) "History as Social Memory", in *Memory: History, Culture and the Mind*, ed. Thomas Butler (Oxford and New York: Basil Blackwell), 97–113.

Carter, Carolle J. (1977) *The Shamrock and the Swastika* (Palo Alto: Pacific Book Publishers).

Cohen, Gerard Daniel (2011) *In War's Wake: Europe's Displaced Persons in the Postwar Order* (Oxford, New York: Oxford UP).

Dickel, Horst (1983) *Die deutsche Außenpolitik und die irische Frage von 1932–1944* (Wiesbaden: Franz Steiner).

Donovan, Katie (1996) "In Honour of Francis Stuart?", *The Irish Times*, 10 October, 12.
Eagleton, Terry (1998) *Crazy John and the Bishop and Other Essays on Irish Culture* (Cork: Cork UP).
Elborn, Geoffrey (1990) *Francis Stuart: A Life* (Dublin: Raven Arts Press).
Erll, Astrid (2011) "Travelling Memory", *Parallax* 17.4, 4–18.
Erll, Astrid, and Ann Rigney (eds.) (2006) "Literature and the Production of Cultural Memory: Introduction", *European Journal of English Studies* 10.2, 111–115.
Fischer, Joachim (2000) "Nineteenth-Century Irish Travellers to Germany and Their Tales", in *Das schwierige neunzehnte Jahrhundert: Germanistische Tagung zum 65. Geburtstag von Eda Sagarra im August 1998*, ed. Jürgen Barkhoff et al. (Tübingen: Max Niemeyer), 535–546.
Foster, R. F. (2007) *Luck and the Irish: A Brief History of Change, 1970–2000* (London: Allen Lane).
Gefter Wondrich, Roberta (2000) "Exilic Returns: Self and History outside Ireland in Recent Irish Fiction", *Irish University Review* 30, 1–16.
Hahn, Hans-Joachim (2007) "'Die, von denen man erzählt hat, dass sie die kleinen Kinder schlachten': Deutsche Leiderfahrung und Bilder von Juden in der deutschen Kultur nach 1945: Zu einigen Texten Wolfgang Weyrauchs", in *A Nation of Victims? Representations of German Wartime Suffering from 1945 to the Present*, ed. Helmut Schmitz (Amsterdam and New York: Rodopi), 51–70.
Hallberg, Edith, and Christoph Houswitschka (2005) "'The Silent Grey Foreign Country which Called Itself Germany' in the Novels of Hugo Hamilton, Nicholas Shakespeare and Others", in *Literary Views on Post-Wall Europe: Essays in Honour of Uwe Böker*, ed. Christoph Houswitschka et al. (Trier: Wissenschaftlicher Verlag), 83–98.
Hamilton, Hugo (2007) *Die redselige Insel: Irisches Tagebuch*, transl. Henning Ahrens (Munich: Luchterhand).
Hamilton, Hugo (2006) *The Sailor in the Wardrobe* (London: Fourth Estate).
Hamilton, Hugo (2006 [1991]) *The Last Shot* (London et al.: Harper Perennial).
Hamilton, Hugo (2005) "After a 60-Year Guilt Trip, You Can Mention the War", *The Irish Times*, 30 April, http://www.ireland.com/newspaper/newsfeatures/2005/0430/pf3420134830WK30HITLER1.html (accessed 20 March 2016).
Hamilton, Hugo (2005) "Rescuing Germans from Their Past", *The Irish Times*, 15 October, 7.
Hamilton, Hugo (2004) "I'm a Kraut, and I'm Proud", transl. Wieland Freund, *Die Welt*, 12 June, http://www.welt.de/data/2004/06/12/289835.html (accessed 26 May 2016).
Hamilton, Hugo (2004) "The Loneliness of Being German", *The Guardian*, 7 September, http://www.guardian.co.uk/print/0"5009679-103532,00.html (accessed 20 March 2006).
Hamilton, Hugo (2003) *The Speckled People* (London: Fourth Estate).
Hamilton, Hugo (2003) *Unschuldsgefühle*, transl. Hans-Christian Oeser (Berlin: DAAD Künstlerprogramm).
Hamilton, Hugo (1998a) "Thanks for Nothing, Michael Flatley", *The Guardian*, 6 September, http://www.guardian.co.uk/World_Report/Story/0,,324845,00.html (accessed 24 July 2006).
Hamilton, Hugo (1998b) "Hostages to Fortune", *The Irish Times*, 8 August, B1.
Hamilton, Hugo (1997a) "Letter to the Editor: Francis Stuart", *The Irish Times*, 4 December, http://www.ireland.com/newspaper/letters/1997/1204/pfarchive.97120400105.html (accessed 24 July 2006).

Hamilton, Hugo (1997b) "Morals in Our Pockets", *The Irish Times*, 6 May, http://www.ireland.com/newspaper/features/1997/0506/pfarchive.97050600070.html (accessed 20 March 2006).

Hamilton, Hugo (1996) "Understanding Francis Stuart", *Writing Ulster* 4, 69–76.

Hamilton, Hugo (1989) "What Is this Freedom the Silent Herds Want so Badly?", *The Irish Times*, 10 November, 6.

Hugo Hamilton Papers, National Library of Ireland, Dublin: MS 48,106–MS48, 170.

Keane, Damien (2004) "Francis Stuart to America, 9 June 1940", *The Dublin Review* 14, 53–56.

Kiely, Kevin (2007) *Francis Stuart: Artist and Outcast* (Dublin: The Liffey Press).

LaCapra, Dominick (2001) *Writing History, Writing Trauma* (Baltimore: Johns Hopkins UP).

Larkin, Philip (1985 [1964]) *The Whitsun Weddings* (London: Faber & Faber).

Lorrequer, Harry (1847) "A Chapter of Continental Gossip: A German Grand Ducal City", *The Dublin University Magazine* 29.173, 541–543.

Margalit, Avishai (2002) *The Ethics of Memory* (Cambridge, MA and London: Harvard UP).

Maxton, Hugh (1970) "Francis Stuart: The Long-Distance Winner", *Hibernia*, 28 August, 20.

McCann, Fiona (2008) "A Question of Identity", *The Irish Times*, 6 June, 18.

McCartney, Anne (2000) *Francis Stuart: Face to Face: A Critical Study* (Belfast: Institute of Irish Studies, Queen's University).

McCormack, W. J. (1982) "Black List Past", *The Connacht Tribune*, 26 November, VI.

Mitscherlich, Alexander, and Margarete Mitscherlich (1975) *The Inability to Mourn: Principles of Collective Behavior*, transl. Beverley R. Placzek (New York: Grove Press).

Murry, John Middleton (1954 [1936]) *Shakespeare* (London: Jonathan Cape).

Natterstad, J. H. (1991) "Locke's Swoon: Francis Stuart and the Politics of Despair", *Eire-Ireland: A Journal of Irish Studies* 26.4, 58–75.

Natterstad, J. H. (1974) *Francis Stuart* (Lewisburg and London: Bucknell University Press & Associated UP).

Nora, Pierre (2002) "The Reasons for the Current Upsurge in Memory", *Tr@nsit* online, http://www.iwm.at/index.php?option=com_content&task=view&id=285&Itemid=463 (accessed 1 December 2008).

O'Donoghue, David (1998) *Hitler's Irish Voices: The Story of German Radio's Wartime Irish Service* (Belfast: Beyond the Pale).

O'Keeffe, Timothy (1972) "A Survivor", *The Guardian*, 24 August, 7.

O'Toole, Fintan (1996) "The Survivor", *Writing Ulster* 4, 77–84.

Pageaux, Daniel-Henri (1988) "Image/Imaginaire", in *Europa und das nationale Selbstverständnis: Imagologische Probleme in Literatur, Kunst und Kultur des 19. und 20. Jahrhunderts*, ed. Hugo Dyserinck and Karl Ulrich Syndram (Bonn: Bouvier), 367–379.

Piette, Adam (1995) *Imagination at War: British Fiction and Poetry*, 1939–1945 (London: Papermac).

Rigney, Ann (2012) "Transforming Memory and the European Project", *New Literary History* 43.4, 607–628.

Rigney, Ann (2005) "Plenitude, Scarcity and the Circulation of Cultural Memory", *Journal of European Studies* 35, 11–28.

Roth, Andreas (2001) "Francis Stuart's Broadcasts from Germany, 1942–44: Some New Evidence", *Irish Historical Studies* 32.127, 408–422.

Rothberg, Michael (2009) *Multidirectional Memory: Remembering the Holocaust in the Age of Decolonization* (Stanford, CA: Stanford UP).

Scally, Derek (2007) "A Homeland Sculpted by Love", *The Irish Times*, 22 August, B7.

Schmitz, Helmut (2007a) "Introduction: The Return of Wartime Suffering in Contemporary German Memory Culture, Literature and Film", in *A Nation of Victims? Representations of German Wartime Suffering from 1945 to the Present*, ed. Helmut Schmitz (Amsterdam and New York: Rodopi), 1–30.

Schmitz, Helmut (2007b) "Historicism, Sentimentality and the Problem of Empathy: Uwe Timm's Am Beispiel meines Bruders in the Context of Recent Representations of German Suffering", in *A Nation of Victims? Representations of German Wartime Suffering from 1945 to the Present*, ed. Helmut Schmitz (Amsterdam and New York: Rodopi), 197–222.

Stuart, Francis (1994 [1948]) The Pillar of Cloud, introd. Hugo Hamilton (Dublin: New Island Books).

Stuart, Francis (1980) "A Season in Hell: Review of All Quiet on the Western Front by Erich Maria Remarque", *Hibernia*, 31 January, 14.

Stuart, Francis (1976) "Extracts from a Berlin Diary Kept Intermittently between 1940 and 1944", *The Irish Times*, 29 January, 10.

Stuart, Francis (1971) *Black List, Section H* (Carbondale and Edwardsville: Southern Illinois UP).

Stuart, Francis (1958) *Victors and Vanquished* (London: Victor Gollancz).

Stuart, Francis (1950) *The Flowering Cross* (London: Victor Gollancz).

Stuart, Francis (1938) "Letter to the Editor: Suffering Foreigners", *The Irish Times*, 13 December, 8.

Stuart, Francis (1938) "Letter to the Editor: 'Suffering Foreigners'", *The Irish Times*, 19 December, 10.

Francis Stuart Papers, Ulster University, Coleraine: 17 diaries (March 1942–August 1977) and 1 notebook labelled "Notes on Shakespeare and Other Subjects, August 1942".

National Archives of Ireland, Dublin: DFA 10/A/72 and DFA 10/A/72/A.

Stuart, Madeleine (1984) *Manna in the Morning: A Memoir, 1940–1958* (Dublin and Buckinghamshire: The Raven Arts Press & Colin Smythe).

Taberner, Stuart (2009) "Memory-Work in Recent German Novels: What (if Any) Limits Remain on Empathy with the 'German Experience' of the Second World War?", in *Germans as Victims in the Literary Fiction of the Berlin Republic*, ed. Stuart Taberner and Karina Berger (Rochester, NY: Camden House), 205–218.

Webb, W. L. (1975) "Hunting Stuart", *The Guardian*, 16 April, 10.

Wilde, Lady Jane Francesca (2009 [1884]) *Driftwood from Scandinavia* (Charleston, SC: BiblioLife).

Johanna-Charlotte Horst (LMU Munich)

Damaged Words and Closed Houses: Everyday World and Memory Narratives in Georges Perec

> La littérature concentrationnaire [...]. Nous restions étrangers à ce monde; c'était un fragment d'histoire qui s'était déroulé au-delà de nous. (Perec 1992: 93)[1]

> Écrire par fragments: les fragments sont alors des pierres sur le pourtour du cercle: je m'étale en rond: tout mon petit univers en miette; au centre quoi? (Barthes 1975: 96)[2]

As a young man, Georges Perec was involved in the current controversy over Marxism and the related question of how to change society. In this political debate, his crucial interest had always been aesthetics. He and some comrades planned a periodical under the telling title *La Ligne générale*.[3] Following Georg Lukács' footsteps, they wanted to formulate a Marxist aesthetic as a new program of artistic production. For Lukács, literature's task was – broadly speaking – to envision a regained unity in the presently fragmented world of capitalism.[4] Along these lines literature appears as potentially capable of trans-

1 "We remained strangers to that world, which was a fragment of history that had unfolded somewhere beyond us." (Perec 1997: 252)

2 "To write by fragments: the fragments are then so many stones on the perimeter of a circle: I spread myself around: my whole little universe in crumbs; at the center, what?" (Barthes 1977: 92–93).

3 This title is taken from a film of the Soviet film-maker Sergei Eisenstein who is famous for his montage technique.

4 See Lukács 2009: 65: "Die Komposition des Romans ist ein paradoxes Verschmelzen heterogener und diskreter Bestandteile zu einer immer wieder gekündigten Organik [...] das letzte vereinende Prinzip [muss] die inhaltlich deutlich gewordene Ethik der schöpferischen Subjektivität sein." / "The composition of the novel is the paradoxical fusion of heterogeneous and discrete components into an organic whole which is then abolished over and over again [...] the ultimate unifying principle therefore has to be the ethic of creative subjectivity, an ethic which the content reveals." (Lukács 1971a: 84) In order to understand how closely Perec followed Lukács, see Perec 1992: 51: "Ce que nous appelons œuvre d'art, ce n'est justement pas cette création sans racines qu'est l'œuvre esthétiste, c'est au contraire, l'expression la plus totale des réalités concrètes: si la littérature crée une œuvre d'art, c'est parce qu'elle ordonne le monde, c'est parce qu'elle le fait apparaître dans sa cohérence, c'est parce qu'elle le dévoile, au-delà de son anar-

https://doi.org/10.1515/9783110556858-009

forming the existing social structures. Perec, however, soon became aware that Lukács' ideas on socialist literature tended to turn it into an instrument of ideology.[5] The two major categories of Lukács' thought – history and society – nevertheless kept his attention. What the following discussion intends to demonstrate is how these categories were reshaped in Perec's writing and, accordingly, how literary realism evolved in a different way than initially projected. To put it briefly, two conceptual shifts can be specified. On the one hand, there is the Marxist idea of history turning into a memory project with an increasing focus on the problem of trauma; on the other hand, the preoccupation with the socialist concept of society leads to an inquiry into what Perec calls the "infra-ordinaire." So the master narrative[6] of class struggle – bringing history and social structures into a necessary historical process culminating in communism[7] – comes into conflict with the two emerging narratives of memory and everyday life in Perec's writing. What actively 'makes' sense is thus transformed through a dynamic of dispersal into a narrative that explicitly does not 'make' sense any more.

1 From Second Nature to the "infra-ordinaire"

In the 1960s, Perec cooperated with a group of sociologists who strove to push Marxism forward by investigating the structures of everyday life.[8] This group in-

chie quotidienne, en intégrant et en dépassant les contingences qui en forment la trame immédiate, dans sa nécessité et dans son mouvement." / "What we call a work of art is precisely not the kind of creation that has no roots as in the case of *l'art pour l'art*. On the contrary, it is the most total expression of concrete realities: if literature creates a work of art it does so because it puts the world in order, because it shows it in its coherence. Leaving the world's daily anarchy behind, it reveals the world's necessity and development by integrating and exceeding the contingencies that form the world's immediate appearance." (Translation mine, J.-C. H.)

5 For Perec's occupation with Marxist theories, see the first chapter in James 2009: 39–65 with the telling title "Mastering History".

6 Lyotard coined the term "master narrative" or "grand narrative" in *Les Problèmes du savoir dans les sociétés industrielles les plus développées*, a work originally commissioned by the *Conseil des universités du Québec*, later republished under the title *La Condition postmoderne*. For the notion of the Marxist concept of history as a master narrative see in particular the fourth chapter (Lyotard 1979: 16–19).

7 Wolff 2011: "Marx sees the historical process as proceeding through a necessary series of modes of production, characterized by class struggle, culminating in communism."

8 Lefebvre 1994: 142–143: "So etabliert sich in der modernen Welt eine Alltäglichkeit, die den Erfordernissen gesellschaftlicher Praxis im Schein entspricht; tatsächlich hat sie sich aber 'von oben' installiert, durch die ausgeweitete Kapazität der Produktion und des Marktes. Sie geht ein in den Markt, in den verallgemeinerten Austausch und damit in ein ungeheures System

cluded distinguished figures such as Henri Lefebvre, Michel de Certeau, Roland Barthes, Paul Virilio, and Jean Duvignaud. The two latter edited a journal called *Cause Commune* to which Perec now and then contributed articles. Their primary goal was bringing to light invisible social structures that nonetheless, or rather by virtue of their hidden status, play an oppressing role. Such structures have been referred to as "Second Nature", a term originally coined by Aristotle and revived in particular by Lukács and Theodor W. Adorno. Since Lukács' *Die Verdinglichung und das Bewußtsein des Proletariats* looms large in Perec's early essays, the notion of Second Nature, as it is specifically developed here, seems to have crucially influenced the young writer.

Throughout Lukács' work the concept is invested with multifarious meanings. In *Die Theorie des Romans,* the Second Nature makes up a "world of convention" (Lukács 1971a: 62) in which social structures have become naturalized to an extent that they can no longer be questioned. Lukács strives to demonstrate their profound lack of legitimation: they are something "frail",[9] fundamentally detached from the "interiority of the soul" (Lukács 1971a: 62).[10] In *Die Verdingli-*

---

von Äquivalenzen, die allen Austausch regulieren [...]. [E]ine Revolution im Marxschen Sinne verändert das Leben, sie formt die Alltäglichkeit um." / "So in the modern world a daily routine has been established that corresponds with the requirements of social practice. But in fact it was installed 'from the top' by the extended capacities of production and market. The quotidian goes down in the market, in the generalized exchange and thereby in the enormous system of equivalences regulating every exchange [...]. A revolution in Marxist sense changes the life, it transforms the daily routine." (Translation mine, J.-C. H.) For this debate, see also Gardiner 2006.

9 See Lukács 2009: 48: "Wo keine Ziele unmittelbar gegeben sind, verlieren die Gebilde, die die Seele bei ihrer Menschwerdung als Schauplatz und Substrat ihrer Tätigkeit unter den Menschen vorfindet, ihr evidentes Wurzeln in überpersönlichen, seinsollenden Notwendigkeiten; sie sind etwas einfach Seiendes, vielleicht Machtvolles, vielleicht Morsches, tragen aber weder die Weihe des Absoluten an sich, noch sind sie die naturhaften Behälter für die überströmende Innerlichkeit der Seele. Sie bilden die Welt der Konventionen [...]." And furthermore: „Sie [the world of convention] ist eine zweite Natur; wie die erste nur als Inbegriff von erkannten, sinnesfremden Notwendigkeiten bestimmbar und deshalb in ihrer wirklichen Substanz unerfaßbar und unerkennbar." / "Where no aims are directly given, the structures which the soul, in the process of *becoming-man*, encounters as the arena and sub-stratum of its activity among men lose their obvious roots in supra-personal ideal necessities; they are simply existent, perhaps powerful, perhaps frail, but they neither carry the consecration of the absolute within them nor are they the natural containers for the overflowing interiority of the soul. They form the world of convention [...]." And furthermore: "It [the world of convention] is a second nature, and, like nature, it is determinable only as the embodiment of recognised but senseless necessities and therefore it is incomprehensible, unknowable in its real substance." (Lukács 1971a: 62)

10 Adorno 1997: 356 comments in "Die Idee der Naturgeschichte" the passage about the Second Nature in Lukács' *Theorie des Romans* as follows: „Diese Tatsache der Welt der Konventionen, wie sie geschichtlich produziert ist, der uns fremd gewordenen Dinge, die nicht entziffert werden *chung und das Bewußtsein des Proletariats*, however, Second Nature becomes a synonym for reification which, in turn, conceptualizes a core feature of capitalism. When social relationships are dictated by the "reign of commodity", every process is rendered alienated and reified.[11] Lukács (1971b: 87) describes capitalist society as "a world of objects and relations between things" whose laws can be recognized yet nonetheless persist as "invisible forces that generate their own power" (Lukács 1971b: 87). Under such conditions individuals are torn or fragmented within themselves.[12] As David Frisby (1983: 78) emphasizes, the question is, "how 'true life' and structures of meaning can emerge out of this chaos". Lukács' late *Ästhetik* suggests an answer by entrusting art with a decisive potential: conceived as emancipation from the particular, it is endowed with the power to enable an experience of wholeness that has become impossible in the alienated quotidian under capitalism.[13]

Inspired by other thinkers, in particular by Roland Barthes and his *Mythologies*,[14] Perec later gradually revised Lukács' ideas about history, society, and the role of art.[15] Yet the notion of fragmented reality retained its profound impact

können, aber als Chiffern [sic] begegnen, das ist der Ausgang der Problematik, die ich hier vortrage." / "This fact of a world of convention as it is historically produced, this world of estranged things that cannot be decoded but encounters us as ciphers, is the starting point of the question with which I am concerned here." (Adorno 1984: 118)

11 Lukács 1978: 174: "Denn nur als Universalkategorie des gesamten gesellschaftlichen Seins ist die Ware in ihrer unverfälschten Wesensart begreifbar. Erst in diesem Zusammenhang gewinnt die durch das Warenverhältnis entstandene Verdinglichung eine entscheidende Bedeutung sowohl für die objektive Entwicklung der Gesellschaft wie für das Verhalten der Menschen zu ihr; für das Unterworfenwerden ihres Bewußtseins den Formen, in denen sich diese Verdinglichung ausdrückt; für die Versuche, diesen Prozeß zu begreifen oder sich gegen seine verheerenden Wirkungen aufzulehnen, sich von dieser Knechtschaft unter der so entstandenen zweiten Natur zu befreien." / "The commodity can only be understood in its undistorted essence when it becomes the universal category of society as a whole. Only in this context does the reification produced by commodity relations assume decisive importance both for the objective evolution of society and for the stance adopted by men towards it. Only then does the commodity become crucial for the subjugation of men's consciousness to the forms in which this reification finds expression and for their attempts to comprehend the process or to rebel against its disastrous effects and liberate themselves from servitude to the 'second nature' created." (Lukács 1971b: 86)

12 Lukács 1978: 178: "Zweitens bedeutet dieses Zerreißen des Objektes der Produktion notwendig zugleich das Zerreißen seines Subjektes." / "In the second place, this fragmentation of the object of production necessarily entails the fragmentation of its subject." (Lukács 1971b: 89)

13 Lukács 1972: 36.

14 Barthes' *Mythologies* can also be considered as an approach to everyday-life that reshapes the idea of Second Nature as conceived in Marxist thought.

15 Also see Bellos 1993: 146.

specifying a representational demand for that layer of reality Perec wishes to make visible. In a short, but very dense text entitled "Approches de quoi?" Perec (1989: 11) writes:

> Interroger l'habituel. Mais justement, nous y sommes habitués. Nous ne l'interrogeons pas, il ne nous interroge pas, il semble ne pas faire problème, nous le vivons sans y penser, comme s'il ne véhiculait ni question ni réponse, comme s'il n'était porteur d'aucune information. Ce n'est même plus du conditionnement, c'est de l'anesthésie. Nous dormons notre vie d'un sommeil sans rêves.[16]

The imperative to question the habitual implies something symptomatically overseen that needs to be challenged. Perec thus articulates his distrust towards a layer of the real that is hidden not only from public discourse, but even from collective consciousness. What appears natural, and therefore unchangeable, has a profound effect on social life precisely by virtue of this quality. According to Perec, the scandal does not lie in epic events, but actually in this unarticulated layer of reality. The change of attitudes to put in practice is hence not towards the social contradictions at large and towards overcoming them, but the very banal. One must awake from the 'anesthetic sleep' in order to see what is excluded from the official system of representation. Returning to Lukács, we could rephrase this demand in Marxist terms: social transformation will require the shaping of a consciousness for those reiterating patterns that constitute the actual social scandal. However, in contrast to Lukács' view that art must envision society in its regained wholeness, Perec calls for texts giving a detailed description of exactly that stratum of reality that naturally eludes any totality. As Michael Sheringham (2006: 268) underscores, for Perec the inquiry into the everyday is always linked to the question of practice.[17] A socially committed impetus is thus still articulated. "Approches de quoi?" states further:

> Ce qui se passe vraiment, ce que nous vivons, le reste, tout le reste, où est-il? Ce qui se passe chaque jour et qui revient chaque jour, le banal, le quotidien, l'évident, le commun,

16 "To question the habitual. But that's just it, we're habituated to it. We don't question it, it doesn't question us, it doesn't seem to pose a problem, we live it without thinking, as if it carried within it neither questions nor answers, as if it weren't the bearer of any information. This is no longer even conditioning, it's anaesthesia." (Perec 1997: 206)

17 Sheringham writes: "But if we use Perec's own criterion – of trying to make the everyday visible, not as an objective reality but as something in which we participate – we can see the stylistic and enunciative richness of TELP [that is *Tentative d'épuisement d'un lieu parisien*, J.-C. H.] as an indication of the sheer multiplicity of the channels with which we engage with the world."

> l'ordinaire, l'infra-ordinaire, le bruit de fond, l'habituel, comment en rendre compte, comment l'interroger, comment le décrire? (Perec 1989: 11)[18]

The rest is excluded from the official regime of representation so that it is hard to find words for its description.[19] In order to grasp this concealed layer of life, new words or a new order of representation need to be invented: hence the logical necessity for the neologism "infra-ordinaire". In this regard Perec's agenda appears to resist blind submission under an always already existing order of discourse which – keeping up with Lukács – could be reasonably identified as part of Second Nature.

Instead of sketching a better society as Lukács requested, Perec shows how to observe one's surroundings without prejudice, i.e. without knowing in advance what one will see.[20] This mode of observation draws attention to a variety of singular details: e.g. a bus stopping and driving on, a man getting into a car.[21] There is one text with the revealing heading "Tentative d'inventaire des aliments liquides et solides que j'ai ingurgités au cours de l'année mil neuf cent soixante-quatorze". It is simply a ten-page list of the meals Perec had within the indicated period of time.[22] There is no story, no plot, nothing that might be called an event. Figuratively spoken, the elements of the real are scattered all over. Even if there is a narrative order, it is none that would align or systematize the observed into a storyline. Thus, the projected "prise sur le concret"[23] (Perec 1992: 28) is realized differently from its conceptualization in the footsteps of Lukács. To avoid the predicament of either ending up in total chaos or being dominated by constraints, Perec sets up a rule: the radical refusal to plot or any "meaningful" narrative. The resulting "description minutieuse"[24] (Perec 1990: 90) juxtaposes singular elements without dissolving them into a coherent whole. Like this, it becomes im-

---

18 "What's really going on, what we're experiencing, the rest, all the rest, where is it? How should we take account of, question, describe what happens every day and recurs every day: the banal, the quotidian, the obvious, the common, the ordinary, the infra-ordinary, the background noise, the habitual?" (Perec 1997: 205–206.)

19 For the political dimension of language, see Rancière 2000 and Marcuse 1964: 69–92. From a different point of view, this is also discussed in Stockhammer 2014.

20 A relation between the quotidian and a specific way of impartial seeing came up in phenomenological debates as well; see e.g. Waldenfels 2005: 34–55.

21 Sheringham 2006: 261–271.

22 The English title is "Attempt at an Inventory of the Liquid and Solid Foodstuffs Ingurgitated by Me in the Course of the Year Nineteen Hundred and Seventy-Four". Perec praises the art of enumeration in *Penser/Classer* (Perec 2003: 164–165).

23 "grip of the concrete" (Translation mine, J.-C. H.).

24 "meticulous description" (Perec 1997: 128).

possible to extract an ideology from the "infra-ordinaire". On the contrary, it insists on a radical resistance to ideology. With Adorno (1977: 179) one could argue that here exists a modality of artistic practice "whose mere guise is enough to disrupt the whole system of the rigid coordinates that govern authoritarian personalities." Political protest is thus realized on the level of formal criteria capable to resist the rhetorical machines of official politics.

2 Closed houses

An essay from 1963 programmatically entitled "Robert Antelme ou la vérité de la littérature" uses the word "quotidienneté" in connection with the debate on the representation of trauma. Here Perec states:

> [S]on refus du gigantesque et de l'apocalyptique participe, en fait, d'une volonté délibérée, qui gouverne l'organisation de son récit jusque dans ses moindres détails, et lui donne sa coloration spécifique: une simplicité, une quotidienneté jusqu'alors inconnue, et qui va jusqu'à *trahir* la 'réalité' afin de l'exprimer d'une manière plus efficace, afin de nous interdire de la trouver 'insupportable'. (Perec 1992: 94)[25]

An efficient method to address the reality of an entirely indescribable situation thus consists in foregrounding not the most horrible things, but precisely the contrary: that is, the very banality of the quotidian. Here Perec's ideas on memory, writing history, and trauma intertwine with what he will later term the "infra-ordinaire", and what this passage still calls "everydayness". The most horrible event eludes our grasp to the extent that its very obscurity is what makes it unbearable. The only possible approach is hence to explain the banal and thereby showing indirectly the traumatic by its effects on everyday life.

"La Rue Vilin" – one of the texts collected in the volume *Infra-ordinaire* – again brings together the issues of the everyday and memory. This short piece comprises six passages written from 1969 to 1975 describing the same street in Paris. [26] Before his parents' deaths during World War II – his father was killed in battle, his mother probably gassed in a concentration camp – Perec lived

25 "But his rejection of anything outsized or apocalyptic is in fact part of a determination that governs the organization of his story right down to its smallest details, and which gives it its specific colouring: a desire for simplicity, for a previously unknown everydayness, which goes so far as to *betray* the 'realité' in order to express it more effectively and prevent us from finding it 'unbearable'." (Perec 1997: 252)

26 The extensive but not completed memory project *Lieux* is based on a similar procedure of writing (Lejeune, 1991: passim).

with them in this street. As the text progresses, the passages become shorter. The final one condenses into the single graffiti line saying: "TRAVAIL=TORTURE." Confirming the poetological demands in "Approches de quoi?", the text consists of detailed observations. Meticulous descriptions are provided of the houses in the Rue Vilin, of other streets crossing, of encounters with residents, of changes taking place during a day as well as on the longer-term scale of two years. There is no discernable plot to structure the different visits apart from the sequence of house numbers on the route which the observer takes each time. Only minor changes in their repetitive order or skipping a house may qualify as narrative events. At first glance, the observer does nothing but 'neutrally' pin down what comes into his view. Yet, in fact, a second layer of meaning is traceable, encoded in elements that function as keys to the underlying memory project: the street's shape is described as an "SS"; a resident mistakes Perec for a policeman in charge of the local riots between Jews and Arabs: "Alors, vous venez nous détruire?" (Perec 1989: 24)[27]; old houses that are still intact are called "survivances".[28] The narrator's involvement is thus somehow concealed in the text.

Once, he talks to a woman who remembers his mother. While the episode is related in exactly the same tone as everything else, the reader assumes that the narrator does not reveal his identity to his interlocutor. Likewise, the house where he lived as a child is specified only in brackets although this is the most significant piece of information in the text. Obviously, the point of taking this walk is an encounter with this house, yet it is being merely passed by and never really explored. Fear of approaching the past too closely, or of a barrier that cannot be crossed, seems to take hold. In a mnemonic reading, the houses can be understood as rhetorical *loci*, as fixed elements containing what shall be remembered.[29] However, they somehow cannot be entered; they appear cryptic to the narrator.[30] A place where the past is kept, but to which there is no access fails in its mnemonic function. Standing in front of his childhood home without finding any entrance, the narrator epitomizes the impossibility of memory. Perec mentions again and again certain "terrains vagues" (Perec 1989: 31)[31] in the street, spaces that are empty without any kind of public function. In contrast to the houses' closed doors these totally empty places symbolize even more radically the irrevocable loss of access to the past. He knows where to go and does come across some hints at his childhood, but there is no impetus for an actual

27 "So you've come to knock us down?" (Perec 1997: 213)
28 "survivors" (Perec 1997: 214).
29 See Barthes 1970 for the debate on mnemonic rhetoric.
30 See Derrida 1986 for the debate on the cryptic in memory.
31 "waste ground" (Perec 1997: 217).

reconstruction of the events that took place precisely here. The section from 1972 is very laconic on this aspect. It merely says: "24 toujours intact" (Perec 1989: 29).[32] The question remains what "intact" refers to. It may either state the survival of the house itself, or also indicate its function as an intact closure keeping the visitor out.

Next to these loci, writing is another paradigmatic means of memory. There are several mentions of graffiti and billboards informing about various businesses and services. Among other things, in the Rue Vilin one can see advertisements for cafés and restaurants, for a paint store, a furniture dealer, a hairdresser's. Some of these no longer correspond to the actual shops around, but are mere props: this is, for example, the case with some letters written on the wall of house number 24 that read "COIFFURE DAMES". The reference is to a business Perec's mother once ran here: "encore des traces de peinture et au-dessus, pas encore tout à fait effacée, l'inscription COIFFURE DAMES" (Perec 1989: 18).[33] These letters on the wall are quoted at two other instances in the text, first in majuscules and then uncapitalized. The latter reads: "Au 24: coiffure dames (pas le magasin, seulement la trace de l'enseigne peinte sur le mur)" (Perec 1989: 27).[34] This inscription is not yet entirely faded; it is still readable, although the letters are gradually vanishing from the wall. In other cases, whole words are missing. All the writing encountered in the street appears, in one way or another, damaged. Following the logic of this interpretation, the narrator's memory is both as inaccessible as the closed houses are and as damaged as the inscriptions. The *loci* and the words, i. e. the houses and the letters on them, are "wounded" to an extent that they can no longer produce speaking images from the past.

3 Impossible narrations

The original meaning of trauma is 'wound' in the sense that something is no longer complete – a 'whole' – but rendered broken or damaged. Trauma means fragmentation, so that a traumatic experience can never be fully grasped: there are only disparate memories repeatedly coming back to consciousness without ever assembling into a coherent picture. For trauma, there exists no system of representation, or more precisely: it can be defined as a crack in a specific representa-

32 "No 24, still intact" (Perec 1997: 216).

33 "still traces of paintwork and above, not yet completely rubbed away, the inscription LADIES' HAIRDRESSER" (Perec 1997: 210).

34 "At No 24, ladies' hairdresser (not the shop, simply traces of the shop sign painted on the wall)." (Perec 1997: 215)

tional system. By analogy to a physical wound tearing organic tissue, one could capture the traumatic experience as working fundamental rupture into the texture of a text or a narrative.[35] With recourse to Freud, we can say that trauma disrupts narrative order: it is a shock manifesting itself as suspension of the usual spatio-temporal setting. If we are to remember things, they need to be put into some sort of order.[36]

In an interview about his practice of memory, Perec explains that one needs to circumnavigate things in order to get them placed.[37] What resists any order or syntax are the times he had shared with his parents. His father's death becomes tangible only after the encounter with the small piece of earth where the corpse was buried. With his mother, there is not even a grave to visit. Her disappearance can thus only be shown, but not told: in the section where the autobiographic novel would have to place the mother's death, the reader finds only a blank page with nothing but triple dots signifying ellipsis.[38]

The traumatic is also characterized as returning again and again without being cured in the process. As has been shown for the "Rue Vilin", the house number 24 insistently reappears without ever being investigated in detail. This recurring movement hinges on the repetition compulsion caused by the traumatic experience which had abruptly changed Perec's childhood. Cathy Caruth elucidates this aspect of trauma by referring to the latency of experience: i.e. the fact that the subject does not consciously participate in the traumatic event at the very moment of its occurrence. Forgetting is, in this sense, always inscribed into the trauma already: "The historical power of the trauma is not just that the experience is repeated after its forgetting, but that it is only in and through its inherent forgetting that it is first experienced at all." (Caruth 1996: 17). The historical power manifests itself in the trauma's insistence, which never grants comprehensive access to the past. It brings about the literal existence of something that cannot be read or told, and hence also cannot be changed or distorted by any narrative. It is precisely in this sense that trauma can be conceived as 'cryp-

---

35 See Assmann 1999: 264: "Trauma, das ist die Unmöglichkeit der Narration. Trauma und Symbol stehen sich in gegenseitiger Ausschließlichkeit gegenüber; physische Wucht und konstruktiver Sinn scheinen die Pole zu sein, zwischen denen sich unsere Erinnerungen bewegen."/ "Trauma is the impossibility of narration. Trauma and symbol interrelate in mutual exclusion to each other; physical force and constructive meaning seem to be the two poles of our memory." (Translation mine, J.-C. H.)

36 For the notion of "trauma", see Freud 1975: passim.

37 Perec 1990: 84. There it says: "besoin de faire le tour de quelque chose pour le situer." / "the need to define something in order to situate it." (Perec 1997: 124)

38 Perec 1975: 89.

tic'. So, reconsidering the two forms of failing memory – the damaged letters and the closed houses – trauma includes both of them.

Perec's 1975 novel *W ou le souvenir d'enfance* can be regarded as the main œuvre in his memory project. This non-conform autobiography does not attempt to recover a "temps perdu". The narrator time and again attests his lack of childhood memories, thus clarifying that the past seems irretrievably lost.[39] And yet, the praxis of writing itself propels him towards those lost memories while he develops a narrative style articulating as much an insisting will to remember as, conversely, his memory's failure. The childhood story is rendered in two alternating narratives that interrupt and press each other forward, producing, by means of their mutual constraint, the unwritable third story of trauma.[40] Repeated interruptions break each storyline into pieces, fragment the narratives, and damage their unity.[41] In Cathy Caruth's terms this holds true for every trauma narrative. The "double telling" reflects a crucial ambiguity of the underlying event, its two-

---

39 Perec 1975: 17–18: "Je n'ai pas de souvenirs d'enfance. Jusqu'à ma douzième année à peu près, mon histoire tient en quelques lignes: j'ai perdu mon père à quatre ans, ma mère à six: j'ai passé la guerre dans diverses pensions de Villard-de-Lans. En 1945, la sœur de mon père et son mari m'adoptèrent."/ "I have no childhood memories. Up to my twelfth year or thereabouts, my story comes to barely a couple of lines: I lost my father at four, my mother at six; I spent the war in various boarding houses at Villard-de-Lans. In 1945, my father's sister and her husband adopted me." (Perec 2011: 6)

40 In the blurb of *W ou le souvenir d'enfance* Perec 1973 writes: "Il y a dans ce livre deux textes simplement alternés; il pourrait presque sembler qu'ils n'ont rien en commun, mais ils sont pourtant inextricablement enchevêtrés, comme si aucun des deux ne pouvait exister seul, comme si de leur rencontre seule, de cette lumière lointaine qu'ils jettent l'un sur l'autre, pouvait se révéler ce qui n'est jamais tout à fait dit dans l'un, jamais tout à fait dit dans l'autre, mais seulement dans leur fragile intersection."/ "In this book there are two texts which simply alternate; you might almost believe they had nothing in common, but they are in fact inextricably bound up with each other, as though neither could exist on its own, as though it was only their coming together, the distant light they cast on each other, that could make apparent what is never quite said in one, never quite said in the other, but said only in their fragile overlapping." (Perec 2011)

41 See also Roland Barthes' autobiographical text on which I will comment later on: "Dans ce qu'il écrit, il y a deux textes. Le texte I est réactif, mû par des indignations, des peurs, des ripostes intérieures, de petites paranoïas, des défenses, des scènes. Le texte II est actif, mû par le plaisir. Mais en s'écrivant, en se corrigeant, en se pliant à la fiction du Style, le texte I devient lui-même actif; dès lors il perd sa peau réactive, qui ne subsiste plus que par plaques (dans de menues parenthèses)." (Barthes 1975: 47)/ "In what he writes, there are two texts. Text I is reactive, moved by indignations, fears, unspoken rejoinders, minor paranoias, defenses, scenes. Text II is active, moved by pleasure. But as it is written, corrected, accommodated to the fiction of Style, Text I becomes active too, whereupon it loses its reactive skin, which subsists only in patches (mere parentheses)." (Barthes 1977: 43)

fold “crisis”: the one of death – the unbearable experience itself – and the other “of life”, i.e. the unbearableness of survival.[42] According to Caruth, the novel’s narrative pattern is hence not retrospectively designed, but directly shaped by the traumatic quality of its subject matter. In this light, remembrance here significantly departs from the Western notion of descending into an inner self as it is paradigmatically contained in the German ‘Er-Innerung’. For Perec, memory is rather a textual practice, that is, a practice set in train by a configuration of elements coming from without. Writing, therefore, is understood not as the imaginary product of focusing on something deep within, but as a configuration of separate textual elements. In an early passage from *W ou le souvenir d’enfance*, the narrator comments on the motivation behind his writing:

> [...] je ne retrouverai jamais, dans mon ressassement même, que l’ultime reflet d’une parole absente à l’écriture, le scandale de leur silence et de mon silence: je n’écris pas pour dire que je ne dirai rien, je n’écris pas pour dire que je n’ai rien à dire. J’écris: j’écris parce que nous avons vécu ensemble, parce que j’ai été un parmi eux, ombre au milieu de leurs ombres, corps près de leur corps; j’écris parce qu’ils ont laissé en moi leur marque indélébile et que la trace en est l’écriture: leur souvenir est mort à l’écriture; l’écriture est le souvenir de leur mort et l’affirmation de ma vie. (Perec 1975: 63–64)[43]

All the specified characteristics of relating the trauma loom large here: the original narrative is damaged, what is left are only echoes of absent voices; there are fruitless repetitions of the past and even the idea of sealing it up hermetically: “leur souvenir est mort à l’écriture.” Memory appears inextricably linked to writing, yet not so much as a means to keep the past in its right place but, rather, as the only praxis which can approach remembrance: “Le projet d’écrire mon his-

---

42 Caruth 1996: 7: “At the core of these stories [texts by Freud, Lacan and Duras], I would suggest, is thus a kind of double telling, the oscillation between a *crisis of death* and the correlative *crisis of life:* between the story of the unbearable nature of an event and the story of the unbearable nature of its survival. These two stories, both incompatible and absolutely inextricable, ultimately define the complexity of what I refer to as *history* in the texts that I read [...].” And furthermore: “In these texts, as I suggest, it is the inextricability of the story of one’s life from the story of a death, an impossible and necessary double telling, that constitutes their historical witness.” (Caruth 1996: 8)

43 “[...] for I shall ever find in my very reiteration is the final refraction of a voice that is absent from writing, the scandal of their silence and of mine. I am not writing in order to say that I shall say nothing, I am not writing to say that I have nothing to say. I write: I write because we lived together, because I was one amongst them, a shadow amongst their shadows, a body close to their bodies. I write because they left in me their indelible mark, whose trace is writing. Their memory is dead in writing; writing is the memory of their death and the assertion of my life.” (Perec 2011: 42)

toire s'est formé presque en même temps que mon projet d'écrire" (Perec 1975: 45).[44] So in response to the question why he is writing, the narrator capitalizes on the mere fact of having once lived together, of having been physically close to his passed-away parents. This corporeal co-presence, however, has left a trace not on his body, but in his "écriture", which can refer both to that which is written and the act of writing as such. In this sense the written text is about his parents' death and, at the same time, an expression of their child's life; so the double telling is caused by the simultaneity of an absence and a presence.

4 Damaged Words

Perec describes the writing of this memory narrative as essentially dissociated writing:

> Désormais, les souvenirs existent, fugaces ou tenaces, futiles ou pesants, mais rien ne les rassemble. Ils sont comme cette écriture non liée, faite de lettres isolées incapables de se souder entre elles pour former un mot, qui fut la mienne jusqu'à l'âge de dix-sept ou dix-huit ans, ou comme ces dessins dissociés, disloqués, dont les éléments épars ne parvenaient presque jamais à se relier les uns aux autres [...]. (Perec 1975: 97)[45]

Radically opposed to longhand, in the child's handwriting characters are disconnected.[46] Every single letter remains a fragment not integrated into an intact word. This passage on the writing and scribbling child can be read as an image for the adult author's work. Attempting to reclaim his childhood, Perec indeed returns, yet not to the very experience, but to the practice of his childhood's writing. In this sense, the disconnected letters directly represent an incoherent autobiographical narrative. Just like words used to break into pieces for the child, the adult's narrative disintegrates into disparate parts. The writing process becomes a series of disruptions producing damaged words and rebus-like images. The

44 "The idea of writing the story of my past arose almost at the same time as the idea of writing." (Perec 2011: 26)

45 "From this point on, there are memories – fleeting, persistent, trivial, and burdensome – but there is nothing that binds them together. They are like that unjoined-up writing, made of separate letters unable to forge themselves into a word, which was my writing up to the age of seventeen or eighteen, or like the dissociated, dislocated drawings whose scattered elements almost never managed to connect up [...]." (Perec 2011: 68)

46 By transferring Gerhard Neumann's comment on Franz Kafka's scribblings, we can shed light on Perec's scribblings: "Kritzeln, das ist Zeichnen und Überschreiben zugleich, Umreißen und Löschen, Kontur und Blendung." (Neumann 2012: 57) / "Scribbling is drawing and overwriting at the same time, it is outlining and deleting, shaping and dazzling." (Translation mine, J.-C. H.)

pieces, it seems, need to be put together into a whole in order to make sense. The question is just how to proceed with such reconstruction. Since we know about Perec's acquaintance with psychoanalytic discourse,[47] a link to Sigmund Freud's discussion of the rebus in dreams seems plausible. Freud suggests reading these with a focus not on their "Bilderwert", but on their "Zeichenbeziehung", i.e to regard elements of the rebus not as images, but as letters. So, also in Freud, understanding results not from the imaginary, but from the work on letters, that is, writing and reading. A passage in Roland Barthes's autobiographic *Roland Barthes par Roland Barthes*, published in the same year as *W ou le souvenir d'enfance*, closely resembles the description of Perec's sketches. When trying to copy ancient Persian drawings "détail par détail", Barthes ended up with a series of fragments failing to assemble into a coherent image or anything like a composition.[48] Notably, this memory is located in a passage entitled "Le cercle des fragments", which demonstrates the book's creative logic: a succession of more or less alphabetically ordered fragments allowing Barthes to resist a linear narrative of his life even more radically than Perec.

In *W ou le souvenir d'enfance,* the focus on the act of writing reappears yet again in another context. The narrator is looking at old photographs not reprinted in the book, thus asking the reader to imagine what the pictures might show.[49] Most of the photographs have notes on their backside, yet these are

---

47 Among other things the essay "Les lieux d'une ruse" in *Penser/Classer* (Perec 2003: 59–71).

48 "N'ayant pratiqué en peinture que des barbouillages tachistes, je décide de commencer un apprentissage régulier et patient du dessin; j'essaye de copier une composition persane du XVIIe siècle ('Seigneur à la chasse'); irrésistiblement, au lieu de chercher à représenter les proportions, l'organisation, la structure, je copie et j'enchaîne naïvement détail par détail; d'où des 'arrivées' inattendues: la jambe du cavalier se retrouve perchée tout en haut du poitrail du cheval, etc. En somme, je procède par addition, non par esquisse; j'ai le goût préalable (premier) du détail, du fragment, du *rush*, et l'inhabileté à le conduire vers une 'composition': je ne sais pas reproduire 'les masses'." (Barthes 1975: 97) / "Never having done more in the way of painting than some '*tachiste*' daubing, I decide to begin a patient and regular apprenticeship in drawing; I try to copy a Persian composition of the seventeenth century ('Nobleman Hunting'); irresistibly, instead of trying to represent the proportions, organization, and structure, I copy and naïvely connect detail to detail; whence unexpected 'conclusions': the horseman's leg turns out to be perched right on top of the horse's breastplate, etc. In other words, I proceed by addition, not by sketch; I have the antecedent (initial) taste for the detail, the fragment, the *rush*, and the incapacity to lead it toward a 'composition': I cannot reproduce 'the masses'." (Barthes 1977: 93–94.)

49 Reading the same passage, Christelle Reggiani talks about "une série d'*ekphrasis*" (Reggiani 2003: 81). But also according to Reggiani, the photographs do not evoke a working memory, but actuate rather the process of writing. She speaks about "la genèse effectivement photographique de l'écriture" (Reggiani 2003: 89) / "the actually photographic genesis of writing" (Translation

all fragmentary in one way or another. One note is damaged because Perec had cut off a section of the picture, another is scribbled in disconnected letters. In this latter case, Perec suspects the handwriting of his mother who had received no higher education. Concerning a photograph showing his father, the narrator states: "[...] au dos de la photo de mon père, j'ai essayé d'écrire, à la craie, un soir que j'étais ivre, sans doute en 1955 ou 1956: 'Il y a quelque chose de pourri dans le royaume de Danemark.' Mais je n'ai même pas réussi à tracer la fin du quatrième mot." (Perec 1975: 45)[50] Why did Perec try to put this quote on the backside of his father's picture? And more importantly, why didn't he finish it? The text suggests alcohol to be the reason. But more programmatically, Hamlet's phrase might somehow be performed in the act of writing. By reference to this drunken night, the sentence regains its meaning; the reader is implicitly asked to reconstruct the damaged bit into something like "Il y a que" or "Il y a quel". At which letter in the word "quelque" the writer had stopped remains untold. There are as many options as letters in "quelque". So even the shape of the fragmented becomes vague itself. In this passage, the prevailing order of reading and writing is reversed. Here the narrator does not show the fragmented, but the intact phrase. Thus the reader – confronted with a somehow fragmented storyline throughout the book – has at this point to fragment the sentence in its wholeness for getting an image of the real note. So what remains is not a remembered event, but merely a quotation from a well-known drama that can be reproduced as unity. Intactness of memory seems to be provided only in conveying something known by heart.

5 'By heart' from without

Just as those notes on the back, descriptions of the photographs' content likewise reflect the fragmentary nature of Perec's memory. Next to the rhetorical *loci* and the praxis of writing, images and particularly photographs figure prominently among the instruments of memory. A crucial concern for Perec, however, is to understand just how looking at old photographs can serve this function. Here again there is an obvious parallel to Barthes who begins his autobiographic text with photographs which he briefly comments: "Lorsque la méditation (la

mine, J.-C. H.). [For the debate about ekphrastic writing, see Nicola Creighton's contribution to our book.]

50 "[...] on the back of the photograph of my father, one evening when I was drunk, probably in 1955 or 1956, I tried to chalk: 'There is something rotten in the state of Denmark.' But I didn't even manage to scrawl to the end of the fourth word." (Perec 2011: 26) sidération) constitue l'image en être détaché, lorsqu'elle en fait l'*objet* d'une jouissance immédiate, elle n'a plus rien à voir avec la réflexion, fût-elle rêveuse, d'une identité [...]." (Barthes 1975: 5)[51] At the latest since Descartes, "méditation" figures as the paradigmatic state of constituting identity out of oneself. For Barthes, "méditation" is conversed into "sidération", i.e. into a state of petrifaction caused by astonishment. Whereas for Barthes this closure articulates itself in the pure enjoyment of the images, Perec's photographs rather mark a gap between past and present while constituting the paradox of a disconnecting connection. In the interview quoted above Perec elaborates on his memory project: "Cette autobiographie de l'enfance s'est faite à partir de descriptions de photos, de photographies qui servaient de relais, de moyens d'approche d'une réalité dont j'affirmais que je n'avais pas le souvenir." (Perec 1990: 84)[52] Strictly according to the text, the photos do *not* transport the narrator into his past. They are not his 'Madeleine', but a "relais" rather mechanically operating on the memory. *Le Grand Robert* provides several meanings for "relais". On the one hand, it can signify a gap in various respects: the space between a rampart and a moat, an opening left in the new wallpaper for future changes, a coastline emerging with receding tide. On the other hand, it can refer to a place where things are being exchanged: dogs during a hunt, horses while travelling by carriage, runners in a relay race, workers taking shifts. Finally, "relais" can also be the place where one stops to rest. Conceived as "relais", the photographs thus do not provide essences of the past from which it could be unpacked. Rather, they are empty spaces where potentially anything could pass. Instead of insinuating the one truly original story, the pictures serve as points of departure to in-

51 "When consideration (with the etymological sense of seeing the stars together as significant constellation) treats the image as a detached being, makes it the *object* of an immediate pleasure, it no longer has anything to do with reflection, however oneiric, of an identity [...]." (Barthes 1977: 3) In contrast to the English translation of this passage I understand "sidération" in the more common sense of this word, namely as "numbness by astonishment". See Kawashima 2011 for a more detailed analysis of the function of photographs in *Roland Barthes par Roland Barthes*.

52 "The autobiography of my childhood was done from descriptions of photos, from photographs that served as a relay, as a means of approaching a reality of which I used to declare I had no memory." (Perec 1997: 124) Also see Perec 1975: 26. There it says: "Même si je n'ai pour étayer mes souvenirs improbables que le secours de photos jaunis, de témoignages rares et de documents dérisoires, je n'ai pas d'autre choix que d'évoquer ce que trop longtemps j'ai nommé l'irrévocable [...]." / "Even if I have the help only of yellowing snapshots, a handful of eyewitness accounts and a few paltry documents to prop up my implausible memories, I have no alternative but to conjure up what for too many years I called the irrevocable [...]." (Perec 2011: 12)

terchangeable narratives. Earlier in his work, Perec had experimented with writing family histories from photo albums of people he did not know. In contrast to the memory project based on his own family's pictures, making up multiple narratives was no problem. [53]

In *Unclaimed Experience*, Caruth (1996: 22) elaborates on the notion of departure inherent to traumatic experience. The point is to conceive of compulsive repetition as caused by a departure that is always too early to "claim experience". Trauma and forgetting thus directly coincide in the retreat from the site of the event – a retreat too precipitous to retain accessible memories. In the sense of the "relais", the photographs could be understood as a site of perpetual departure according to precisely this aspect of traumatic experience.[54] Figuratively speaking, they do not function as a memorial but, on the contrary, a kind of void where nothing is to be found and which is quickly left behind.

In *La Chambre claire*, Barthes defines photographs as radically flat. They defy 'deep' readings in the sense of unveiling an underlying layer of meaning that might unpack or complement what is seen on the surface. Barthes quotes a passage from Maurice Blanchot into which the term 'Auswendigkeit' seems to be latently inscribed. According to Blanchot, photographs always remain on the very outside foreclosing any intimacy and, at the same time, they are inaccessibly enigmatic. In short: the visible remains concealed behind the evident. Descriptions to the images in *W ou le souvenir d'enfance* obviously have an analogous effect. The narrator does not seem capable to make any in-depth comments apart from basic facts: where might the pictures have been taken, who was the photographer. Next to this information probably provided by his aunt, he merely states what anybody could see. The only not-too-obvious detail noted is his und his mother's carefully styled hair on one of the images. This could have triggered a sequence of memories since his mother, as mentioned above, was in fact a hairdresser. Perec's recollection of his mother's job, however, relies on someone else's testimony. He doesn't remember this detail himself. Remnants of the past thus systematically come from the outside: the commonplace inwardness of 'Erinnerung' turning out to be an 'Auswendigkeit' as discussed with regard to the Shakespeare quote.[55] So the narrator's memory seems to function exclusively by heart from without.

53 Perec 1990: 85.

54 Caruth 1996: 20 – 21. There it says: "The trauma in Freud's text, is first of all a trauma of leaving, the trauma of *verlassen*."

55 Interestingly in French and also in English, the "Auswendigkeit" reposes on "Innerlichkeit": "savoir par cœur" and "to know by heart". For the debate on memory as "Auswendigkeit", also see Haverkamp 1990 and von Koppenfels 2000.

> J'ai des cheveux blonds avec un très joli cran sur le front (de tous les souvenirs qui me manquent, celui-là est peut-être celui que j'aimerais le plus fortement avoir: ma mère me coiffant, me faisant cette ondulation savante). Je porte une veste (ou une brassière, ou un manteau) de couleur claire, fermée jusqu'au cou, avec un petit col surpiqué. J'ai des grandes oreilles, des joues rebondies, un petit menton, un sourire et un regard de biais déjà très reconnaisables. (Perec 1975: 74)[56]

This passage makes remarkable use of the device of enumerating already discussed with regard to the "infra-ordinaire". The photograph seems to assemble fragments that resist integration into a narrative. The individual elements in this sense acquire the status of leftovers, or props. In my reading, I would like to suggest that this writing technique symptomatically reflects the pictures' inaccessibility. The photographs do not resonate with an inner sense of self to be reclaimed, but merely display an impenetrable surface. Like the house wall of Rue Vilin 24, the images do not invite the visitor to enter and explore what they contain, but serve the opposite function of a protective, i.e. concealing layer. In a sense, the narrator stands anaesthetized in front of the petrified appearance of what is to be represented.

Here is a similar pattern to Lukács' notion of Second Nature in capitalist society. The power of conventions or, in his later phrasing, the reification determining every social relationship, impinge on the subjects in the same anaesthetizing way as the closed walls of the houses and the photographs' surfaces. We can draw a parallel from Lukács' argument on capitalism to the problem of trauma and memory: experiences remain inaccessible and incomprehensible because their original constitution cannot be reconstructed. Tellingly, Lukács' definition of Second Nature also involves the forgetting of history, i.e. – to stretch the parallel even further – Second Nature appears as cryptic as trauma.[57] One's own history is covered by another History:

> "Je n'ai pas de souvenirs d'enfance" : je posais cette affirmation avec assurance, avec presque une sorte de défi. L'on n'avait pas inscrite à mon programme. J'en étais dispensé :

56 "I have fair hair with a very pretty forelock (of all my missing memories, that is perhaps the one I most dearly wish I had: my mother doing my hair, and making that cunning curl). I am wearing a light-coloured jacket (or sleeved vest or coatee), buttoned up to the neck, with a little quilted collar. I have big ears, puffy cheeks, a small chin, and a lopsided grin and sidelong glance which are already quite recognizable." (Perec 2011: 49)

57 See Adorno 1997: 358. There it says: "Wenn Lukács das Historische als Gewesenes in Natur sich zurückverwandeln läßt, so gibt sich hier die andere Seite des Phänomens: Natur selber stellt als vergängliche Natur, als Geschichte sich dar." / "If Lukács demonstrates the retransformation of the historical, as that which has been, into nature, then here is the other side of the phenomenon: nature itself is seen as transitory nature, as history." (Adorno 1984: 119)

une autre histoire, la Grande, l'Histoire avec sa grande hache, avait déjà répondu à ma place : la guerre, les camps. (Perec 1975: 17)[58]

In another passage already mentioned, Perec reflects on his mother's writing skills – how she mixes up upper-case and lower-case letters as if she did not know for sure about their difference. In line with the hypothesis that writing is crucially linked to memory, one could hold that the mother's memory collapses the distinction between her private place and the one given by officials. The story of her life is literally buried under the big events of official historiography. Inquiries into her own narrative always return answers given by others already. Accordingly, autobiographic narration cannot be arranged by the narrator, but 'auswendig'. The narrator always remains outside – in front of the closed houses – working only with leftovers, with damaged words whose fragments can never be reassembled into an intact unit. The only option left is to arrange a narrative that exposes its constitution from pieces coming from without. Thus, the memory narrative must result in a historiography of gaps and cracks.

Works cited

Adorno, Theodor W. (1977) "Commitment" in *Aesthetics and Politics*, ed. Fredric Jameson, transl. Francis McDonagh (London: Verso), 177–195.
Adorno, Theodor W. (1984) "The Idea of Natural History", transl. Bob Hullot-Kentor, *Telos* 60, 111–124.
Adorno, Theodor W. (1997) *Philosophische Frühschriften*, ed. Rolf Tiedemann (Frankfurt/M.: Suhrkamp).
Assmann, Aleida (1999) *Erinnerungsräume: Formen und Wandlungen des kulturellen Gedächtnisses* (Munich: C. H. Beck).
Barthes, Roland (1957) *Mythologies* (Paris: du Seuil).
Barthes, Roland (1970) "L'ancienne rhétorique. Aide-mémoire", *Communications* 16, 172–223.
Barthes, Roland (1975) *Roland Barthes par Roland Barthes* (Paris: du Seuil).
Barthes, Roland (1977) *Roland Barthes by Roland Barthes*, transl. Richard Howard (New York: Hill & Wang).
Bellos, David (1993) *Georges Perec: A Life in Words* (Boston: David R. Godine).
Caruth, Cathy (1996) *Unclaimed Experience: Trauma, Narrative, and History* (Baltimore: Johns Hopkins UP).

58 "'I have no childhood memories': I made this assertion with confidence, with almost a kind of defiance. It was nobody's business to press me on this question. It was not a set topic in my syllabus. I was excused: a different history, History with a capital H, has answered the question in my stead: the war, the camps." (Perec 2011: 6)

Derrida, Jacques (1986) "Foreword: Fors: The Anglish Words of Nicolas Abraham and Maria Torok", transl. Barbara Johnson, in Abraham, Nicolas, and Maria Torok *The Wolf Man's Magic Word: A Cryptonymy*, transl. Nicholas Rand (Minneapolis: U of Minnesota Press), xi–xlviii.
Freud, Sigmund (1972) *Die Traumdeutung*, ed. Alexander Mitscherlich, Angela Richards and James Strachey (Frankfurt/M.: S. Fischer).
Freud, Sigmund (1975) "Jenseits des Lustprinzips", in *Psychologie des Unbewußten*, ed. Alexander Mitscherlich, Angela Richards and James Strachey (Frankfurt/M.: S. Fischer), 213–272.
Frisby, David (1983) *The Alienated Mind: The Sociology of Knowledge in Germany 1918–33* (New Jersey: Humanities Press).
Gardiner, Michel E. (2006) "Marxism and the convergence of utopia and the everyday", *History of the Human Sciences* IXX, 1, 1–32.
Haverkamp, Anselm (1990) "Auswendigkeit: Skizzen zum Gedächtnis der Rhetorik", *Rhetorik – Ein internationales Jahrbuch* 9, 84–102.
James, Alison (2009) *Constraining Chance: Georges Perec and Oulipo* (Evanston, Ill.: Northwestern UP).
Kawashima, Kentaro (2011) *Autobiographie und Photographie nach 1900: Proust, Benjamin, Brinkmann, Barthes, Sebald* (Bielefeld: transcript).
Koppenfels, Martin von (2000) "Dante in- und auswendig: Primo Levis Gedächtnisfuge", *Poetica* 32, 203–225.
Lefebvre, Henri (1994) "Alltäglichkeit", in *Historisch-kritische Wörterbuch des Marxismus* I, ed. Wolfgang Fritz Haug (Hamburg: Argument).
Lejeune, Philippe (1991) *La Mémoire et l'Oblique: Georges Perec autobiographe* (Paris: P.O.L).
Lukács, Georg (1958) *Wider den mißverstandenen Realismus* (Hamburg: Claasen).
Lukács, Georg (1969[2]) *The Meaning of Contemporary Realism*, transl. John and Necke Mander (London: Merlin Press).
Lukács, Georg (1971a) *The Theory of the Novel: A historico-philosophical essay on the forms of great epic literature*, transl. Anna Bostock (London: Merlin Press).
Lukács, Georg (1971b) *History and Class Consciousness: Studies in Marxist Dialectics*, transl. Rodney Livingstone (London: Merlin Press)
Lukács, Georg (1978[5]) *Geschichte und Klassenbewußtsein: Studien über marxistische Dialektik* (Darmstadt: Luchterhand).
Lukács, Georg (1972) *Ästhetik*. Vol. 1 (Darmstadt: Luchterhand).
Lukács, Georg (2009 [1916]) *Die Theorie des Romans: Ein geschichtsphilosophischer Versuch über die Formen der großen Epik* (Bielefeld: Aisthesis).
Lyotard Jean-François (1979) *Les Problèmes du savoir dans les sociétés industrielles les plus développées* (Quebec: Les presses du Service des Impressions en régie du Bureau de l'Éditeur officiel du Québec).
Marcuse, Herbert (1964) *One-Dimensional Man: Studies in the Ideology of Advanced Industrial Society* (London: Routledge & Kegan Paul).
Neumann, Gerhard (2012) *Franz Kafka: Experte der Macht* (Munich: Hanser).
Perec, Georges (1975) *W ou le souvenir d'enfance* (Paris: Denoël).
Perec, Georges (1989) *L'Infra-ordinaire*, ed. Maurice Olender (Paris: du Seuil).
Perec, Georges (1990) *Je suis né*, ed. Maurice Olender (Paris: du Seuil).

Perec, Georges (1992) *L. G.: Une aventure des années soixante*, ed. Maurice Olender (Paris: du Seuil).
Perec, Georges (1997) *Species of Spaces and Other Pieces*, ed. and transl. John Sturrock (London: Penguin).
Perec, Georges (2003) *Penser / Classer*, ed. Maurice Olender (Paris: du Seuil).
Perec, Georges (2011) *W or The Memory of Childhood*, transl. David Bellos (London: Vintage).
Rancière, Jacques (2000) *Le Partage du sensible: Esthétique et politique* (Paris: La Fabrique-éditions).
Reggiani, Christelle (2003) "Perec: une poétique de la photographie", *Littérature* 129, 77–106.
Sheringham, Michael (2006) *Everyday Life: Theories and Practices from Surrealism to the Present* (Oxford: Oxford UP).
Stockhammer, Robert (2014) *Grammatik: Wissen und Macht in der Geschichte einer sprachlichen Institution* (Berlin: Suhrkamp).
Waldenfels, Bernhard (2005[3]) *In den Netzen der Lebenswelt* (Frankfurt/M.: Suhrkamp).
Wolff, Jonathan (2011) "Karl Marx", *The Stanford Encyclopedia of Philosophy*, ed. Edward N. Zalta, http://plato.stanford.edu/archives/sum2011/entries/marx/ (accessed 24 May 2015).

Isabel Capeloa Gil (UCP Lisbon)

The Sovereign's Broken Voice: On the Cinematic Politics of Representation

Can voice be seen? And is sound visible? In the opening shot of Michel Hazanavicius' *L'artiste* (2011), the viewer is presented with the close-up of a man in pain, head crushed by two electrical rods, mouth open wide, crying. The meaning of the shout becomes clear in the title card: "I won't talk! I won't say a word!" The two torturers, who resemble scientists in their white pristine coats, insist and inflict upon the suffering man yet another electrical discharge. "Speak!" they order, but to no avail. This scene from the award-winning *L'Artiste* provides a visual metaphor to film's deep-seated conflict between voice and image, revealing that even in silent movies, if not heard, voice can always be seen. In this comedy about the trials of the transition from silent to sound film, human voice becomes the location of a strategic resistance before the technological transformation of moving pictures.

The unwillingness to submit to the power of technology, that is, of becoming recorded and synchronized voice, inscribes a mark of resistance to the apparatus. The change from silent into sound film was highly contentious not only regarding technological conditions, but in conceptual and cultural terms as well, as film historians argued. At a time when cinema was still struggling to find a place amongst the system of art, the shift brought about a further theoretical debate amongst early film theorists, namely between those who opposed sound and those who considered the organic unity of sound and image as part and parcel of the modern film experience. Years before the synchronization of sound in film, Hugo von Hofmannsthal addressed the allure of film as deriving particularly from its mimic, i.e. silent, dimension:

> The fact that these images are mute is one more allure, they are as mute as dreams. And deep down, without knowing it, these people fear language; they fear in language the workings of society; [...] This language of the literate and half-literate, either spoken or written, is strange. It scratches the surface, but it does not awake what lies beneath. There is too much algebra in language, each letter hides a cipher, the cipher is short for reality. All of this points towards other things, to power, to power modes in which one is invested, but all this is too indirect; the connections too abstract. [...] All of this leaves a sense of lack behind, and again this feeling of being part of a machinery. And they all know of a different power, a real one, the only one that is real: that of dreams. (Hofmannsthal 1979: 142)

This passage, included in a piece published in the Viennese newspaper *Neue Freie Presse* on 27 March 1921, entitled "The Substitute of Dreams" ("Ersatz für

https://doi.org/10.1515/9783110556858-010

die Träume"), reflects Hofmannsthal's life long interest for the pantomimic arts,[1] while connecting a deep-seated mistrust of language with social critique and an early presentation of film's psychological apparatus as a mode of resisting social machinery. In this programmatic assumption, silent film becomes a machine against the machine, an adversarial mode of using technology against its misuse of the subject. Or, as in Hazanavicius' shot, an enabler of resistance for the *homo mediatus* – the actor – against the final collapse of the subject before the apparatus.

Sound movies did in fact introduce an element of irritation into this adversarial understanding of silent film's edenic technology. In fact, as early as 1921, Willy Haas argued that silent film was a signpost of movies not having yet reached a technologically mature stage. Without the abilities to synchronize sound, film was a mere mechanical art form, only good for crafts workers (Haas 1921: 155). The introduction of sound, or rather the optimization of synchronization, not only upgraded cinema's technological core, but promoted as well the perception of a growing penetration of bodily materiality into the otherwise distanced image projected on screen. Thus, Walter Benjamin in "The Work of Art in the Age of Technological Reproducibility" considered that to meet the demands of the microphone was "to preserve one's humanity in the face of the apparatus" (Benjamin 2006: 111). Sound was seen as a bodily intervention, a marker of the inextricable enfleshment of voice, in the realm of technology. Later, Rudolf Arnheim would defend the collapse of distinction between sound and image. In *Film als Kunst*, he deemed there was no such thing as "sound film", because film and sound constituted an organic unity that was to be addressed solely as "cinema" (Arnheim 1931: 311).

In fact, the question of voice in film exceeds the problems of sound versus silent cinema. If the technological problems of synchronization open up the discussion of larger issues, that results by and large from the fact that the actor's voice has traditionally occupied a central position in the mode of cinematic representation, controlling narrative and the advancement of action. It is thus fair to argue that the discomfort of Jean Dujardin's character in *L'Artiste* speaks to a larger concern in the film's discursive network, articulating the resistance of the *homo mediatus* with a wider anxiety with respect to cinematic voice and

---

1 See for instance the essays "Die unvergleichliche Tänzerin" (1906) or "Über die Pantomime" (1911). The interest in mime is furthermore expressed in the 1898 piece "Friedrich Mitterwurzer", where Hofmannsthal proclaims a love for all the arts that are practiced "in silence", see Gil 1993 and 2004. He was also involved in a number of failed film projects, the most famous of which would be *Das fremde Mädchen*, with dancer Grete Wiesenthal; a project for a Lillian Gish film is also reported. See Hofmannsthal 2006 and Hiebler 2003: 427–430.

the illusion constructed by the apparatus about the wholesome dimension of the subject's representation in film. As modern and later postmodern philosophical discourse underlined the collapse of unified subjectivities, cinema seemingly drew from the illusion of a body glued together by smokes and mirrors. But this is probably unfair, as film also used editing and framing to promote a dismembering of the visual homogeneity of the human body. Indeed as a multimodal art form that uses visuals, accoustics, but also architecture, theatre or dance, cinema works conflictual devices into a joint perceptual envelope (Elsaesser and Hagener 2010: 10).

In the following, this article discusses the conflictual relation between voice and sovereign power in film and particularly the role of damaged or broken voice in the cinematic narrative. Agreeing with Rick Altman that the collapse between voice, body and image structures cinematic representation and conditions its particular mode of seeing (Altman 1980: 70), it moves on to ask how this collapse configures social and cultural concerns over the possibilities of subjective and collective voice in contemporary societies. At a time when the subject can neither move nor speak, lisps, stutters, or aphasia reflect the fundamental collapse in the structure of representation. In Alexander Sokurov's *The Sun* (2004) and Tom Hooper's *The King's Speech* (2011), speech impediments are conflictual devices in the cinematic narrative that speak through the sovereign's broken voice to a wider crisis of power. Following the turn to embodiment in film perception, I argue that more than a metaphor of a foundational lack in the subjectivity of power, voice is an ambivalent element that not only discloses the wound in self-representation, but works to suture it as well.

Voice is taken here as the sign of a wider embodiment of the social, the sexual and the political, where physiology meets metaphor at the crossroads between the invisibility of silence and the visible sensoriality of the utterance. Considering that in film the relation between the visible and the audible is not without tensions, George VI's stutter in Tom Hooper's film or Hirohito's speech flaw in Sokurov are also perceptual interruptions that the visual force field of cinema both reveals and works to contain. They promote a discussion about damaged voice in historical conflict situations, like World War II, and how technologies, such as radio, testify to the challenges faced by the modern *homo mediatus*, deemed to rely on technology to be, i. e. to have a voice. In addition, they evince in the royal characters' speech flaws the crisis in power and the pervasive sense of lack at the root of modern subjectivity in the aftermath of war. I contend that the crisis of voice seen here is largely indicative of the foundational lack in sovereign subjectivity in the twentieth century and that it is a sign of the wider crisis of political voice in the conflict-torn western world after 9/11.

1 Voice and the acoustic unconscious

Voice has been an integral part of the cinematic mode of representation even before moving lips became audible. With voice, I refer to the materiality of a sound emanating from human throat, to "the vibration of a throat of flesh" in Adriana Cavarero's words (2005: 2), but also to the culturally, politically and socially mediated utterance, that is, to voice as matter (*phoné*)[2], to a voice that matters (*phoné semantiké*), and to the ways in which it matters. Both as matter and symbol, as possibility and discourse, voice is inextricably linked to cinema's particular *Dasein.*[3] It neither subverts the artistic dimension of the moving image nor is it merely redundant or subsidiary to the fulguration of the visible, but voice, and sound, more generally, are part and parcel of the multisensory appeal of cinematic representation.

The difficulty of synchronization in the early stages of sound film is keenly illustrated in the comical disjuncture of body and voice in the famous scene from *Singing in the Rain,* when silent film actress Lina Lamont (Jean Hagen) is dubbed by the unknown, but talented, Kathy Selden (Debbie Reynolds).[4] The moment when Hagen's voice is revealed as a playback of Reynolds' speaks to the fundamental collapse between image and sound, body and voice, as structuring the very mode of cinematic representation. More than fostering an organic whole subsumed under the aegis of the image, film is a complex structure that works from the strains, the tensions and gaps amongst the visible and the acoustic, the image and the body, the human and the non-human, the apparatus and the operator. This is why cinema is multisensory rather than strictly visual. Cinematic visuality exceeds the mere dimension of the visible, working with the acoustic to truly perform a multisensory vocation, thereby addressing senses other than seeing that work the two-dimensional structure of the moving image to produce a complex layered narrative, disclosing how cinema's many languages are: on the one hand, made to matter, that is to signify, and on the other, how they effectively *matter* upon the bodies within and without the screen.

Over the past thirty years, particularly in the wake of the classical study by Michel Chion, *La Voix au cinema* (1982), a new interest in cinematic voice and

2 Aristotle defines the human in *Politics* as an animal with a voice (*zoon logon echon, Politics,* 1253a9–19), but what distinguishes him from other animals and makes him a political being is the capability to communicate with meaning, to own a *phoné* inhabited by *logos*, or as the philosopher puts it in *Poetics*, to own a signifying voice (*phone semantiké*, 1457a5–30).

3 Elsaesser and Hagener's shift towards a sensory film theory turns cinema into "a life form in its own right" (2010: 7).

4 For a discussion of the scene, see Elsaesser and Hagener 2010: 129.

sound has emerged.[5] Acknowledging a caveat in sound analysis, namely that filmic sound hermeneutics are traditionally dominated by human voice and suffer by and large from a noticeable "vococentrism", Chion suggests that in sound diegesis there is voice and then everything else (1999: 5). The anthropocentric nature of sound analysis then reflects two forms of bias: on the one side, the centrality of the actor's body in the cinematic economy, on the other the onto-phenomenological subsuming of voice to language and meaning, of *phoné* to *logos*. In other words, phonocentrism in film reflects the bias of logocentrism in western cultural-philosophical tradition, a bias that stands at the root of Deconstruction's critique of the logos.[6]

The consequence of this move for film studies is reflected in the apparent support of sound film for the gluing of voice and language with meaning and truth. In this economy, human voice would be essentialized in the transparent hoax of the image as a by-product that not only gives a body to the image, but subsumes acoustics to the grand logic of the visual. This could be one picture, but it is not the whole picture, as film history has taught us, because both mainstream films and art cinema have questioned the illusion of wholeness between image and sound and between voice and subjectivity. In the *Wizard of Oz*, for instance, the disjunction of the Wizard's voice and image places puppetry at the core of the cinematic representation. Voice becomes an uncanny surplus, because its source can never be seen. It stems in fact from an undisclosed unseen interior (Dolar 2006: 70), suggesting that in film voice is essentially ventriloquism, as Steven Connor as argued (2000: 15). This is precisely what Michel Chion has named the acousmatic[7] presence in film, a sound that is heard without its source actually being seen – as most filmic sound is usually recorded *ex post* and synchronized with the image – and actually defining a zone within the cinematic economy that is "[f]luctuating, constantly subject to challenge by what

5 To name just a few, see the psychoanalytical approach to voice and power, particularly by Slavoj Žižek and Renata Saleci (1996) as well as Mladen Dolar (2006); Adriana Cavarero's (2005) phenomenological approach and Don Ihde's media phenomenology (2007), Nick Couldry's media sociological discussion (Couldry 2010) and Steven Connor's cultural-hermeneutical analysis (2000).

6 Jacques Derrida questions the overlapping of logos with voice and consciousness (1973: 80) and Cavarero, reading Derrida, questions the destination of voice as language, as meaning (2005: 46 and 213–220).

7 According to Chion, acousmatics defined a pedagogical practice of a Phytagorean sect, who trained students' to listen to the master's voice for five years and thus getting acquainted with its modulation and identity before being allowed to look at him, so the master's image would not distract them from the message. The term means literally "invisible sound" (Chion 1999: 19).

we might see" (Chion 1999: 22). Breaking the illusion of an authentic voice, glued to an adequate body, movies have on several instances reflected on the trials of visible voice as permanent tension and deferral in the logic of representation.

Clearly, if sound, and more specifically, voice, introduce tension and antagonism into the visible, that is because they enhance certain parts of the shot, whilst undermining others, because they work in excess of the visible or under the visible or because they hide their origin even when seemingly disclosing it[8]. Acoustics brings an element of enigma into the cinematic economy. Rick Altman therefore places sound and voice as part of the image while simultaneously challenging the visual narrative, opening up meaning rather than providing closure: "*The image, in terms of sound, always has the basic nature of a question.* Fundamental to the cinema experience, therefore is a process [...] whereby the sound asks *where?* And the image responds *here!*" (Altman 1980: 74) Arguably, as in the following examples, voice does get to ask the question, but the image does not always respond satisfactorily.

Over the past decade the cinematic representation of political voice in film has achieved a remarkable notoriety, following or rather keeping pace with theory's rising interest in the topic. Either in the obscene display of the screaming Hitler in Oliver Hirschbiegel's *Der Untergang* (2004), in João Canijo's uncanny voice-over of the softspoken Portuguese autocrat Salazar in *Fantasia Lusitana* (2010), or from Aleksandr Sokurov's power tetralogy about the three dictators Hitler, Lenin and Hirohito (*Moloch*, 1999; *Taurus*, 2000; *The Sun,* 2004), and more recently, *Faust* (2011), to which even the euphoric pop-nationalism of Tom Hooper's *The King's Speech* (2011) may be added, it becomes clear that the cinematic interest in political voice resonates with a wider perception of the crisis in public voice. Arguably, the growing sensibility towards the tensions of voice in its relation to image speaks to the increasing failure of citizens in western democracies to have a voice and to make it matter.

The articulation of voice with political power has been treated at length by psychoanalysis, mainly by the Lacanian school. Studies on authoritarian regimes, such as those by Mladen Dolar, have signaled that the dictator's voice suggestively embodies an obscene maternal *jouissance* that feeds the citizens unto death as an uncanny mother does (qtd. after MacCannel 1996: 80). Fascist voice calls for a reply, it seeks an auditor, it is an *appeal* (ibid.). Yet, the reply to this uncanny voice may in this economy become the simple echo of the listener's nothingness (81). The psychoanalytical approach to authoritarian voice builds

8 This is why for psychoanalysis, there cannot be a disacousmatization of the image (Dolar 2006: 18).

from the long-standing relation between the representation of voice and sovereignty. Indeed the vocal relevance of political sovereignty is supported by the clear acceptance or rather acknowledgement on the part of the subjects of the power of voice and in voice. This carries a deep entanglement of physiology with political representation. Arguably, in the vocal emission authority and exposure are tightly knit together. Because the sovereign nature of voice is relational, the speaking sovereign is exposed to the power of the Other as the legitimation of his/her authority requires the other to listen. Whilst exerting the authority of voice s/he is subject to the Other's willingness to listen. Mladen Dolar argues that this is the conundrum of the ruling voice:

> [...] by using one's voice one is also "always-already" yielding power to the Other; the silent listener has the power to decide over the fate of the voice and its sender; the listener can rule over its meaning, or turn a deaf ear. The trembling voice is a plea for mercy, for sympathy, for understanding, and it is the power of the listener to grant it or not. (Dolar 2006: 80)

The authority and even tyranny waged by the sovereign speaker requires an answer that may come as the resonant surrender to the power of speech, or on the other hand suggest that the Other's recognition, although demanded, may be denied. The plea, the appeal to the Other, may be an attempt to dominate him/her, but the listener has the power to deny this plea. The equation was reconsidered with the rise of reproducible technologies, when sovereign voice became deeply dependent on recording (radio, film, television and now social networks) and mediation. Technologically mediated voice reveals the ambivalence and conflicts at the core of the political representation and produces an acoustic unconscious in the mind of the receiver, while simultaneously intensifying the exposure of the sovereign. Clearly, they both reinforce the sovereign's power by expanding her/his ubiquity, and expose her/his innermost fragility. The sovereign's fragile voice then becomes a symbol of the dismembering of the sovereign's symbolic body and that of the nation.

Speech impediments, lisps and stutters, damaged voice in a word, inspire two film productions by Aleksandr Sokurov and Tom Hooper on the trials of ruling voice in the age of the apparatus. Strikingly distinct, Sokurov's *The Sun* and Hooper's *The King's Speech* look back to voice both as value and discursive practice, as physiological matter and diegetic marker to literally 'show voice' and ask what this visibility of speech does to the representation of authority.

2 The sovereign's broken voice

More than the acousmatic enigma of the uncanny hidden voice that haunts the screen in *The Wizard of Oz*, the cinematic representations of voice I am interested in addressing doubly present the already discussed collapse between voice and body. Aleksandr Sokurov's *The Sun* (2004) and Tom Hooper's *The King's Speech* (2011) deal, albeit in radically different ways, with the sovereign's damaged voice and the connection between an acoustic unconscious, technology, and power. The background of Sokurov's voice critique and Hooper's collective co-opting of damaged voice is set by two historical events: King George VI's address to the nation once war with Germany was declared, on 3 September 1939; and Emperor Hirohito's surrender and renunciation speeches in 1945 and 1946, respectively. Sokurov's film is the third part of his power tetralogy (*Moloch, Taurus, The Sun, Faust*), character-studies of absolute rulers. While Hitler is the subject of *Moloch* (1999), and *Taurus* (2001) deals with a wheel-chair bound Lenin in his death throes, in *The Sun* the director presents a clearly more humane and sympathetic view of a twentieth-century ruler. Hirohito is for Sokurov "the symbol of a constructive finale" (Sokurov 2013), because by choosing surrender he does not doom his people to non-existence. The lisping, reluctant voice of Emperor Hirohito (Issey Ogata) or George VI's (Colin Firth) stammer reveal the sovereign's body out of control, articulating the "damaged life" (*Minima Moralia*) that marks the condition of mankind in modernity, sovereign and commoners alike. Hirohito's reluctant articulation, the incontrollable facial spasms and lip smacks express the body's resistance to the ritualized imperial biopolitics, arguably presenting the emperor as a puppet in the imperial ventriloquism of power. Indeed, the emperor's speech impediment suggests a body that is spoken, but does not speak. A sovereign unable to rule in the state of exception of unconditional surrender, a voice that relinquishes its appeal/*appel*, to the *objet petit a* of radio. Other than the metaphorical crisis of sovereignty portrayed by the collapsed voice, Sokurov's refined acoustical visibility and Hooper's phobic technoeuphoria are related in the attention paid to the role of the discursive networks created by voice gadgetry in the first half of the twentieth century, particularly radio, although there are in both films plenty of other voice devices, gramophones and telephones, to go about. The less potent the human voice, the more do these gadgets speak. As surrogates to defective voices, these sound technologies occupy the sovereign's vacant seat. The voice's daunting appeal becomes mere exposure.

George VI's speech defect is elaborated in the film as an inspirational metaphor for the overcoming of fear and hardship that is to test the nation during

WWII, with the King's Speech functioning as a heroic premeditation of Britain's overcoming of the trials and hazards dealt to them by history. In a Freudian mode, one could say, as the individual, so the nation: the King's Speech becomes a surrogate to the collective mind and truly promotes a collective acoustical unconscious. On the other hand, Sokurov's film blends Hirohito's voice and the unseen, but symbolically present speeches into a unique narrative about the transformation of the subject. Unlike in Hooper's film, here the radio speeches instruct the narrative but do not become visible. In the end, unlike George VI's, the god emperor's voice cuts across the social pact between the sovereign and the nation. Reduced to its elemental materiality, it represents itself alone. The abdication of divinity that comes with the exposure of voice shocked Japanese listeners, then, and also impacted the reception of Sokurov's film in Japan. Indeed, Hirohito's visible voice still upsets Japanese viewers.[9]

On 14 August 1945, Emperor Hirohito gave his surrender address on national radio (*Gyokuon-hōsō*), astonishing his subjects unprepared, as they were, to listen to the voice of a god. The unconditional capitulation of Japan was later signed aboard the USS Missouri on 2 September 1945 by the emperor's dignitaries. The radio broadcast reacted to the Hiroshima and Nagasaki bombings, and the emperor claimed that surrender arose from the need "to save the millions of our subjects, and to atone ourselves before the hallowed spirits of our imperial ancestors". Hirohito and his dignitaries viewed the radio broadcast as a more emphatic and sympathetic way of reaching the disgruntled and suffering Japanese subjects. Considering radio as mostly a one-way propaganda instrument, the address aimed at persuading a passive audience in the most direct of forms. Radio broadcast had acquired a reputation in forming the minds and souls of audiences, perceived as soft and passive, and was a privileged means of political action. Mussolini first addressed audiences via wireless communication in 1925, the same year King George VI's inaugural radio address for the Empire Exhibition was broadcasted. Nazi Germany used radio broadcasting as a privileged means of reaching households, and President Roosevelt, fully aware of this potential, introduced the Fireside Chats in his first term (1933 and 1934) to foster a stronger connection between the White House and American citizens. The growth in the number of radio receivers all over the world deepened awareness about the power of wireless communication. As Nelson Ribeiro argues, "Radio broadcasting made it possible to sense [...] the vibrations of emotion in

9 The filmmaker received death threats for having dared to represent the figure of the Japanese emperor (Szaniawski 2006: 13).

a voice, with the objective, just like in public speaking, of persuading listeners" (2011: 53).

In Japan, however, the effect of perceiving the emperor's voice over the radio was twofold and none of them positive. Although photographs of Hirohito in state attire or in civilian clothes circulated widely among citizens, the sense of embodiment that came with the broadcast shocked many subjects. Because a god does not have a body, the incarnation suggested by vocal transmission was met with awe on the one side, with horror on the other. In fact, as the Emperor's voice echoed across the radio waves, many Japanese held their swords and were ready to commit collective suicide, known as the Honorable Death of the Hundred Million.[10] Although some suicides did indeed take place, the Emperor sought to prevent the act, claiming that he dared "to pave the way to a grand peace", and warned listeners to beware of "any outbursts of emotion that might engender needless complications, [and] any fraternal contention and strife that might create confusion". Clearly, Hirohito used the symbolic body of the sovereign to convey a unique voice that spoke to the hardship of his countrymen, but did not represent the collective and general voice of the imaginary nation. In a second transmission, on 1 January 1946, already under American occupation, Hirohito rejected "the notion that the emperor is a living god" and the idea that "the Japanese are superior to other races destined accordingly to rule the world". Arguably radio gives birth to a new man, to a literal *homo mediatus*, whose very nature is negotiated with the apparatus. Technology, by allowing the emperor to be reconciled with his humanity, improves upon the flawed and lacking subjectivity as a prosthetic surrogate.

The cinematic techniques employed by the two directors to embody voice in film are strikingly distinct. Aleksander Sokurov instructed the actor Issey Ogata to make the strain and disjuncture of articulation visible, turning human voice into an interruption of the visible. Whilst seemingly upholding the law of narrative coherence, the film enacts on the montage level the hiatus produced by the human voice. In *The Sun*, montage reflects the fragility of the narrative focalization, which is that of the damaged subject. As the filmmaker says in an interview to Jeremi Szaniawski: "When I solve the question of construction, of the dramatic structure of my film, I make recourse to one voice only, one inner principle." (2006: 18) Unlike the other dictator films, *The Sun* allows for the transformation of the emperor from god to human.[11] This transformation is equivocal, non-linear

10 A military contingent captured the Imperial Palace the day before the broadcast in an effort to prevent the Emperor from making the surrender speech.

11 For Sokurov, although the end must remain open, the key to the film is the denoument. "The beginning is narrow and the end full of meanings." (Szaniawski 2006: 18)

and conflictual. For Sokurov, this can only be achieved through a skillful montage that does not submit to the story:

> The distinction between the world of my films and the world of the scripts on which I base them is that these are two totally different worlds. [...] I add a scene, I modify others and also the settings because life in film is another life. If the film is based on the principle of the story, the narrative, it is not art. Art is 'the other life'. (Szaniawski 2006: 18)

The emperor's diegetic hesitant speech brings an element of irritation to the veil of the visible. If the obscene of the capitulation address and the abdication speech remain invisible, off frame – the film cuts at the moment when Hirohito decides to accept defeat, and in the closing sequence glues a visit to the destroyed city to the aftermath of divine recanting –, as a matter of fact, a suggestive work with non-diegetic sound allows for the acoustic embodiment of the horrible to work as an uncanny presence embodied in the whizzing sound of radio waves. Because the incapable human voice cannot be glued, and veiled by the visible, it remains an element of resistance to the imaginary wholeness of the image. In fact, it is even silenced by the sound of things that buzz, displacing the human from its central position in filmic diegesis and reclaiming it as a supplement to the narrative of sovereign voice.

In the opening sequence, the emperor is locked in his bunker served by his chamberlain (Shiro Sano) and his assistant. The emperor's meal is performed as the ritualized serving of a god. Avoiding eye contact, the two servants seemingly submit to the logic of a divinity that cannot be regarded in the face. The camera focuses on the curious ritualized gestures of the servants, initially avoiding the capture on frame of the invisible Other being served. The emperor appears in a back shot, which then cuts into a frontal position. The great hidden Other is now revealed. Placed in the middle of the frame, the scene invokes the hoax of the Wizard of Oz, a harmless, tiny, quite common man, with spectacles. The ritualized gestures clash with the everyday sounds that invade the shot and do indeed question the hallowed space of the room. In this economy, human voice does not hold center stage. The emperor is silent, and lets himself be spoken by the assistant who functions as the god's translator, a voice by proxy. The ambivalence between the ritual, the common body of the sovereign, and the acoustical dissonances is further enhanced when the emperor speaks. His first words are an order: "Turn on the radio, please." The receiver submits to the logic of imperial power positions, tuning in first to a radio station playing military marches and then to Radio Tokyo, a propaganda broadcast in English aimed for American ears. The receiver provides a radiophonic corporeality (Connor 2000) to the discourse of *bushido* that is antagonized by the emperor's behavior.

The emperor's reluctant symbolic *Gestalt* is deconstructed by the collapse of voice and body, which the cinematic techniques work to enhance by focusing on the unwilling mouth gestures, the lisp, the lip smacks, an opening for a voice that is trapped inside a resistant body. As the film progresses, the speech impediment is negotiated with the humanization of the character. The two radio speeches provide the symbolical cues for the character's development, yet they remain as hidden signifiers in the narrative progression, only evoked and even intruding the diegesis in the acoustic reverberations of whizzing sound waves.

As the film progresses and the attacks on Tokyo increase, the emperor's fragility becomes climatic. Left alone in his quarters and curling upon himself, the emperor's body regresses into a symbolical womb and is reborn, with no voice and shedding tears. The suffering body is no longer godlike. This is the body that is then moved by the ailments of the population caused by the fire showers over Tokyo and by the nuclear holocaust in Hiroshima and Nagasaki.

The meeting with General MacArthur is a double mimicry of the opening sequence. The shot of Hirohito walking into the American Headquarters speaks against the entrance of the chamberlain in the emperor's bunker. It is now MacArthur who holds the sovereign position, he is the great hidden Other, shot from the back as Hirohito comes into frame. This reenactment of the first meeting between Hirohito and MacArthur reproduces what political scientist Douglas Lummis called the "wedding photo" moment (Lummis 1981: 18, see Fig. 1). In the sexually charged power relations between the two countries, Hirohito's attire and tiny figure before the obnoxious General displays the feminization of Japan before the hypermasculine US. In his memoir *Reminiscences,* MacArthur actually invokes a similarly charged scene in his recollection of the meeting with the Emperor at the American Embassy on 27 September 1945. He recalls the gesture of lighting the emperor's cigarette that in classical Hollywood cinema usually reflects a gendered relation of seduction, when a man lights the woman's cigarette (Wagner-Pacifici 2005: 107).

Sokurov picks this moment up with a topical close-up of the two-men's faces suggesting a loving sexual embrace, as MacArthur blows smoke into the emperor's face. Then again, by using English and speaking the Other's voice, the emperor's willing submission suggests his fragility and absolute exposure to the power of the victor, foregrounding the ultimate acknowledgement of his human, flawed dimension. The awareness of the Other that forces him not only to speak, but also to hear, the awareness after all of the dialogical and always incomplete, enigmatic and uncanny nature of voice resounds in the final decision to renounce divinity. As with the speech of 14 August 1945, the address to the nation on 1 January 1946, although not visually displayed, is welded into the cinematic narrative through condensation and allusion. Faithful to the stated intent of

Fig. 1: Gen. Douglas MacArthur and Emperor Hirohito at the American Embassy in Tokyo on 27 September 1945. Photo by US Army photographer Lt. Gaetano Faillace.

placing the character at the center, Sokurov's camera penetrates the unconscious, to expose visually the internal workings of the psyche. In the end, the god is human, the sovereign becomes an uncomfortable family man, the spectator is appeased by the return to normality. Conflict is over... or maybe not.

Tom Hooper's film, on the other hand, aims to bridge the unwholesome gap between the damaged sovereign with a stammer and the auditors both on and off frame. The film works to sew the open wound in the collective imaginary created by the absence of a sovereign voice, arising first by the demise of George V and then Edward VIII's abdication. The father's voice, the voice of sovereignty must undergo the test of the apparatus as the opening sequence populated by a cohort of mechanical surrogates, microphones, tape recorders and radios noticeably shows. The radiophonic apparatus, I argue, speaks to modern fears about the reification of the real and the emancipation of the object which, having acquired a life of its own, is definitely independent from the tyranny of the subject. Indeed this is a technology of gender, embodying the discursive anxiety of the incompetent/impotent sovereign, a powerful phallic surrogate to the pervasive sense of lack inhabiting a masculinity in crisis. It is by submitting to the object's force field, that is, by truly becoming a *homo mediatus*, and by relinquishing voice to the apparatus, that power may be restored. Ultimately, by letting "the microphone do its job", as King George V repeatedly tells his son after the 1934 Christmas radio address, the sovereign relinquishes voice to the puppet master, the acousmatic ghost in the machine, to radio as the ventriloquist of power. The voice that is thus spoken exposes the sovereign to the power of the Other, it actually makes the sovereign dependent on the Other's responsiveness to his power in a phonological master-slave dialectics of sorts.

Following the traditional line of classical narrative film, and at times despite the edgy dialogue, *The King's Speech* remains a popular tale about the recovery of manliness, about the mending of the sovereign's damaged voice and of film, gramophone, microphone as discursive networks that structure the national community of feeling. *Mutatis mutandis*, and returning to Rick Altman's insightful assertion, in Sokurov voice and sound ask, and the image tentatively responds, whilst in Hooper's film image and voice are not made to ask, but to tell, and the audience is meant to respond (Altman 1980: 70)

Sokurov's film as Tom Hooper's build from key historical radio broadcasts to construct a critique of sovereign voice, in *The Sun*, and an acousmatic euphoria, in *The King's Speech*. The critique of sovereign voice discusses its role in the construction of sovereignty, whilst producing a visual meta-critique on the cinematic use of sound and the tradition of placing voice at the center. This emperor who finds it hard to speak, the man who was mostly spoken for, presents a critique of phonocentrism, displacing human voice to a subsidiary role in the acoustic system and forcing it to relinquish its meaning making potential to the non-diegetic sounds (sound of the writing brush, the whizzing sound of radio, birds chirping, objects moving), hence producing an alternative synaesthesia of sound and image constructed against the grain of voice.

Thus, inviting us to see voice as a fundamental marker of the cinematic mode of embodiment, the films in their inalienable difference speak to the crisis of sovereign voice in our conflict torn twenty-first century and to film's seismic ability to premediate the challenges ahead while presenting two narratives in conflict regarding the possibilities of democratic voice. In what I call the conservative acousmatic euphoria of *The King's Speech* resonates the traditional orientation towards the hidden voice as a carrier of authority structuring the construction of a collective sense of identification. While the critique of sovereign voice creates distance between screen and spectator, and fosters an interruption in the logic of identification, the acousmatic euphoria aims to bridge the gap and foster a maternal *jouissance* that will reconstruct in the relation between film and audience the imminent collapse of voice. Rather than asking whose voice, as Sukorov's film does, and what it does, Hooper's acousmatic euphoria mends the damage and places univocality back to the center. Conflict is over, but only on screen.

Works Cited

Altman, Rick (1980) "Moving Lips: Cinema as Ventriloquism", in *Yale French Studies* 60, 67–79.

Aristotle (1984) *The Complete Works of Aristotle,* revised Oxford translation, ed. Jonathan Barnes, vol. 2 (Princeton, NJ: Princeton UP).

Arnheim, Rudolf (1931) *Film als Kunst* (Berlin: Rowohlt).

Benjamin, Walter (2006) *Selected Writings.* Vol. 3: 1935–1938, ed. Howard Eiland, Howard and Michael W. Jennings (Cambridge, MA: Harvard UP).

Cavarero, Adriana (2005) *For More Than One Voice: Toward a Philosophy of Vocal Expression* (Stanford, CA: Stanford UP).

Chion, Michel (1999) *The Voice in Cinema* (New York: Columbia UP).

Connor, Steven (2000) *Dumbstruck: A Cultural History of Ventriloquism* (Oxford: Oxford UP).

Couldry, Nick (2010) *Voice Matters* (London: Sage).

Derrida, Jacques (1973) *Speech and Phenomenon*, transl. David Allison (Evanston: Northwestern UP)

Dolar, Mladen (2006) *A Voice and Nothing More* (Cambridge, MA: MIT Press).

Elsaesser, Thomas, and Malte Hagener (2010) *Film Theory: An Introduction Through the Senses* (London: Routledge).

Gil, Isabel (1993) "Caos e Metamorfose: Uma Leitura da Dança na Obra de Hugo von Hofmannsthal", in *Runa* 20: 2 (1993), 151–160.

Gil, Isabel (2003) "'*Schweig und tanze!*' Textos no Limite da (Re)Presentação. A Palavra e o Gesto no Drama de Franz Werfel, Eberhard Pannwitz e Hugo von Hofmannsthal", *Dedalus* 9, 91–117.

Haas, Willy (1921) "Sprechbühne und Lichtbühne: Brief eines Filmwesens an ein Theaterwesen", *Die neue Schaubühne* (Oct. 1921), 153–155.
Hiebler, Heinz (2003) *Hugo von Hofmannsthal und die Medienkultur der Moderne* (Würzburg: Königshausen & Neumann).
Hofmannsthal, Hugo von (1979) *Gesammelte Werke: Reden und Aufsätze II 1914–1924*, ed. Bernd Schoeller (Frankfurt/M.: Fischer).
Hofmannsthal, Hugo von (2006) *Sämtliche Werke XXVII: Ballette, Pantomime, Filmszenarien*, ed. Gisela Bärbel Schmid and Klaus-Dieter Krabiel (Frankfurt/M.: S. Fischer).
Ihde, Don (2007) *Listening and Voice: Phenomenologies of Sound* (Buffalo: SUNY Press).
Lummis, Douglas (1981) "Genshiteki na nikko no nakadeno hinatabokko", *Shiso no Kagaku* (June 1981), 18.
MacCannell, Juliet M. (1996) "Facing Fascism: A Feminine Politics of Jouissance", in *Lacan, Politics, Aesthetics*, ed. Willy Apollon and Richard Feldstein (Buffalo: SUNY Press), 65–99.
Neumark, Norie, Ross Gibson, and Theo van Leuwen (eds.) (2010) *Voice: Vocal Aesthetics in Digital Art and Media* (Cambridge, MA: MIT Press).
Pauleit, Winfried, et al. (eds.) (2009) *Das Kino träumt: Projektion, Imagination, Vision* (Stuttgart: Bertz + Fischer).
Ribeiro, Nelson (2011) *BBC Broadcasts to Portugal in World War II: How Radio was Used as a Weapon of War* (London: Edwin Mellen).
Shell, Marc (2005) *Stutter* (Cambridge, MA: Harvard UP).
Sokurov, Aleksandr: "The Sun", in *The Island of Sokurov*, http://www.sokurov.spb.ru/isle_en/feature_films.html?num=82, consulted 30-04-2013.
Szaniawski, Jeremi (2006) "Interview with Aleksandr Sokurov", *Critical Inquiry* 33: 1, 13–27.
Wagner-Pacifici, Robin (2005) *The Art of Surrender: Decomposing Sovereignty at Conflict's End* (Chicago: U of Chicago Press).
Winthrop-Young, Geoffrey (2010) *Kittler and the Media* (London: Polity Press).
Žižek, Slavoj, and Renate Saleci (eds.) (1996) *Gaze and Voice as Love Objects* (Durham, NC: Duke UP).

Ana Mijić (University of Vienna)

"Hurt Identities?" The Postwar Bosnian Narrative of Self-Victimization

In summer 2009, many Bosnian cities were plastered with posters showing the image of Radovan Karadžić and the slogan: "We believe that you are not guilty. Happy birthday, President." During the war in Bosnia-Herzegovina (1992–1995), Karadžić had been the head of the so-called *Serbian Republic in Bosnia and Herzegovina (Republika srpksa)*. In 1996 the *International Criminal Tribunal for the former Yugoslavia* (ICTY) issued an international arrest warrant for the Bosnian Serb leader who had been charged with genocide – amongst other cases, the Srebrenica massacre – and crimes against humanity. Twelve years later, in August 2008, Karadžić was captured and turned over to the ICTY. The posters, wishing the war crimes suspect a happy birthday, were put up by the *Serbian National Movement Izbor je naš* [The Choice is Ours]. The movement's former president gave a public statement on this "congratulation-campaign":

> In this way we are showing that we have not forgotten the person who deserves the credit for establishment of Republika Srpska and defense of the Serbian people. We have undertaken this action in order to show that we have not forgotten him. We wished him a happy birthday, which is a civilized act. We are hoping that Radovan Karadžić will be glad to see this [...] Radovan Karadžić is a political visionary, humanist and peacemaker. He fights for the truth. So, help us God, The Hague Tribunal will render a verdict of not guilty after it sees the evidence he presents. (BIRN BiH – Balkan Investigating Reporting Network)

Six years ago, something quite similar could be observed when the former Croatian General Ante Gotovina was found guilty of war crimes committed in 1995 during and in the aftermath of the so-called *Operacija Oluja* (Operation Storm), and sentenced to twenty-four years in prison. Operation Storm was a military action carried out by the Croatian Armed Forces to regain control of the Croatian Krajina region around Knin that had been occupied by Serbs since 1991. According to the UNHCR, during this operation and its aftermath a total of 500 Serbs were killed and 200,000 Serb civilians displaced (Human Rights Watch 1996). Gotovina's conviction, however, sparked Croatian protests worldwide. People in tears, ripped EU-flags, pictures of the convict subtitled with *Heroj* [hero], and a huge lack of understanding could be observed not only in Zagreb, Split, and Zadar, or in various Bosnian cities like Mostar, but also in Berlin, Stuttgart, New York, Sydney, or Melbourne, and obviously in The Hague.

https://doi.org/10.1515/9783110556858-011

The verdict dealt a blow to the self-image of Croatia as victim of war crimes rather than a culprit; The Hague did not want to recognize the purely defensive character of the *Domovinski Rat – their* Homeland War. Then, on 12 November 2012, the ICTY overturned the sentences of Gotovina and with it – at least according to the perception of the Croatian people – the sentences of Croatia. This verdict of not guilty was extraordinarily significant for the Croats, as it was seen as the final evidence for their own victimhood. Not surprisingly, the Serbian reaction was less enthusiastic. From their point of view, no one was held responsible for the murder of several hundred people and the displacement of thousands of civilians. Furthermore, with the acquittal of Gotovina, the Serbs lost their only significant Croatian equivalent to Radovan Karadžić and Ratko Mladić; once again, they had to take the part of the prime aggressor, of the sole responsible for the bloodshed during the war.

Phenomena like these, i.e. this special kind of collective identification, cannot be explained only by referring to the peculiar character of nationalism in the Balkans. They should rather be seen as an expression of the specific socio-historical constellations of this post-war region. Despite the fact that there have been great achievements since the end of the war, Bosnia-Herzegovina is still characterized by precarious political, economic, and social structures. Consistently, politicians, journalists, and scholars state that Bosnia is still a problem: not only for the International Community, but also for the Bosnian people themselves. On a regular basis social scientists publish "disillusioning findings" and international politicians express their concerns about the difficult and complex situation in the country. The following analysis is more specific: it is based on a research project which aimed to analyze the social construction of the "Self" and with it, the social construction of "others" in the post-war Bosnia-Herzegovina (Mijić 2014).

A hermeneutical analysis of interviews which were conducted in different regions in Bosnia-Herzegovina between 2007 and 2009 reveals that ethnic identifications still play a significant role; it indicates that *conflicting narratives* about the past and the future, about in-group and out-group make it difficult to create continuity and to cope with discontinuities in one's own biographical development. But the analysis also shows that despite these difficulties the construction of a positive self-image is still possible: the maintenance of one's own 'we'-ideal is strongly intertwined with processes of self-victimization.

1 The situation in post-war Bosnia-Herzegovina

The violent conflict officially ended with the ratification of the Dayton Peace Agreement in December 1995. Approximately 100,000 people were killed, over two million displaced. Until today, many Bosnians have not returned to their hometowns, but are living in those regions where their 'own' ethnic community constitutes the majority. This ethnic segregation is institutionalized by the peace talks actually. One frequent point of criticism regarding the Dayton Peace Agreement is the fact that the agreement sealed the division of Bosnia into the Serbian dominated *Republika Srpska* (with app. 49 % of the territory) and the *Federation of Bosnia and Herzegovina*[1] – each with its own political structure and administrative organization. The Federation itself is divided into ten largely ethnically – either Bosniak or Croatian – homogeneous cantons. Some politicians and scholars even claim that, in the end, the Dayton Peace Agreement has legitimized the euphemistically so-called "ethnic cleansing" (Lovrenović 1999: 198). Dayton was successful in ending the physical violence, but it has also created one of the most complicated, ethnically divided, and therefore unstable political systems worldwide. Actually, the present situation in Bosnia and Herzegovina is often described – by using Clausewitz's famous characterization upside down – as an extension of war by political means (Lovrenović 2010: 151–154; Ćurak 2004; Ćurak 2002; Džihić 2008).

The belief in one's own absolute truth has not been banned from the public space. Ethno-nationalistic parties still dominate the political landscape of the fragile state. In ethnically divided schools one-sided '(hi)stories' are told and taught, and the media landscape is also divided along ethnic lines. Due to a law, which intended equal participation of the three constitutive nations, people are in fact forced to declare themselves either as Bosniak, Croat or Serb; thus, until today, in Bosnia-Herzegovina one can hardly find any Bosnians. This obviously has consequences with respect to one's own personal identity, which is to a large extent ethnicized. But despite all these complications, the Bosnian people are still bonded to each other due to the fact that they are sharing one language and one state – not the least because international pressure provides no realistic exit options. The observation of this dilemma, i.e. the coexistence of proximity and distance between the different ethnic communities of the country, was the initial point of my research into identities in post-war Bosnia-Herzegovina.

---

1 In fact, there is a third political unit, the so-called *Brčko District*, which formally belongs to both entities.

2 Identities in post-war Bosnia-Herzegovina

During the war between 1992 and 1995, the conflicting parties constructed identities which were characterized by intensive and powerful ethnic in-group/out-group differentiations, i.e. by hierarchies of 'us' and 'them', combined with positive attributions towards the in-group and pejorative attributions towards the members of the out-group. To put it with the German sociologist Norbert Elias, there is "group charisma" on the one side and "group disgrace" on the other (Elias 1990: 16–18): the own ethnic group is characterized as morally superior, as more civilized, as 'better', whereas the others are seen as morally inferior and barbaric. Simply put, it is an in-group-/out-group differentiation that goes far beyond simple *otherness*.

After the end of war, people were confronted with an entirely novel situation; due to new and (mainly) externally induced normative standards which delegitimize ethnic mobilization, and due to the fact that they have to continue living together in one state (i.e. beyond their own ethnic communities), they are forced to perform new definitions of ethnic boundaries, or, to frame it with a sociological classic, a new "definition of the situation" (Thomas 1928), which challenges the respective group charisma as well as the others' group disgrace. For this reason, it can be assumed that there is a structural tension between conflicting narratives about what is 'real' and about the characteristics of the different identities. In fact, my research project focuses on a (qualitative) empirical analysis of the genesis and the persistence of self-attribution and the characterization of others in the context of accelerated social transformation processes that are characterized by this structural tension.

I endeavor to find out to what extent this tension between different narrations of reality affects the social construction of the individual self. Moreover, it has been investigated how members of the "conflicting parties", i.e. the members of the respective ethnic groups – under these circumstances – create a consistent self or *we*-image, respectively, i.e. how they deal with the described ambivalence.

3 The social construction of (ethnicized) realities

The theoretical foundation of the analysis is the social constructivism approach of Peter L. Berger and Thomas Luckmann. In *The Social Construction of Reality*

(1966), with which they have developed a new sociology of knowledge,[2] the authors define reality "as a quality appertaining to phenomena, that we recognize as having a being independent of our own volition (we cannot 'wish them away'), and [...] 'knowledge' as the certainty that phenomena are real and that they possess specific characteristics" (Berger & Luckmann 1967: 1). But where do these realities come from? As the title of the book suggests, the authors are of the opinion that these realities are socially created by humans who themselves are at the same time social products of these very realities. Berger and Luckmann base their work on a fundamental (dialectical) proposition: *"Society is a human product. Society is an objective reality. Man is a social product"* (Berger & Luckmann 1967: 61; italics in the original). With this assumption they systematically tackle one – if not the – fundamental question of social theory: the question of how to understand the relation between individual and society. With their theory, they are strictly arguing against the tendency to reify social reality, i.e. to define social structures as something independent from the social actions of individuals. In fact, humans are constructing reality socially and, at the same time, internalizing this constructed or created realities within the lifelong process of socialization as their own realities.[3] During this, the individual does not only learn how others see the world, s/he learns also that this is how the world quite simply *is*, and: who s/he is:

---

2 While classical theories (Karl Marx, Max Scheler, Karl Mannheim) typically were focused on scientific and theoretical knowledge and ideology respectively, Berger and Luckmann argue that the problem of ideas (including ideology) constitutes only part of the larger problem of the sociology of knowledge. Reality, the objective as well as the subjective reality, is constructed by knowledge. Insofar "the sociology of knowledge must concern itself with everything that passes for knowledge in society" (Berger & Luckmann 1967: 14–15).

3 Knowledge is in fact the basis and the tool for the social construction of realities, without which no meaningful creation of realities would be possible. It is the core of the fundamental dialectic of society as it "'programmes' the channels in which externalization produces an objective world. It objectifies this world through language and the cognitive apparatus based on language, that is, it orders it into objects to be apprehended as reality. It is internalized again as objectively valid truth in the course of socialization. Knowledge about society is thus a *realization* in the double sense of the word, in the sense of apprehending the objectivated social reality, and in the sense of ongoingly producing this reality" (Berger & Luckmann 1967: 66). Considering this background, it is quite consistent that there are two different perspectives on social reality: on the one hand, they understand society as an objective reality, which includes the institutionally defined constructs around us (Berger & Luckmann 1967, ch. 2). On the other hand, they conceive society as subjective reality, which is the personal acquisition of reality (Berger & Luckmann 1967, ch. 3).

> Identity is, of course, a key element of subjective reality and, like all subjective reality, stands in a dialectical relationship with society. [...] Societies have histories in the course of which specific identities emerge; these histories are, however, made by men [and women] with specific identities. If one is mindful of this dialectic one can avoid the misleading notion of "collective identities" without having recourse to the uniqueness, *sub specie aeternitatis*, of individual existence. (Berger & Luckmann 1967: 173)

In other words, identity or the self is always a social self (Mead 1934; Goffman 1959; Cooley 1964). Without society there is no identity, without social narratives about who I am there is no self, and without social narratives about who 'we' are there is no such thing like ethnicity. This constructivist perspective on ethnicity challenges the so-called "primordialist" assumptions, which argue that ethnic membership is acquired through birth and therefore represents a 'given' characteristic of the social world. A further proponent of this constructivist perspective was Max Weber who offered this definition of ethnicity:

> We shall call 'ethnic groups' those human groups that entertain a subjective belief in their common descent because of similarities of physical type or of customs or both, or because of memories of colonization and migration [...] It does not matter whether or not an objective blood relationship exists. (Weber 1978: 389)

With the publication *Ethnic Groups and Boundaries* in 1969, the Norwegian anthropologist Fredrik Barth in particular initiated an important constructivist change in the research about ethnicity. There are at least three central insights of Barth's theory (Verdery 1994: 34–35). First, ethnicity should be seen as a form of social organization, i.e. a form of "organizing cultural differences" (Verdery 1994: 35). Second, this implies that "the critical focus of investigation [...] becomes the ethnic boundary that defines the group not the cultural stuff that it encloses" (Barth 1969: 15). It is the dichotomization, i.e. the presence of boundaries, not the cultural content, which determines in-group and out-group (Verdery 1994: 35). As Barth states (1969: 14): "It is important to recognize that although ethnic categories take cultural differences into account, we can assume no simple one-to-one relationship between ethnic units and cultural similarities and differences." Third, and furthermore, ethnicity or ethnic identity "should be seen as based on ascription and self-ascription, rather than on 'possessing' a certain cultural inventory" (Verdery 1994: 35).

While positioned in opposition to primordialist ideas of a fixed nature of ethnicity, the constructivist approaches do not deny that "the subjective belief in a common descent" (Weber) could become objective facticity and has immediate consequences on identity construction. In fact, one of the central questions of the book *The Social Construction of Reality* is "[h]ow is it possible that subjective meanings become objective facticity?" (Berger & Luckmann 1967: 18)[4] But the significance of ethnic belonging or ethnic boundaries for the construction of the self depends to a great extent on the social context (Wimmer 2008). It could be assumed that the war and the violence in South-Eastern Europe raised the importance of ethnicity, and that ethnic belonging became a central component of the Self, so that in the end hardly anyone was capable of freeing himself or herself from the fiction of an "irreducible ethnic identity" – to put it in the words of the Canadian historian Michael Ignatieff (1994). This extraordinarily strong bond between 'I' and 'we' explains the potential vulnerability of identity when the group-charisma is challenged. In fact, there is always a connection between I and we, as for instance Norbert Elias states: "A person's we-image and we-ideal form as much part of a person's self-image and self-ideal as the image and ideal of him- or herself as the unique person to which he or she refers as I" (Elias 1976: xliii). This connection should be imagined as a kind of a balance between two different components of identity: the I-identity and the we-identity. Which component is stronger depends on the specific socio-historical context, but "as long as individuals are regarded merely as we-less I's, and the role of the we-I balance and of the we-ideal and we-identity in individual feeling and behavior is misunderstood", some social phenomena like the difficulties regarding the integration of European countries – this is the topic Elias wrote about – or the integration of Bosnia-Herzegovina (BiH) "will remain inaccessible to analysis" (Elias 2001: 221).

Considering this, it should be asked how people deal with situations where their respective we-ideal is called into question? To answer this question, about 30 narrative interviews with people of different ethnic belonging have been conducted in different regions in BiH. These interviews were analyzed by means of the so-called objective hermeneutics, a reconstructive approach following German sociologist Ulrich Oevermann (1979, 1981, 2002). This method aims to reconstruct

> [l]atent structures of meaning that underlie social practices and subjective meanings. These structures are the outcome of and provide the meaning context for the social coordination of practice. They are latent – not restricted to the actor's discursive knowledge – and independent of their subjective intentions and meanings (and in this sense 'objective'). (Lueger et al. 2005: 1147)

4 With this question, Berger and Luckmann are connecting the approaches of Max Weber and Émile Durkheim.

4 (Self-)charismatization through (self-) victimization

The analysis confirmed the assumption that people in post-war Bosnia-Herzegovina have to deal with a certain reality crisis. Its central source seems to be a kind of interpretatory uncertainty due to not only different, but also conflicting or contradictory perspectives of, and with it conflicting narratives about, reality. Furthermore, the analysis shows that there is one central pattern of how people deal with such a dilemma.

People in Bosnia-Herzegovina still strongly identify with their respective ethnic group. The construction of personal identity is to a large extent affected by the identification with the ethnic in-group, which is typically perceived as the central victim of war and the post-war constellations. Self-victimization seems to be a self-evident solution of the post-war crisis. It enables people to handle the dilemma between the old interpretation patterns – i.e. hierarchical ethnicity – and the new, externally induced normative standards. Self-victimization is a convincing strategy to maintain a positive self-image in the light of external delegitimization, since it fulfills some important functions.

As the Israeli social psychologist Daniel Bar-Tal and his research associates point out, self-victimization creates a sense not just of differentiation, but also of superiority. It describes the out-group in pejorative and delegitimizing terms and defines "them" as responsible for the violence. Simultaneously it presents the in-group – as already mentioned – as the only victim of the conflict (Bar-Tal et al. 2009: 244). Furthermore, self-victimization can be considered a fundament for in-group solidarity and unity, since

> it implies a threat to the collective's well-being and even to its survival. It heightens the need for unity and solidarity, which are important conditions for survival in view of the continuous harm caused by the rival. Collective victimhood may serve as 'social glue', bonding members of the collective together on the basis of the present threat and past 'chosen traumas'. (Bar-Tal et al. 2009: 245)

One of the most important functions of self-victimization is moral justification. The responsibility for the physical violence is typically passed on to the out-group, and the violence of the in-group towards the out-group is usually legitimized by referring to its irreducibly defensive character (Bar-Tal et al 2009: 244). Another central objective of self-victimization is the gaining of international support:

> Victims are not blamed for the outbreak of the conflict and the violence that follows, as they are suffering from the unjustified violence of the aggressor. This is crucial in obtaining the backing of worldwide public opinion and increasing the likelihood of moral, political and material support. (Bar-Tal et al. 2009: 246)

All of this most likely leads to "competitive victimhood" between two or more sides in the conflict or in the aftermath of a conflict (ibid.). Each conflicting party is making great efforts to persuade the in-group, the adversarial out-groups, and the third party – the international community – that it is an innocent victim. It is actually a fight over "moral social identity", which not only focuses on one's own in-group victimhood, but also on the competition of which group is suffering most (Bar-Tal et al. 2009: 247).[5]

Considering these benefits, it is unsurprising that societies are trying to maintain the sense of victimhood over time and to assimilate it into the society's collective memory (ibid.). But the claimed 'victim' status also has to be recognized by others. Referring to the initially mentioned example, the peoples in the Balkans, for instance, have quite clear expectations of the ICTY. The Tribunal should confirm that one's own ethnic group is an innocent victim and therewith not guilty. If they fall short of expectations, i.e. if the 'national heroes' suddenly become murderers, perpetrators, culprits, it is seen as an assault on the personal identity. Their strong identification with the defendants makes the people believe that the Tribunal does not focus on individual responsibility, but on the collective guilt of the whole ethnic group. From this point of view, General Ante Gotovina, for example, does not stand for the individual, the person Gotovina. His conviction as well as his acquittal stand for the conviction and the acquittal of the Croatian people. In this respect, the ICTY can be considered as a battlefield for the protection of one's own identity and with it of one's own reality.

Self-victimization indeed stabilizes a positive self-image, since it strengthens the group-charisma. But self-victimization does not guarantee that others recognize this identity. Particularly among the three main ethnic groups in BiH – the three constitutive nations – such a recognition could not be expected, because all of them perceive themselves as the sole or at least as a central victim of war. This could be seen as a kind of zero-sum game. However, due to the social and spatial proximity of the conflict parties, people are not able to avoid the re-

5 A quantitative analysis shows that a majority of the interviewed Bosnians – 89% of the Bosniaks, 80% of the Serbs and 73% of the Croats – are of the opinion that their group fought only defensive wars (Kostić 2008: 395) and define the respective armed forces (Armija BiH, Vojska RS, HVO) as defender (ibid.).

alities of the (ethnic) others. In order to defend their particular 'truth' about the past, they are implementing specific strategies.

5 Strategies for maintaining self-victimization

The hermeneutical analysis of the in-depth interviews exposed some patterns, which seem to enable the individuals to maintain their reality perspective as well as a positive self-image despite their permanent confrontation with the conflicting narratives. Four of these strategies are illustrated below: the tabooization strategy, the moral alchemy, the double relativization, and the subjectifying of war.

5.1 Tabooization

Due to pragmatic considerations, the knowledge about the war often is not mobilized in interethnic communication. The following interview passage exemplifies this omission:

> After a short period, just a few months after the end of war, we began to visit each other. As if nothing had happened [...] As if this hole had never existed. As if the lines had never existed. (Interview 1, ll. 82–86)

Such an "as-if" strategy for the benefit of the normalization process seems to be quite reasonable – at least *prima facie*. A second glance shows that this strategy supports a reproduction of ethnic boundaries, and makes them even denser:

> I go there and sit with my former friends. We sit together and talk about this and that. We make jokes about this and that. But it doesn't feel right, it isn't the same anymore. Somehow we have fallen out. The topics we are talking about aren't the same anymore. (Interview 1, ll. 88–91)

When conversations about the reality of the past just take place among like-minded people, it could be expected that this reality will be set in stone. Thus "tabooization" has an impact on societal orientations regarding interethnic relations:

> [I]n situations where there is competition between different reality-defining agencies, all sorts of secondary-group relationships with the competitors may be tolerated, as long as

> there are firmly established primary-group relationships within which *one* reality is ongoingly reaffirmed against the competitors. (Berger & Luckmann 1967: 152)

This explains why there are multifarious economic and other non-personal relationships between members of the different ethnic groups, while personal or intimate relationships like friendships or marriages are condemned or at least have to be justified.

5.2 "Moral Alchemy"

Self-victimization is characterized by the dichotomy of victim and perpetrator. But in the light of the permanent confrontation with alternative realities, the interpretation that the respective ethnic out-groups are just perpetrators is hardly sustainable. To solve this problem, agents simply question the truth or the *Wahrhaftigkeit* [truthfulness] – to use a Habermasian term – of alternative narrations. The dichotomy of victim and perpetrator becomes a dichotomy of true victim and a created, constructed, and invented victim. Following US sociologist Robert K. Merton, this process could be described as "moral alchemy":

> Through a faultlessly bisymmetrical prejudice, ethnic and racial out-groups get it coming and going. The systematic condemnation of the out-grouper continues largely irrespective of what he does. More: through a freakish exercise of capricious judicial logic, the victim is punished for the crime. Superficial appearances notwithstanding, prejudice and discrimination aimed at the out-group are not a result of what the out-group does, but are rooted deep in the structure of our society and the social psychology of its members. To understand how this happens, we must examine the moral alchemy through which the in-group readily transmutes virtue into vice and vice into virtue, as the occasion may demand. (Merton 1996: 119)

5.3 Double relativization as identity stabilizer

Occasionally, people recognize that members of their own ethnic in-group could have committed (war) crimes. It would stand to reason that such a recognition supports a no longer idealized image of one's own we-image. But what is actually happening is the effort to relativize in-group crimes by comparing them to out-group atrocities. The Croats, for example, try to relativize the responsibility of Ante Gotovina by referring to the crimes committed by Karadžić and Mladić:

> All people who have committed war crimes have to be punished. But, all of us know what Karadžić has done. He has issued the command to go to Srebrenica and to massacre, to kill. How many? 12,000 people. That's not nearly the same. Croatia was an internationally recognized state when Operation Storm took place! With recognized borders. Recognized by the West, by all powers. A recognized state. Even if you go there to clean up... The people there didn't want to recognize the Croatian government. You have to do something with these people. When a criminal wants to rob a bank you have to go there to prevent it. That's the same thing. [...] In my opinion Gotovina is not guilty. (Interview 1, ll. 416–421)

This double relativization – i.e., the relativization of one's own we-ideal, which itself is relativized – in the end supports the stabilization of the we-ideal.

5.4 Personification of war

Many interviewees describe the war not as something made by humans. They characterize it rather as something that abolished and antagonized the "innocent" human beings. The following interview sequence illustrates this strategy of personifying war:

> When Tito died, when Yugoslavia fell apart, this dammed war came and did what it did: it made us all enemies. (Interview 2, ll. 8–9)

The war is seen as an event completely independent from human action – like a natural disaster – or even as an active subject. War can thus not be seen as a matter of ethical considerations, and no responsibility has to be attributed to human action (Hoch 1999: 38). The social function of this interpretation pattern is obvious: by personifying the war, the agents not only distance their own ethnic in-group from any responsible action in order to protect their own we-ideal. Furthermore, the same possibility is offered to the respective ethnic out-group. It seems to be quite reasonable to assume that this 'outsourcing' of war could be seen as the lowest common denominator which the parties can agree on. Primarily those people who were successfully and persistently socialized in the socialist system of former Yugoslavia seem to come back to this definition of the situation, since this interpretation is often attended by the cultural phenomenon of *Yugo-nostalgia:* "I was born in 1953 in the Socialist system, where life was easygoing and beautiful – I don't know how to describe it – without any physical or mental burdens. During the Tito years, life was beautiful." (Interview 2, ll. 1–2) Personifying the war makes it easier to disconnect the present from the war-torn past and connect with the Yugoslav *Vorvergangenheit* – the Yugoslav past before the war. This mechanism as well as the tabooization of the war-torn past in interethnic communication are conducive to a normalization of everyday relations between members of the different ethnic groups – even if only in a cursory way. By applying these strategies, people are repressing the past and reshaping it rather than dealing with it in a constructive way. The moral alchemy and mechanism of the double relativization, in contrast, are more disintegrative strategies of interaction with manifest conflict potential and are applied by Bosnians who are not interested in a normalization of the situation. They are not willing to repress the past, but neither are they willing to question their version of it, according to which their own ethnic group is just a victim of the atrocities of the others.

5.6 Conclusion

As the hermeneutical analysis reveals clearly, the pattern of self-victimization seems to be a widespread mechanism for protecting a positive self-image in post-war Bosnia-Herzegovina. But it is certainly not a regionally limited phenomenon; in fact it is a globally observable strategy of people and groups involved in conflicts and struggles about social and political values and beliefs. As German psychoanalysts Alexander and Margarete Mitscherlich aptly point out: "In each instance the evil is externalized. It is sought for on the outside, and it strikes one from the outside." (Mitscherlich & Mitscherlich 1975: 46)

The interpretation pattern of self-victimization as well as the mentioned strategies to maintain the self-perception as a victim could be reconstructed in all conducted interviews regardless of the respondent's ethnic belonging. The discovered strategies can also be identified within the political discourse – but only the disruptive ones. The political landscape in Bosnia-Herzegovina is still dominated by nationalist powers who are not interested in normalizing the situation, or in supporting the formation of a Bosnian identity beyond ethnic self-ascription. Those politicians who are arguing beyond an ethnic in-group/out-group differentiation have hardly any chance to participate in the political process. Playing the ethnic card and stroking the fundamental fears of people guarantee their (re-)election, since this most effectively mobilizes the population. Similar to the notion of warlords, one could probably speak of 'post-war lords' in this case.

Their efforts in maintaining the ethnic dimension as the decisive element of politics are paradoxically supported by the Dayton Peace Treaty, as demonstrated over and over again. In the course of the first Bosnian Census since the end of war, the Bosnian population was asked about their national affiliation in October 2013. They should declare themselves as Bosniaks, Croats, Serbs, or as members of a national minority – i.e. as Bosnians. In the months before the census, the political and religious leaders of the different ethnic groups started a major offensive of ethnic mobilization. Their arguments were congruent. Since the political reality of Dayton distributes political power along ethnic criteria only to the three constitutive peoples of Bosnia-Herzegovina (the Bosniaks, Croats, and Serbs), ethnic leaders insist on the duty of each member of the respective in-group to declare herself or himself Bosniak, Croat, or Serb. Otherwise they would risk again to fall victim to the despotism of the others. The final results show that a majority of the Bosnians had fulfilled their duty (Agency for Statistics of Bosnia and Herzegovina 2016). In the end, as long as the conflicting narratives about the past and the future as well as the self-perceptions as victims are predominant, Bosnian society – or more precisely: the Bosnian societies – will not be able to take responsibility for their own destiny.

Works cited

Agency for Statistics of Bosnia and Herzegovina (2016): Census of Population, Households and Dwellings in Bosnia and Herzegovina, 2013. Final results, http://www.popis2013.ba/popis2013/doc/Popis2013prvoIzdanje.pdf (accessed 2 August 2017).

Bar-Tal, Daniel, Lily Chernyak-Hai, Noa Schori, and Ayelet Gundar (2009) "A Sense of Self-Perceived Collective Victimhood in Intractable Conflicts", *International Review of the Red Cross* 91.874, 229–258.

Barth, Fredrik (ed.) (1969) *Ethnic Groups and Boundaries: The Social Organization of Culture Difference* (Oslo: Universitetsforlaget).

Berger, Peter L., and Thomas Luckmann (1967) *The Social Construction of Reality: A Treatise in the Sociology of Knowledge* (New York: Anchor Books).

BIRN BiH – Balkan Investigating Reporting Network (2009) "Happy Birthday, Mr President Karadzic", http://www.balkaninsight.com/en/article/happy-birthday-mr-president-karadzic (accessed 1 February 2014).

Cooley, Charles H. (1964) *Human Nature and the Social Order* (New York: Scribner's).

Ćurak, Nerzuk (2002) *Geopolitika kao Sudbina: Slučaj Bosna. Postmodernistički Ogled o Perifernoj Zemlj* (Sarajevo: Fakultet Političkih Nauka).

Ćurak, Nerzuk (2004) *Dejtonski Nacionalizam: Ogledi o Političkom* (Sarajevo: buybook).

Džihić, Vedran (2008) "Ethnonationalismus und Ethnopolitik als bosnisches Schicksal: Den geschichtlichen und aktuellen Widersprüchen Bosniens und Herzegowinas auf der Spur", *Kakanien Revisited*, http://www.kakanien.ac.at/beitr/fallstudie/VDzihic1.pdf (accessed 3 December 2012).

Elias, Norbert (2001) *The Society of Individuals*, ed. Michael Schröter (New York: Continuum).

Goffman, Erving (1959) *The Presentation of Self in Everyday Life* (New York et al.: Doubleday).

Hoch, Martin (1999) "Vater aller Dinge? Zur Bedeutung des Krieges für das Menschen- und Geschichtsbild", *Mittelweg 36* 8.6, 30–48.

Human Rights Watch (1996) "Impunity for Abuses Committed During "Operation Storm" and the Denial of the Right of Refugees to Return to the Krajina (UNHCR)." http://www.unhcr.org/refworld/docid/3ae6a7d70.html (accessed 10 December 2012).
Ignatieff, Michael (1994) *Blood and Belonging* (Toronto: Penguin Books).
Kostić, Roland (2008) "Nationbuilding as an Instrument of Peace? Exploring Local Attitudes towards International Nationbuilding and Reconciliation in Bosnia and Herzegovina", *Civil Wars* 10.4, 384–412. http://www.tandfonline.com/doi/abs/10.1080/13698240802354482 (accessed 11 April 2013).
Lovrenović, Ivan (1999) *Bosnien und Herzegowina* (Vienna: Folio).
Lovrenović, Ivan (2010) "Dvadesetjedna teza", in *Bosna i Hercegovina: Buducnost nezavrsenog rata* (Zagreb: Novi Liber), 149–233.
Lueger, Manfred, Karl Sandner, Renate Mayer, and Gerhard Hammerschmid (2005) "Contextualizing Influence Activities: An Objective Hermeneutical Approach", *Organization Studies* 26.8, 1145–1168. http://oss.sagepub.com/cgi/doi/10.1177/0170840605055265 (accessed 24 February 2014).
Mead, George Herbert (1934) *Mind, Self and Society* (Chicago: U of Chicago Press).
Merton, Robert K. (1996) *On Social Structure and Science*, ed. Piotr Sztompka (Chicago: U of Chicago Press).
Mijić, Ana (2014) *Verletzte Identitäten: Der Kampf um den Opferstatus im bosnisch-herzegowinischen Nachkrieg* (Frankfurt/M. and New York: Campus).
Mitscherlich, Alexander, and Margarete Mitscherlich (1975) *The Inability to Mourn: Principles of Collective Behavior* (New York: Grove Press).
Oevermann, Ulrich (1981) "Fallrekonstruktion und Strukturgeneralisierung als Beitrag der objektiven Hermeneutik zur soziologisch-strukturtheoretischen Analyse." Manuscript, http://www.gesellschaftswissenschaften.uni-frankfurt.de/uploads/391/8/Fall rekonstruktion-1981.pdf (accessed 3 December 2010).
Oevermann, Ulrich (2002) "Klinische Soziologie auf der Basis der Methodologie der objektiven Hermeneutik: Manifest der objektiv hermeneutischen Sozialforschung." Manuscript, http://publikationen.ub.uni-frankfurt.de/volltexte/2005/540/pdf/Manifest Word.pdf (accessed 30 December 2010).
Oevermann, Ulrich, Tilman Allert, Elisabeth Konau, and Jürgen Krambeck (1979) "Die Methodologie der objektiven Hermeneutik und ihre allgemeine forschungslogische Bedeutung in den Sozialwissenschaften", in *Interpretative Verfahren in den Sozial- und Textwissenschaften*, ed. Hans-Georg Soeffner (Stuttgart: Metzler), 352–434.
Thomas, William I, and Dorothy Swaine Thomas (1928) *The Child in America, Behavior Problems and Programs* (New York: A. Knopf)
Verdery, Katherine (1994) "Ethnicity, Nationalism, and State-Making", in *The Anthropology of Ethnicity. Beyond "Ethnic Groups and Boundaries"*, ed. Hans Vermeulen und Cora Govers (Amsterdam: Het Spinhuis), 33–58.
Weber, Max (1978) *Economy and Society* (Berkeley: U of California Press)
Wimmer, Andreas (2008) "The Making and Unmaking of Ethnic Boundaries: A Multilevel Process Theory", *The American Journal of Sociology* 113.4, 970–1022.

Clemens Ruthner (Trinity College Dublin)

Collateral Roadkill: The Conflicted Death of "Central Europe" *en route* to Sarajevo and Brussels*

> Central Europe is hardly a geographical notion. It is not easy to trace its boundaries on the map even if, while walking the streets of its cities, we do not doubt of its survival, whether that be in my native Wilno, or the differently baroque Prague or medieval-Renaissance Dubrovnik. The ways of feeling and thinking of its inhabitants must thus suffice for drawing mental lines which seem to be more durable than the borders of states. (Miłosz 1986: 101)

As the Romanian writer Mircea Cărtărescu states, "[t]here are many Europes in space and time, in dreams and in memories, in reality and in the imagination" (2004: 66). Among them, 'Central Europe' – or, using the more loaded German term *Mitteleuropa* – is a debated concept, a discourse of regional belonging, cohabitation (*Zusammenleben*), and conflict that emerged within a (Post)imperial context and continues to haunt us, mostly as a trope of melancholy, nostalgia, and lost significance, but also as a shared "structure of feelings" (Williams 1977: 131–134), as the opening quote by Czesław Miłosz insinuates. In a similar vein, the Serbian journalist, writer, and diplomat Dragan Velikić (1953–) conjures the proverbial hybridity of the region which proves to be a battlefield as well. In his novel *The Bremen Case*, Central Europe is called "a swamp of pedigrees, coats of arms and flags, [...], strange combinations of first and last names in the telephone directories – this amorphous territory where wars are waged because of accents and borders, where epics are forged [...]" (Velikić 2002: 35)[1] – and "traditions" "invented" (Hobsbawm & Ranger 1983), one should add: *Mitteleuropa* as a discourse mainly works retrospectively nowadays, creating a transnational space of memory between "geopolitics and geopoetics" (Živković 2015).

In the following, a brief sketch shall be given of what defines that region of Central Europe in histori(ographi)cal terms, using Maria Todorova's approach as a point of departure. I will then present four *Mitteleuropa* narratives[2] of supranational belonging stemming from historians, politicians and writers (František

* This text is the extended version of a talk given at Trinity College Dublin twice, at the international workshop *Narrative/s in Conflict* and at the public *EuroVisions* lecture series of the Trinity Long Room Hub Arts and Humanities Research Centre on the occasion of the Irish EU presidency, both in 2013. I am also grateful to Yvonne Živković (Cambridge) for our exchange of thoughts.

1 Translation mine, as it will be in all cases where no English version was available.

2 On narrative as a central device of culture, see Müller-Funk 2008 and 2012.

https://doi.org/10.1515/9783110556858-012

Palacký, Friedrich Naumann, István Bibó, and Milan Kundera) to reveal their hidden agendas. As a next step, the question will be raised as to what extent concepts of Central Europe have died out not only in the violent Yugoslav Succession Wars of the last decade of the twentieth century, but also in the enlargements of the European Union in 1995 and 2004, leaving us with 'post-narratives' of sorts (Lebbeus Woods and Jean-Luc Nancy). Finally, I will ask if there is any life – or at least: undead potential – left in such a macro-regional identity nowadays. Space and time constraints, however, made it impossible to provide much more than a rough, anecdotic and sketchy first outline of a vast and interesting topic.[3]

1 Narratives: what makes a region (Central Europe with Maria Todorova et al.)

A major discursive frontline behind any notion of Central Europe seems to be the scholarly and political assessment of its (mainly) Habsburg past (e.g. Schmitz 2011: 13), which often just reproduces the two conflicting narratives of the era in question: on the one hand, the nationalist verdict that the multi-ethnic *k. u. k.* ("*kaiserlich und königlich*" / "imperial and royal") "double monarchy" Austria-Hungary, which Robert Musil (1978: 31–35) in his epoch-making novel *Der Mann ohne Eigenschaften* (*The Man without Qualities*, 1930–42) called "Kakanien", was a *Völkerkerker*, a "Prison of Peoples", and, on the other hand, the unionist credo of *Viribus Unitis* – 'united we stand stronger!'[4]; from the latter emerges what the Triestine scholar Claudio Magris (1963, 1988) calls the "Habsburg Myth"[5] (also see Cole 2004), which retrospectively takes the Dual Monarchy for a multicultural predecessor, if not a role model for the European Union. However, both narratives are like two sides of the same coin, and there even seem to be hidden connections between them. As the later Austrian vice-chancellor Erhard

---

3 For more comprehensive surveys and discourse analyses of *Mitteleuropa*, see e.g. Meyer 1955, Le Rider 1994, Stirk 1994, Brechtefeld 1996, Čede & Fleck 1996, Marjanović 1998, Baumann & Hauser 2002, Svatek 2015, and Živković 2015.

4 The only battleship the Austro-Hungarian navy ever had bore the same name. Literally, the motto means 'With United Strength / Forces'.

5 Its defining traits are summarized by Živković (2015: 18) as follows: "1) the myth of transnational togetherness and harmonious plurality amongst the many nationalities in the Empire, 2) the influence of the bureaucratic mentality on everyday life, and 3) an all-pervading hedonism ('Gemütlichkeit') which puts distraction and sensual pleasures at the center of social interactions."

Busek put it in 1986: "From being a 'Habsburg Eater', there are obviously broad roads leading to Habsburg nostalgia, too."[6]

But there should be a third way of narrating the imperial past, tested by the informal research network *Kakanien Revisited*, which was set up by Wolfgang Müller-Funk, myself and other researchers around the turn of the Millennium: a critical narrative that was supposed to overcome, or at least bypass, the fallacies of the former two. Facing the lack of a better fitting term, we called it a *postcolonial* approach to late Habsburg history and culture/s, which critically tried to deconstruct the other two narrative streams, having learned its lessons from Edward Said, Homi Bhabha, Gayatri Spivak and other cultural theorists (see Müller-Funk, Plener and Ruthner 2002).[7]

This is particularly important since, as I would like to show in the following, most discourses on Central Europe as a region are also informed by, if not translations of, the aforementioned pro- and anti-Habsburg narratives (cf. Schmitz 2011: 14). They begin to emerge in eras when the legitimacy of the old multi-ethnic empire(s) was severely challenged by rather new forms of collective identity, especially nationhood, in the nineteenth and twentieth centuries (Höhne 2011: 145); thus notions of "regional belonging" are often formulated as counter-concepts to nationalism(s) and the nation-state (Boldt 1988: 104; Schmitz 2011: 23). What those (post)imperial / transnational ideas about a shared political space in Central Europe also have in common is that many – if not most of them – were formulated against the backdrop of an imminent crisis, for example war/revolution, foreign occupation, or the virtual aftermath of a (declining) political system, which I am tempted to call their post/apocalyptic undertone. Thus, they are mostly manifestations of a quest for a supranational construct that goes beyond the shortcomings of the binary of old/new empires versus the new (or "reborn") nation-states.

But let us begin with a first claim: Central Europe as a geographical term has always been invested with a strongly fluctuating meaning. As Jörg Brechtefeld observes,

> [t]he German term 'Mitteleuropa' never has been merely a geographical term; it is also a political one, much as Europe, East and West, are terms that political scientists employ as synonyms for political ideas or concepts. Traditionally, 'Mitteleuropa' has been that part

6 "Vom 'Habsburger-Kannibalismus' führen offenbar breite Straßen zur Habsburger-Nostalgie" (Busek 1986: 78).

7 The current *Kakanien Revisited* team has won a Croatian research grant recently in order to conduct comparative post/imperial studies into the Habsburg and Yugoslav pasts, led by Croatian Germanist Marijan Bobinac, University of Zagreb.

> of Europe between East and West. As profane as this may sound, this is probably the most precise definition of Mitteleuropa available. (Brechtefeld 1996: 1–2)

Any meaningful construction of Central Europe, however, is more than just another version of this floating signifier. It also *per definitionem* escapes a clear-cut definition since after all, Central Europe appears as a "liminal" (Foteva 2014: 1,4)[8] threshold between the East and the West as well as between the North and the South of the continent; a transitional contact zone in the middle of the old Continent, which has brought Otto Forst de Battaglia to call this entity "Zwischeneuropa", "In-between-Europe" (Schmitz 2011: 12). But what lies "in-between"? If you use the Google image search for finding maps of the region, you will notice that almost none of the results resembles another, depending on which countries are included and which ones are left out: all of Germany? Which parts of the Balkans? And what about the Baltic States? The second phenomenon that strikes the observer is that any attempt at circumscribing and visualizing Central Europe conjures the specter of the old borders of vanished regional empires, for instance when it comes to the old (Habsburg) dividing line between Western and Eastern Ukraine. In a way, the region can also be defined as a conflict zone, or overlap, respectively, of homogenizing (neo-)nationalist spatial orders versus the remnants of the old, multiculturaly rhizomic clusters of imperial spaces, and hypermodern forms of Transnationalism.[9]

Thus, one does better to accept the liminality and *différance* (to use Derrida's term) of the region and its term. Instead of an accurate demarcation – which is falling prey to the old fallacy that geography is something 'neutral' and 'objective' – it is advisable to go for a historical and discursive working definition instead that accepts the protean nature of its object. There are prominent precursors for this; according to Maria Todorova, for instance, every region can be seen "as the complex interplay of numerous historical periods, traditions and legacies" (2005: 61). Following this approach, at least four historical factors could be mentioned that constitute Central Europe as the crossroads of the continent:[10]

8 For a discussion of the concept of "liminality" and its use in cultural theory, see Ruthner 2012 and Achilles, Borgards & Burrichter 2012. – Those to whom the term sounds too vaguely anthropological and too ahistorical are welcome to replace it by the historiographical concept of *borderlands* (as it was underlying, in one of its most extreme versions, Tim Snyder's recent book *Bloodlands* for example), cf. recently in Rieber 2014; also see Harboe Knudsen & Demant Frederiksen 2015. (Special thanks to my colleague Balázs Apor for his intervention.)

9 I owe this observation to Wolfgang Müller-Funk with gratitude.

10 Todorova lists three "unique features" of what she calls "Eastern Europe": that the region is 1) "the outcome of the legacies of recent multinationals dynastic empires – Ottoman, Habsburg,

1) Central Europe has been the area where all major religious and linguistic communities of Europe meet and intersect, i.e. Orthodox/Catholic/Protestant Christianity, Judaism and Islam, or Germanic, Romance and Slavic plus several smaller languages, respectively; this exposure to each other has been confrontational at times, but it has also led to the formation of remarkable culturally hybrid spaces such as Silesia, Istria, or Transylvania.

2) Another connector is the region's post-imperial situation, which is also post-totalitarian, and in many cases post-communist. Central Europe is basically defined by the territories of some (but not all) successor states of four Continental empires: Germany, Austria-Hungary, the Russian Empire/the Soviet Union, the Ottoman Empire, plus their historical – multi-ethnic – legacies; characteristically, in this respect, some of the successor states themselves (such as Czechoslovakia and Yugoslavia) appear as copy cats of some aspects of the old empires and share some problematic traits with them.

3) Within and across the multi-ethnic empires, transnational minorities acted as a sort of 'glue' between the ethno-linguistic communities, most prominently the Eastern (*Ashkenazi*) Jews and the ethnic Germans in most parts of the region (Schlögel 1986): communities that have been destroyed through genocide, or "ethnic cleansing", respectively, as a consequence of National Socialism, Soviet-style Communism, and the Second World War.

4) Central Europe has been exposed to almost never-ending political, economic, societal and cultural changes in the last hundred years much more than any other part of the continent; it has been the venue of major wars and other acts of organized political violence, among which the two World Wars and the Holocaust are the most notorious, but certainly not the only ones. Thus, as a consequence of its specific imperial past(s) and aftermath(s), Central Europe can be characterized by the experience of belated industrialization (Todorova 2005: 71) and nation-building plus multiple transition, or transformation, respectively; in the process, it was to become an extreme laboratory of Europe's Modernity, or the "Versuchsstation des Weltuntergangs", the lab of the apocalypse, as the Viennese publicist Karl Kraus (1914: 2) called it shortly before the outbreak of the First World War. The question remains whether this creates a special Central European path through history, a "Sonderweg", as the French scholar Jacques Le Rider (1994: 17) put it.

However, I am not interested in conducting area studies here. I would rather like to take advantage of an observation by the German scholar Walter Schmitz

---

Romanov", 2) an area "of belated industrialization" which has 3) "by-passed the Renaissance and Reformation" (2005: 71–72).

who states that the spatial term ("die Raumvokabel") 'Central Europe' emerges at the intersection of *several* discourses that generate meaning (2011: 26 and 14). This makes it relevant to investigate what their respective implications are: who utters the term in which context, against which backdrop, and with what agenda? And, as a consequence of what was said before, a distinction should be made between the region and its respective geopolitical representation. Thus, in the following mini-case studies, I shall call discursive constructions of a Central European region and its identity *Mitteleuropa* in order to differentiate between geography and geo-political narratives. Scrutiny reveals, however, that, as already was adumbrated, geopolitical concepts and maps mutually reinforce each other. 'Central Europe' as a region thus seems to be the virtual conflation of all *Mitteleuropa* narratives available historically, constituted through their mutual difference.

It will also be claimed that any historical version of *Mitteleuropa*, a discourse which emerges in the nineteenth century and is gradually abolished with the EU accession of the Central European countries in 1995 and in 2004, receives its philosophical tension and lines of development from its underlying narrative that might conflict with others. As will be shown, some of the stories told about the region are driven by imperial ambition, others by post-imperial melancholy.

I will now try to filter out four of these narratives and their leitmotifs to show how they create specific versions of the *Mitteleuropa* discourse;[11] what they all have in common are specific tropes or *topoi*. Quite often, for instance, the 'story' presented is triggered by describing the psychological and political situation sketch of the small Central European nations as being 'between a rock and a hard place', i.e. Germany and Russia.[12] Secondly, the narratives tend to formulate the necessity or historical given-ness of a sort of community across religious and ethno-linguistic borders, which creates brackets between those small countries. Thirdly, they usually come up with a positive or negative genealogy of sorts with regard to the Habsburg Empire. And fourthly, 'Central Europe' is a label often used by those countries or regions that do not desire to be part of 'Eastern Europe' for political reasons: a discursive tool to – at least symbolically – create

---

11 There may indeed be more than four narratives, but due to spatial constraints, I will concentrate on some essentials here and refer to Jacques Le Rider's authoritative book (1994) on the subject matter for more details. There is also a smaller competitor and counter-concept of the *Mitteleuropa* discourse, namely *Stredni Evropa* (East Central Europe), a term coined by the Viennese professor and later Czech president Tomáš Masaryk (1922: 45–48), meaning the small, non-German speaking countries in the middle of the continent, wherever this might be (cf. e.g. Boldt 1988: 99–100; Živković 2015: 8).

12 Even Naumann's *Mitteleuropa* (1916: 20) quotes this *topos*.

in- and out-groups, and to vote the former out of a political sphere dominated by Russia.

1.1 Narrative #1: solidarity as self-protection (František Palacký, 1848)

The Czech historian and politician František Palacký (1798 – 1876) is regarded as the founding father of a political movement in the mid-nineteenth century called *Austroslavismus*, which used an early version of *Mitteleuropa* discourse to support its ideology. It is formulated against the backdrop of the struggle between Prussia/Germany and Austria for supremacy in the region (Feichtinger 2011: 55).

Very famous are Palacký's words that "if the Austrian State had not existed for ages, it would have been in the interests of Europe and indeed of humanity to endeavor to create it as soon as possible" (2007: 325). This passage stems from a letter sent to the German revolutionary assembly in Frankfurt in April 1848, whose members had tried to win the Czechs over for a future German Empire. In his response, Palacký, however, is skeptical about the benefits of joining such an aspiring nation-state. Instead, he envisages a strong and independent Austrian empire – not a republic! –, which should work as a protective federation for the southern German-speakers and the smaller ethno-linguistic groups of the region particularly vis-à-vis Russia (and Prussia?), allowing for the retention of their individual rights and cultures, "to be the bulwark and guardian of Europe against Asiatic [!] elements of every possible type" (ibid.).

However, in the long run of the "long nineteenth century" (Eric Hobsbawm), Austro-Slavism became outdated, since the Slavic masses favored less moderate versions of nationalism and nation building, with the well-known unhappy ending for the Empire in the First World War. After the breakup of the Austro-Hungarian Monarchy in 1918/19, remnants of Palacký's concept will prevail in the Czech lands as the basis for certain thoughts formulated by T.G. Masaryk and later Milan Kundera. Mixed with other ideas, it also lies at the core of the nostalgic Habsburg Myth (Magris ([1963] 1988) as a sort of symbolic mourning (*Trauer- und Traumarbeit*) for an alleged better past, which finds its exemplary presentation in the works of the German-speaking Jewish writer and Austrian exile from Western Ukraine, Joseph Roth, particularly in his novels *Radetzky-Marsch* (1932) and *Kapuzinergruft* (1938).

1.2 Narrative #2: (liberal) imperialism, backyard policy (Friedrich Naumann, 1916)

In E. Phillips Oppenheim's bestselling WWI spy novel *The Great Impersonation*, one of the characters says: "Austria [...] must already feel her doom creeping upon her. There is no room in middle Europe for two empires, and the House of Hapsburg must fall before the House of Hohenzollern. Austria, body and soul, must become part of the German empire" (1920: 284). This refers to an idea which, shortly before the collapse of the old empires, the Protestant clergyman and liberal politician Friedrich Naumann (1860 – 1919) had come up with: probably the most problematic version of a Central European regional discourse, which has tainted the entire concept until today, since to many ears, it has become synonymous with German expansionism (Marjanović 1998: 17).

Indeed, the leitmotif of Naumann's thinking, promoted in his bestselling book entitled *Mitteleuropa* from 1915, can be called liberal imperialism (cf. Höhne 2011: 149 – 157; Frölich 1996: 183 – 185). It is based on the assumption of an imminent end to the Great War that is favorable to the Central Powers, and discusses its aftermath. According to the author, out of the momentum of the so-far successful military alliances between Germany, Austria and the smaller non-Germanic communities in the region, a future Central Europe should arise: "between the Vistula and the Vosges Mountains, and what extends from Galicia to Lake Constance! You must think of these stretches of country as a unity, as a brotherhood of many members, as a defensive alliance, as a single economic district!" (Naumann 1916: 3)

This new political union "is no chance but a necessity" (Naumann 1916: 5), since "[o]nly very big States have any significance on their own account" (4), which, according to the author, is partly due to the "spirit of large-scale industry" (5), thus motivated by capitalist globalization (*avant la lettre*). In reaction, Naumann comes up with a list consisting of twelve points. They are meant to standardize – or at least, to create supranational compatibility – with respect to military, foreign affairs, infrastructure, currencies and measures, banking / business / national debts, customs / taxes, and legislation (Naumann 1916: 31). However, as the author admits, for the sake of creating such "a kind of super-State over other States, and Empire of Empires, it would be a direct sin against the ideal of this new creation to try to stuff it with tasks that would occupy ten or twenty years" (32). Rather than through cumbersome democratic procedures, "a community of life may develop from above downwards as a result of comradeship in the alliance [of WWI]" (33).

Thus, what seems to be a virtual forerunner of a (Central) European Union, is actually a top-down model dictated by Germany through an alleged military success story. To be found between the lines of this version of *Mitteleuropa* is very evidently German hegemonic thinking, creating a "triple division" of the old Continent (Naumann 1916: 8): not in the sense of Homi Bhabha's (1990) "third space" (Babka et al. 2012), but rather as a buffer zone between the Reich and Russia, comparable to the interference of the United States in their Central American 'backyard'. *Mitteleuropa* as a political entity is to be dominated by Germany behind the scenes, a bit like Prussia did in the Kaiserreich (Frölich 1996: 183–184). It can also be seen as imperialism directed at the interior of the continent to replace exterior colonies (Schmitz 2011: 19); the last brainchild of the previous decades when geopolitics became the hobbyhorse of imperialist professors in Wilhelmine Germany, radicalizing throughout the emergency of the Great War (Meyer 1955: 137–173; Feichtinger 2011: 60–63; Živković 2015: 9–15).

In 1915, however, many readers among Germany's Habsburg allies were not really amused about the proposed "welding together of the German Empire and the Austro-Hungarian Dual Monarchy" (Naumann 1916: 1) under the auspices of Berlin (Feichtinger 2011: 57; Frölich 1996: 183–184; Schwarz 1989: 147). In all fairness it must be added though that out of all late Wilhelmine imperialist concepts, Naumann's is somehow ambivalent, vacillating between "closet hegemonic endeavor and the liberal will to find an arrangement with Germany's neighbors" (Frölich 1996: 85). However, as Živković (2015: 15) states, "the intent towards an intercultural dialogue without hierarchy is precisely what distinguished the Austrian *Mitteleuropa* writers even from humanistically inclined German thinkers such as Naumann." Moreover, the latter's roadmap to a German-dominated Central Europe was to be recycled as a blueprint for Nazi *Lebensraum* policies in the region after his death.

It should not be omitted either that, particularly in the interwar period, there was a revival of the first *Mitteleuropa* narrative particularly among Habsburg nostalgics, along the lines that I have already sketched. All of these thoughts, however, were able to bridge the gap the disappearance of the Habsburg cohesion had left only as a *cultural* idea, but barely in the political realm. In 1924, the *Paneuropa-Union* was founded by the Bohemian aristocrat Richard von Coudenhove-Kalergi (1894–1972) along with Thomas Mann, Otto von Habsburg and other prominent protagonists of a rather conservative orientation, giving voice to the idea of a united Europe. The historical decisions were taken elsewhere though, leading to authoritarian rule not only in many countries of Central Europe, but also throughout the whole continent.

The end of the Second World War left Central Europe completely devastated by the material destructions, casualties and genocides the armed conflicts left behind along with the ethnic cleansings in the wake of the war, which had further destroyed the multi-ethnic setup of the region that had created brackets across political borders.[13] Along with the ideological division in the Cold War that tore the region apart, this interrupted most of the last existing continuities, creating a deep caesura. As Karl Schlögel writes, *Mitteleuropa* was like a vanished image ("wie ein verschwundenes Bild"), left back or even lost in the enormous masses of those being killed or refugees after 1945: "Es ist abhanden gekommen. Es wurde zurückgelassen bei der überstürzten Flucht, bei der nicht Bilder, sondern Menschenleben in Sicherheit zu bringen waren." (Schlögel 1986: 39)

1.3 Narrative #3: criticism of the deadlock (István Bibó, 1946)

Arising from that legacy of the Second World War, the third *Mitteleuropa* narrative is probably the most acceptable nowadays, since it provides a skeptical and at places even polemical analysis with a vague, but peaceful roadmap; it does not come up with wonder-solutions, but it rather seeks reconciliation, as difficult and tiresome as this might be. It is formulated in *The Misery of the Small East* [!] *European States*, a small book written in the middle of the war in 1942/43 and published in 1946 by the Hungarian academic, politician and librarian István Bibó (1911–1979). It tells the story of Central Europe as a series of disasters insofar as it shows and deplores the peculiar consequences of belated national development as much as it warns of ardent nationalisms leading to future catastrophes. As constitutive factors for the Central European "misery", Bibó lists:

> die Vielfalt der territorialen Konflikte, die Bereitschaft, auf gemäßigte und zurückhaltende politische Methoden zu verzichten, den Mangel an demokratischem Geist, die Tendenz zum politischen Irrealismus, die Bereitschaft, sich weniger auf Leistungen als vielmehr auf Rechtstitel und Ansprüche zu berufen, [...], die Verantwortungslosigkeit gegenüber den universellen Fragen Europas, oder auch die Tatsache, dass ihre politischen Entscheidungen nicht von langfristig angelegten und seriösen politischen Konzeptionen geleitet [...] werden. (Bibó 2005: 75)

Perversely, it is this set of negative characteristics that creates a bond of sorts between the Central European countries: their manifold territorial conflicts, political radicalism and irrationalism, the lack of a moderate, democratic political spirit, of long-term concepts and responsibility vis-à-vis the greater whole of Europe, creating policies that are based on diffuse "historical" claims and "entitle-

13 It is a very deplorable fact that the last transnational minority left behind, the Romani, only paradoxically unifies the region in all the racism directed against them.

ment" rather than solid efforts. On the other hand, Bibó's anti-nationalistic narrative also rings the warning bells about the effects of supranational states by exposing the "civilizing mission" of the old regional empires as pure pretense and pretext.[14] He is equally dismissive of keeping the *status quo* at any cost (Bibó 2005: 89) or of hastily forged 'commonwealths' (87).

The Hungarian historian is thus one of the founding fathers of a critical, non-nostalgic, non-nationalist and non-imperialist Central European narrative in postwar Europe that investigates a third way of sorting out the region peacefully beyond empires, nation-states and federations (which must have sounded quite utopian in Cold War Europe). However, his critical potential sometimes threatens to outweigh any possible optimism for the future (for which we cannot really blame the author in the 1940s). Very obviously, the Second World War leaves a question behind, which our next narrator is going to formulate: whether there is any potential left in Central Europe "after Auschwitz, which swept away the Jewish nation of, its map" (Kundera 1984: 11).

1.4 Narrative #4: bridging the divide (the revival of *Mitteleuropa*, Kundera et al., 1980s)

What is significant about narratives on Central Europe is that they seem to be linked with particular situations in late empires or their aftermath, in which the region's intellectuals felt overpowered by historical developments that had led to totalitarian rule, the Second World War, and the genocides of the twentieth century. It does not come as a surprise then that the new heyday of *Mitteleuropa* discourses were the 1980s when the tension of the Cold War between the super powers eased and first cracks in the Eastern Bloc became visible.

At that time, the narrative was revived in a fourth version, stressing the "ideal of a civil society, transnational humanism, and a unifying cultural memory" (Živković 2015: xxiii) by a group of Central European writers and intellectuals, most of whom were acquainted with one other: the Czech exile Milan Kundera (1929–), the Hungarian György Konrád (1933–), the Yugoslav Danilo Kiš

14 "Wenn man sie fragte, warum sie über Völker Herrschaft ausüben wollten, die dies nicht wünschen, dann verwiesen sie auf *archäologische Ausgrabungen, Volkslieder, ethnograpische Motive, Lehnwörter, Flügelaltare und auf die Wirkung ihrer Bücher und Institutionen*, die beweisen sollten, dass das betreffende Volk ohne sie bis heute in der finstersten Barbarei dahinvegetieren würde." (Bibó 2005: 60; italics in the original) – What's interesting here is that Bibó makes empires use the same arguments nation-states would claim for their "invention of tradition", at least according to Hobsbawm & Ranger 1983.

(1935–1989), and the Polish writer Czesław Miłosz (1911–2004), who were supported by a group of liberal conservative politicians around the later Austrian vice-chancellor Erhard Busek (1941–) and other intellectuals in the 'West'. Their shared vision of a shared Central European culture envisages this concept – to use the words of Hungarian writer György Dalos (1943–) – as a sort of "mental Common Market" ("geistiger Binnenmarkt" qtd. after Schmitz 2011: 24), which is meant as an antidote to the East-West divide of the continent, as "Regulativ einer abzulehnenden Wirklichkeit" (21): a way of voting out of the Eastern Bloc and the Cold War at least in the Republic of Letters, "not as a reactionary dream, but as a subversive program" (Živković 2015: xxiii).

Probably the most famous, but also most problematic document in this context is Milan Kundera's *Un Occident kidnappé* (1983) / *The Tragedy of Central Europe* (1984).[15] In this literary essay, the Czech writer in Paris reiterates images of an alleged older division of Europe between "Rome", i. e. the West, and Eastern "Byzantium" (Kundera 1984: 1). It is his endeavor to move the smaller member states of the Warsaw Pact back to the West; in order to achieve this, Kundera paradoxically re-invents the intermediary zone of Central Europe. According to him, the struggle of Czechoslovakia, Hungary, Poland and other countries is not political, but identitary, if not a clash of civilizations, to use Samuel Huntington's notorious formula *avant la lettre:*

> This is why the countries of Central Europe feel that the change in their destiny that occurred after 1945 is not merely a political catastrophe; it is an attack on their civilization. The deep meaning of their resistance is their struggle to preserve their identity – or, to put it another way, to preserve their Westernness. (Kundera 1984: 4)

Kundera is eager to create a sharp contrast between the Sovietized Russians (behind whom he conjures the cliché of Asian despotism[16]) and the Central Europeans by disengaging, for instance, from the notion of a "Slavic soul" (following the Polish-British writer Joseph Conrad in this respect, see Kundera 1984: 5). As a side effect, Kundera's stereotypical image of Russia is sometimes at the brink of racism while his essay manœuvers very consciously in the footsteps of Palacký whom he quotes on the second page already. He pretends to rediscover a common tradition for the region and thus, not surprisingly, also conjures the specter of the Habsburg Empire as a point of departure: "The Austrians had the

---

15 Also see the analysis by Živković 2015: 43–47.

16 For instance, Russia is described as "uniform, standardizing, centralizing, determined to transform every nation of its empire [...] into a single Russian people", whereas Central Europe is characterized by "its passion for variety" (Kundera 1984: 3).

great opportunity of making Central Europe into a strong, unified state. But the Austrians, alas, were divided between an arrogant Pan-German nationalism and their own central European mission [...]" (Kundera 1984: 5).

In spite of these "inadequacies" (5), Kundera's discussion of the Habsburg Monarchy comes to the surprising conclusion that "it was irreplaceable" (5). This rediscovery – or re-invention – of "a common tradition" (Kundera 1984: 7) becomes a device to short-circuit the circles and frontlines of the Cold War in the region. Kundera's narrative is anti-communist, in a version that is meant to appeal to dissident lefties as well as to conservatives and liberals. Reading between the lines, you can find the Habsburg myth, at least in a Palackýian version, as hidden narrative in the corresponding versions of this new *Mitteleuropa* narrative on the other side of the border: there, it was formulated as a sign of hope that Austria and Hungary one day could regain their lost significance (since an important function of most *Mitteleuropa* narratives in Austria and Hungary after 1918 seems to be mourning for the lost grandeur). The undead variant of the Habsburg myth, produced by Kundera and others in a postmodern version that tried to bridge the gap the Iron Curtain had created, however, proved to be quite powerful as a figure of thought, at least as a placeholder for new things to come: "It would be senseless to try to draw its borders exactly. Central Europe is not a state: it is a culture and a fate. Its borders are imaginary and must be drawn and redrawn with each new historical situation." (Kundera 1984: 6)

On 25 January 1990, Palacký's and Kundera's countryman, the Czech(oslovak) president Vaclav Havel, gave a speech at the Polish parliament in the footsteps of the two, stating the historic chance he saw for the region to fill the vacuum left by the dissolution of the Habsburg Monarchy "with something meaningful".[17] And indeed, around and after the changes of 1989 there have been many attempts to forge regional bodies, such as the *Pentagonale*, founded after the *Wende* in November 1989 upon Austrian initiative, consisting of Italy, Austria, Hungary, Yugoslavia and Czechoslovakia. Poland joined in 1991, but after the splitting-up of Czechoslovakia and Yugoslavia the association became meaningless. It was replaced by the *Central European Initiative* in 1993, but due to funding problems, this new supranational project never really got off the ground (it currently has some projects running in the science and university sector, but remains unknown to the wider public and is politically powerless). Other attempts in this direction were

17 Quoted after Schmitz 2011: "uns eröffnet sich zum erstenmal die historische Chance, das große politische Vakuum, das in Mitteleuropa nach dem Zerfall der Habsburger Monarchie entstanden ist, mit etwas Sinnvollem auszufüllen" (30).

Centrope (by the City of Vienna) and the *Visegrad Group* of Poland, Hungary, the Czech Republic and Slovakia, the latter association being rather infamous for having become a gentlemen's club of reactionary, patriarchal, and xenophobic politics with in the EU.

In spite of such attempts to counter-weight German and Austrian hegemony, investors from these countries have swarmed the region since in the 1990s anyway, leaving a bad neo-colonial taste behind in many mouths. As an epitomy of the emerging neo-nationalist reluctance, one could read a toilet graffito in Budapest in 1993, saying: "Hungarian, why are you sad? Becoz Austrian and American gangsters are robbing my country" (qtd. in Breuss et al. 1995: 145).

2 Post-Narratives: the death of *Mitteleuropa?* (Maria Todorova et al.)

As we have seen, *Mitteleuropa* can be approached as a discourse that consists of conflicting narrative elements used or moderated by every version of the discourse. Every narrative, through intertextuality, refers to every other narrative virtually. They co-exist in their opposition to each other, in their *différance*, and their ingredients are pretty much the same, even between Palacký and Naumann, although the point-of-view, or their "protagonist", respectively, is different (Bohemia and Austria versus Germany).

The narratives also share a few more traits. They mostly work retrospectively insofar as after the First World War, they tell a *Verfallsgeschichte*, i.e. the history of gradual decay of the Habsburg Empire and its multiethnic heritage. But they are also "utopian dystopia[n] " (Foteva 2014: 1), as they repeat the mantra of the alleged positive potential to be found in this declining empire, and very often, they are driven by their will to power, i.e. the endeavor to rule or at least to co-rule. Or, in the words of Yvonne Živković (2015: vii), the "inherent dialectics of the *Mitteleuropa* discourse" are "the center versus the margin, nationalism versus transnationalism, the Germans versus the Slavs".

It can be also established, however, that throughout the last decades, those "chimeric" (Schwarz 1989: 153) narratives have become a *quantité negligeable*, and the question remains: what was the reason for their disappearance or falling out of fashion? Here one could claim that the events that terminated any further hopes of a revival of Central Europe as a political entity are basically two. Number one is the EU accession of most Central European countries in 1995 and in 2004. As the aforementioned Maria Todorova writes,

> Central Europe's emancipatory ideology, over which much scholarly ink has been spilled, became after 1989 a device entitling its participants to a share of privileges: accession to the NATO and the front seats for the EU. While the final historical verdict may be that this strategy was a "politically successful representation" with qualified achievements for some, the unintended consequence is that at present "Central Europe" as an idea is dead. (Todorova 2005: 76; see also Schmitz 2011: 33)

Another important place where *Mitteleuropa* obviously died was the gory Yugoslav Succession Wars in the 1990s. The city names of Srebrenica (with its massacre committed on more than 8,000 Muslim men and boys in 1995) and the beleaguered city of Sarajevo have become drastic metonymies for this horrifying outburst of violence and the comeback of genocide to Europe, which nobody had expected to happen again after the end of two World Wars, the Holocaust, and the Cold War. (But maybe the mass killing happened in ex-Yugoslavia exactly *because:* as a re-staging of a massive trauma dating back to a violent past that had not been worked through in the Western Balkans after 1945.)

Thus, after Central Europe, in its South Eastern outskirts, had become an "inhabited ruin" (Sayer & Gafijczuk 2013), any concept of *Mitteleuropa* had to be declared clinically dead eventually, or a lip service meant for literary readings and nostalgic old boys' networks. This death of Central Europe can be further traced and discussed in two more cultural texts that shall be called the post-narratives of *Mitteleuropa* in the following.

2.1 Post-Narrative #1: scars and sutures (Lebbeus Woods, 1997)

The aforementioned Bosnian capital Sarajevo became the site of the longest-lasting siege in modern European history, stretching over more than 1,400 days between 1992 and 1995, in which more than 10,000 people, most of them civilians, and more than 1,000 children were killed by snipers, artillery fire, but also disease and famine. Particularly this Bosnian War left Europe in the position of a helpless bystander, hypnotized and paralyzed by the atrocities which it was unable to stop, because it was still torn and divided along the frontlines of the First World War, and it took particularly the British and the French years to give up their mental alliance with the Serbian aggressor.

As a sort of emblem for this cemetery of Central European belonging I am using here an architectural sketch by the visionary American architect Lebbeus Woods (1940 – 2012) for the reconstruction of Sarajevo (Fig. 2). Woods did not intend to tear down the remnants of houses destroyed in the siege. His "Radical Reconstruction" would repair portions of the buildings' structure, but leave be-

Fig. 2: Sketch from Lebbeus Woods' *Radical Reconstruction* (Woods 1997).

hind a taste of what it looked like as a ruin, and then seal the transition between old and modern parts by a structure that resembles an alien high-tech suture designed by H.R. Giger.

Woods thus meant his sketches to be an architecture that heals wounds, but still displays scars, buildings that reconcile, but still keep people aware of the traumatic past at the same time. An impossible task, like squaring the circle, and needless to say the politicians and inhabitants of Sarajevo did not go for this project. The ruin, as the German sociologist Georg Simmel said in his famous essay from 1907, is "die Gegenwartsform der Vergangenheit" (1987: 128), the present tense of the past, as it were. Similarly, in Woods's architecture of the revamped ruin, the history of Central Europe is structurally symbolized, recalled, welded into sutures and deconstructed at the same time, as it is in the peculiar and half-forgotten EU protectorates of Bosnia-Herzegovina and Kosovo.

2.2 Post-Narrative #2: the loss of the "mêlée" (Jean-Luc Nancy, 1995)

Bosnia-Herzegovina and Kosovo are also markers of the endangered multi-ethnic character of the Balkans and Central Europe after the violent new nation-building processes of the last decades. The two half-baked countries appear as the last bleeding body parts of the corpse formerly called Yugoslavia, half-dead or undead, put into an emergency care unit of the European Community Hospital, with an uncertain future. Their cases are similar to the national draining of other multi-ethnic regions of Central Europe, such as Transylvania in Romania.

In an article that he wrote for beleaguered Sarajevo in March 1993, the French philosopher Jean-Luc Nancy (1940–) sketches a theory of that old identity and hybridity entitled "Eulogy of the Mêlée", which could be inspiring for our further Central European investigation. Nancy celebrates the principle of the "Mêlée" or the "mélange" (to use the well-known Austrian term for a cappuccino), and he mourns its being under siege and subsequent disappearance in the Bosnian War.

His piece of philosophy and cultural theory points at the danger that lies in naming the ingredients of the mix and essentializing them: "To essentialize the mélange is to have already dissolved it, melt it down into something other than itself" (Nancy 2000: 150). It is quite appropriate to read the tension between the "mix" and its essential "ingredients" here as a symbolism for multi-ethnicity and its breakdown in nationalisms of all kinds.

This is probably the strongest diagnosis of the disappearance of the old Central Europe whose mixtures have been taken apart and dissolved. This is not only about the old multi-ethnicity within territories *per se* which is regarded as an obstacle to having clean-cut nation-states. The other side of the national coin is the aforementioned disappearance of the minority groups that floated between and worked as glue across political entities. After the disappearance of the Eastern Jews and the ethnic Germans (and many other smaller groups), the third large transnational community that still exists, the Romani, also derogatorily known as 'Gypsies', is not seen as something that connects the region, but rather as the common scapegoat, focusing all remaining hatred and racism.

On the other hand, we have seen the victory of the nation-state as a prevailing political format for organizing countries, societies, and their relations. This development will not be overcome by any weak *Mitteleuropa* discourse which, behind its false pathos of shared (post/imperial) traditions and a common belonging, still has a hidden agenda of hegemony and dependence, but rather by turbo capitalism and globalization. This brings new migration with it, which is not united through a common feeling of a shared past, but rather of a shared provisional present and a potentially better future. As Nancy states:

> The *mélange*, therefore, *is* not. It happens; it takes places. There is a mêlée, crisscrossing, weaving, exchange, sharing, and it's never a single thing, nor is it never the same. On the one hand, the *mélange* is an 'it happens' rather than an 'it is': displacements, chances, migrations, clinamens, meetings, luck, and risks. (Nancy 2000: 151)

Thus, globalization and migration do not necessarily pose a threat, but rather represent a future potential. In lieu of the old *Mitteleuropa* discourse, the experience of migrants in Europe could create a new cohesion throughout the continent: the experience of their diasporic displacement and their desired integration into meta-motherlands they have moved into along with the memories of their places of origin. A shared present and future rather than the problematic past of the twentieth century: this could be also the positive lesson learned from the so-called 'Refugee Crisis' of 2015.

3 Post-Post-Narrative: in lieu of a conclusion

In light of the events of the "Changes" (*Wende*) of 1989, the demolition of the Iron Curtain, and the following years leading to the EU membership of many Central and South East European states until nowadays, it could be observed throughout my sketch how the narratives of *Mitteleuropa* have somehow come to a closure. The transnational memory discourse (that was often formulated to repress the memories of dictatorship and genocide) was not capable of providing common grounds for action to prevent extreme nationalisms, wars, and violence from happening, nor a vision for a shared future in the twenty-first century. Rather, as has been stated, it has very often been a post-imperial discourse of nostalgia (cf. Boym 2001) and the mourning about lost significance of the former hegemonic centers, using the disguise of equity. The beliefs of the late Otto (von) Habsburg (1912–2011), last crown prince of the homonymous empire, and his circles in Munich, Vienna, and Brussels that the history of Austria-Hungary and the idea of *Mitteleuropa* could provide a role model for a future European Union should thus be renounced. If the EU is to be the new Habsburg Monarchy, even with its utopian potential, then we are really doomed. The narratives of Central Europe will stay, but only as a tool of historical analysis and not as a road map for the future. This is not about neglecting and repressing 'our' 'shared past': it is rather about coming to terms with it and eventually overcoming it.

If we recall the initial quote by Dragan Velikić, Central Europe is not only the Habsburg myth displaying the grandfatherly face of Emperor Franz Josef, but also a huge cemetery full of mass graves and suffering. In this respect, Austrians especially need to better learn their history lesson that the Habsburg Monarchy was not a potential *multi-kulti* paradise, but the cradle of nationalisms and totalitarianisms of all types, the prehistory of ethnic cleansing and genocide.

We can thus agree with Maria Todorova that as a macro-region, Central Europe is dead. The European Union and particularly its new geographical entity colloquially called *Schengen-Land*, however, have resurrected new micro-regional clusters transcending national borders culturally and/or economically, liminal contact zones, many of whom – not surprisingly? – are situated in (Post-Habsburg) Central Europe: the twin-cities of Vienna and Bratislava, for instance, which are scheduled to grow together increasingly in terms of infrastructure, the city of Tr(ie)st(e) and the peninsula of Istria between Italy, Slovenia and Croatia, the border region of Györ, Eisenstadt and Sopron between Austria and Hungary, just to name a few. We have also seen the resurrection of old border-crossing regional identities we have long believed to be dead, such as that of Silesia between Poland, Germany and the Czech Republic, and the emergence of new ones, such as the *Alps-Adriatic-Alliance* or *Centrope*.[18]

The European Union is meant to create new neighbors 'at the same political eye level', a partnership based on political equality rather than on physical borders and post-imperial histories, which always carries and quotes a past of hegemony and domination between the lines. No one should be no one's satellite state ever again. At the same time, concepts are needed to overcome the recently emerged new inequality in EUrope as a consequence of the economic crisis, which has created new hierarchies between creditors and debtors, between teacher's pets and bad students in the Austerity Class of 2009. The recent 'Refugee Crisis' and the anti-democratic tendencies in Hungary and Poland have had similar effects and created anew a rather bad image for the region. This means more than ever in the last decades that looking ahead rather than backwards is advisable, since sticking to old and overcome historical concepts such as *Mitteleuropa* may just indicate a lack of political imagination and/or imminent catastropy: like in the case of one political commentator who, after the shock waves *Brexit* sent to the Continent and Marine Le Pen's threat of becoming French president, instantly conjured the spectre of Friedrich Naumann (cf. Rella 2017).

Works cited

Achilles, Jochen, Roland Borgards, and Brigitte Burrichter (eds.) (2012) *Liminale Anthropologien: Zwischenzeiten, Schwellenphänomene, Zwischenräume in Literatur und Philosophie* (Würzburg: Königshausen & Neumann).
Ágh, Attila (1998) *The Politics of Central Europe* (London: Sage).

---

18 *Alpe-Adria* consists of the Austrian federal states Carinthia, Styria, Burgenland, the Croatian counties Istria, Karlovac, Krapina-Zagorje, Koprivnica Križevci Međimurje and Varaždin, the Association of Cities and Towns of Slovenia and the Hungarian county Vas; *Centrope* of Western Hungary, the districts of Bratislava und Trnava, Southern Moravia, and the Austrian federal states Vienna, Lower Austria, and Burgenland.

Babka, Anna, Julia Malle, and Matthias Schmidt (eds.) (2012) *Dritte Räume: Homi K. Bhabhas Kulturtheorie. Anwendung. Kritik. Reflexion* (Vienna: Turia + Kant).
Baumann, Wolfgang, and Gunther Hauser (2002) *Mitteleuropa: Im geopolitischen Interesse Österreichs* (Graz: Austria-Medien-Service).
Bhabha, Homi K. (1990) "The Third Space", in *Identity: Community, Culture and Difference* (London: Lawrence & Wishart), 207–221.
Bibó, István (2005) *Das Elend der osteuropäischen Kleinstaaterei* [1946] (2nd edn. Frankfurt/M.: Verlag Neue Kritik).
Boldt, Frank (1988) "Mitteleuropa – Aktuelle Visionen seiner zukünftigen Gestalt im Gegenlicht historischer Erfahrungen", in *Mitteleuropa: Traum oder Trauma?* ed. Hans-Peter Burmeister, Frank Boldt and György Mészáros (Bremen: Ed. Temmen).
Boym, Svetlana (2001) *The Future of Nostalgia* (New York: Basic Books).
Brechtefeld, Jörg (1996) *Mitteleuropa and German Politics, 1848 to the Present* (London: Macmillan).
Breuss, Susanne, Karin Liebhart, and Andreas Pribersky (1995) *Inszenierungen: Stichwörter zu Österreich* (2nd edn., Vienna: Sonderzahl).
Busek, Erhard (1986) *Projekt Mitteleuropa* [co-author: Emil Brix] (Vienna: Ueberreuter).
Cărtărescu, Mircea (2004) "Europe Has the Shape of My Brain", in *Writing Europe: What is European About the Literatures of Europe?* ed. Ursula Keller (Budapest: CEU Press), 57–66.
Čede, Peter, and Dieter Fleck (1996) "Der Mitteleuropabegriff: Entwicklung und Wandel unter dem Einfluss zeitspezifischer Geisteshaltung", *Arbeiten aus dem Institut für Geographie der Karl-Franzens-Universität Graz* 34 (1996), 15–26.
Cole, Laurence (2004) "Der Habsburger-Mythos", in *Memoria Austriae,* ed. Emil Brix, Ernst Bruckmüller, and Hannes Stekl. Vol. 1 (Vienna: Verlag für Geschichte & Politik), 473–504.
Droz, Jacques (1960) *L'Europe Centrale: Evolution historique de l'idee de 'Mitteleuropa'* (Paris: Payot):
Feichtinger, Johannes (2011) "Zwischen Mittel- und Zwischeneuropa. Oder: Vom politisch überformten Raum zum heuristischen Konzept", in Lajarrige et al. 2011, 53–73.
Forst de Battaglia, Otto (1954) *Zwischeneuropa von der Ostsee bis zur Adria.* Teil 1 (Frankfurt/M.: Verl. der *Frankfurter Hefte*).
Foteva, Ana (2014) *Do the Balkans Begin in Vienna? The Geopolitical and Imaginary Borders between the Balkans and Europe* (New York et al.: P. Lang).
Frölich, Jürgen (1996) "Zwischen Weltpolitik und Weltkrieg: Friedrich Naumanns Mitteleuropa-Konzept", in *Mitteleuropäische Mythen und Wirklichkeiten,* ed. Peter Gerlich, Krzysztof Glass, and Barbara Serloth (Vienna: Österr. Gesellschaft für Mitteleuropa-Studien).
Gafijczuk, Dariuz, and Derek Sayer (eds.) (2013) *The Inhabited Ruins of Central Europe: Re-imagining Space, History, and Memory* (London: Palgrave Macmillan).
Gauß, Karl-Markus (1991) *Die Vernichtung Mitteleuropas: Essays* (Klagenfurt, Salzburg: Wieser).
Harboe Knudsen, Ida, and Martin Demant Frederiksen (eds.) (2015) *Ethnographies of Grey Zones in Eastern Europe: Relations, Borders and Invisibilities* (London, New York, Haryana: Anthem).

Hobsbawm, Eric J., and Ranger, Terence (eds.) (1983) *The Invention of Tradition* (Cambridge: Cambridge UP).

Höhne, Steffen (2011) "Imperiale Ambitionen und das Recht der kleinen Nationen", in Lajarrige et al. 2011, 143–167.

Kakanien revisited (2001–2013), ed. Peter Plener, Ursula Reber et al., http://kakanien.ac.at [international web platform and internet journal].

Kiš, Danilo (1987) "Variations on the Theme of Central Europe", *Cross Currents* 6, 1–14.

Konrád, György (1986) "Der Traum von Mitteleuropa", in *Aufbruch nach Mitteleuropa: Rekonstruktionen eines versunkenen Kontinents*, ed. Erhard Busek and Gerhard Wilflinger (Vienna: Ed. Atelier), 87–97.

Kraus, Karl (1914) "Franz Ferdinand und die Talente", *Die Fackel*, no. 400–403 (July 10), 1–4.

Kundera, Milan (1984) "The Tragedy of Central Europe", transl. Edmund White, The *New York Review of Books* 31.7 (26 April), 33–38 [original version: "Un occident kidnappé ou la tragédie de l'Europe centrale", *Le Débat*, 27 (1983/5), 3–23].

Lajarrige, Jacques, Walter Schmitz, and Giusi Zanasi (2011) *'Mitteleuropa': Geschichte eines transnationalen Diskurses im 20. Jahrhundert* (Dresden: Thelem).

Le Rider, Jacques (1994) *Mitteleuropa: Auf den Spuren eines Begriffes*, transl. Robert Fleck (Vienna: Deuticke).

Magris, Claudio (1988) *Der habsburgische Mythos in der österreichischen Literatur* [1963], transl. Madeleine Pásztóry (2nd edn., Salzburg: O. Müller).

Marjanović, Vladislav (1998) *Die Mitteleuropa-Idee und die Mitteleuropa-Politik Österreichs 1945–1995* (Frankfurt am Main et al.: P. Lang).

Masaryk, Thomas Garrigue (1922) *Das neue Europa der slavische Standpunkt* (Berlin: Volk und Welt).

Meyer, Henry Cord (1955) *'Mitteleuropa' in German Thought and Action 1815–1945* (The Hague: Nijhoff).

Miłosz, Czesław (1986) "Central European Attitudes", *Cross Currents A Yearbook of Central European Culture*, Vol. 5 (1986), 101–108.

Müller-Funk, Wolfgang (2008) *Die Kultur und ihre Narrative: Eine Einführung* (2nd edn. Vienna and New York: Springer).

Müller-Funk, Wolfgang (2012) *The Architecture of Modern Culture: Towards a Narrative Cultural Theory* (New York and Berlin: De Gruyter).

Müller-Funk, Wolfgang, Peter Plener, and Clemens Ruthner (eds.) (2002) *Kakanien revisited: Das Fremde und das Eigene (in) der österreichisch-ungarischen Monarchie* (Tübingen and Basle: Francke).

Musil, Robert (1978) *Der Mann ohne Eigenschaften: Roman*, ed. Adolf Frisé, 2 vols. (Reinbek: Rowohlt).

Naumann, Friedrich (1916): *Central Europe* [1915], transl. Christabel M. Meredith, introd. W. J. Ashley (London: P.S. King).

Oppenheim, E. Phillips (1920) *The Great Impersonation* (Boston: Little, Brown & Cie).

Palacký, Franz [František] (1971) *Österreichs Staatsidee* (reprint of the Prague 1866 edn., Vienna: Geyer).

Palacký, František (2007) "Letter to Frankfurt, 11 April 1848", in *Discourses of Collective Identity in Central and Southeast Europe*, vol. 2: *National Romanticism: The Formation of National Movements*, ed. Balázs Trencsényi and Michal Kopecek (Budapest: CEU Press),

322 – 329 (also available online, http://books.openedition.org/ceup/2345?lang=en, accessed 23 May 2015).
Petković, Nikola (1996) *The 'Post' in Postcolonial and Postmodern: The Case of Central Europe* (Austin: PhD, Univ. of Texas).
Rella, Christoph (2017) "Werden die Karten neu gemischt?", *Wiener Zeitung*, 25 March 2017.
Rieber, Alfred J. (2014) *The Struggle for the Eurasian Borderlands: From the Rise of Early Modern Empires to the End of the First World War* (Cambridge: Cambridge UP).
Rinner, Fridrun (2011) "Mitteleuropäische Literatur und kulturelle Identität um 1980", in Lajarrige et al. 2011, 75 – 85.
Rogoff, Irit (2000) *Terra Infirma: Geography's Visual Culture* (London and New York: Routledge).
Ruthner, Clemens (2012) "Fantastic Liminality: A Theory Sketch", in *Collisions of Reality: Establishing Research on the Fantastic in Europe*, ed. Lars Schmeink and Astrid Böger (Berlin and New York: De Gruyter), 35 – 49.
Schlögel, Karl (1986) *Die Mitte liegt ostwärts: Die Deutschen, der verlorene Osten und Mitteleuropa* (Berlin: Siedler).
Schmitz, Walter (2011) "Mitteleuropa – Landschaft und Diskurs", in Lajarrige et al. 2011, 11 – 40.
Schwarz, Egon (1989) "Central Europe – What It Is and What It Is Not, in *In Search of Central Europe*, ed. George Schöpflin and Nancy Wood (Cambridge: Polity Press), 143 – 156.
Simmel, Georg (1986) "Die Ruine [1907]", in *Aufsätze und Abhandlungen 1901 – 1908*, Bd. II (= *Gesamtausgabe*, vol. 8), ed. Ottheim Rammstedt (Frankfurt/M.: Suhrkamp), 124–130.
Snyder, Timothy (2010) *Bloodlands: Europe Between Hitler and Stalin* (London: Bodley Head).
Stirk, Peter M.R. (1994) *Mitteleuropa: History and Prospects* (Edinburgh: Edinburgh UP).
Svatek, Petra (2015) "'Mitteleuropa' auf Karten vom 16. bis ins frühe 20. Jahrhundert", in: *Mitteleuropa? Zwischen Realität, Chimäre und Konzept*, ed. Johann P. Arnason, Petr Hlaváček and Stefan Troebst, *Europaeana Pragensia* 7, 9 – 25.
Todorova, Maria (2005) "Spacing Europe: What Is A Historical Region", *East Central Europe* 32.1 – 2, 59 – 78.
Velikić, Dragan (2002): *Der Fall Bremen* [*Slučaj Bremen*, 2001], transl. Aleida Bremer (Berlin: Ullstein).
Westphal, Bertrand (2011) "Jenseits der Nostalgie: Ein geokritischer Zugang zu Mitteleuropa", in: Lajarrige et al. 2011, 411 – 52.
Williams, Raymond (1977) *Marxism and Literature* (Oxford, New York: Oxford UP).
Woods, Lebbeus (1997) *Radical Reconstruction* (Princeton: Princeton Architectural Press).
Živković, Yvonne (2015) *Between Geopolitics and Geopoetics: "Mitteleuropa" as a Transnational Memory Discourse in Austrian and Yugoslav Postwar Literature* (New York: PhD, Columbia University).

Ansgar and Vera Nünning (Univ. of Giessen / Univ. of Heidelberg)

Stories as "Weapons of Mass Destruction": George W. Bush's Narratives of Crisis as Paradigm Examples of Ways of World- and Conflict-Making (and Conflict-Solving?)

1 Narratives of crisis and other weapons of mass destruction, or: the worldmaking power of stories and storytelling[1]

Although the former American President George W. Bush is unlikely ever to be ranked among, or remembered as, one of America's or the world's greatest storytellers, one cannot help admitting that he and his comrades-in-arms displayed a certain degree of creativity, ingenuity, and success in conjuring up and disseminating a number of stories that turned out to be conflict- and worldmaking in a very literal sense despite being largely fictions. Anyone who doubts that narratives can indeed have performative power and worldmaking potential only needs to recall the ideologically charged story that the Bush administration couched in the form of what has come to be called a mini-narration, i.e. the story, or indeed stories, encapsulated in the metaphorically loaded concept of

---

1 In this article we have attempted to adapt and apply theoretical frameworks and analytical concepts that we outlined in a number of earlier publications on narrative worldmaking (A. Nünning 2010; V. Nünning 2010; A. & V. Nünning 2010) and on a narratology of crisis (Nünning 2009, 2012), from which we have also used a number of ideas and formulations. All the translations from German publications are by us. We should like to thank Alexander Scherr and Rose Lawson for their careful proofreading and help with adapting the article to the correct format and stylesheet, and Isabell Dinies for checking the quotations and references. We are also very grateful to Elizabeth Kovach for pointing out a number of important publications (Badiou 2003; Hogan 2009) which we might otherwise have overlooked. Unfortunately, we only came across Adam Hodges's (2011) and Richard Jackson's (2005) excellent books and Michael Frank's (2014) faculty dissertation after completing the first version of the paper upon which this article is based, but we have tried to make amends by incorporating quotations from, and references to, their many valuable insights while revising the text for publication (in the case of Jackson's and Frank's pioneering studies only in the final stages of copy-editing), though not as many as their incisive analyses of Bush's presidential speeches and the language used in "writing the war on terrorism" (Jackson 2005) would have deserved.

https://doi.org/10.1515/9783110556858-013

"weapons of mass destruction". As we will try to show in this article, though the weapons of mass destruction which Bush and Colin Powell claimed to be in Iraq's possession were never found, the stories generated by the Bush administration turned out to be not just propagandistic mass deception, but weapons of mass destruction themselves in that they provided the rhetorical justification for wars in which many soldiers and civilians lost their lives.

By looking more closely at the narrative and rhetorical strategies deployed by the political storytellers in office, we hope to shed some light on the forms and functions of narrative world- and conflict-making, demonstrating that narrative can indeed be, as Wolfgang Müller-Funk recently put it so aptly, "a very powerful – maybe even the most powerful – symbolic 'weapon' in structuring a world that is always, in the end, a cultural one" (Müller-Funk 2012: viii). Numerous accounts and detailed analyses of what has variously been dubbed "America's War on Terrorism" (Christie 2008; Mahajan 2002), "America's War on Terror" (Croft 2006; Ralph 2013), "The Ideological War on Terror" (Aldis and Herd 2007), "Bush's War" (Kuypers 2006), or simply (with or without scare quotes or a question mark) "the War on Terror" (Birkenstein 2010; Brady 2012; Evangelista 2008; Hill 2009; Hodges 2011; Holloway 2008; Jarvis 2009; Naftali 2010; Roger 2013; Schopp and Hill 2009; Shafir 2013; Wade 2010; Welsh 2006) or the "War on Terrorism" (Jackson 2005), to give but a random selection of preferred designations that have also been used as titles of seminal books on the topic at hand, have already been published, mainly from the vantage point of media studies, focussing on media bias (Kuypers 2006) or media technologies (cf. Roger 2013), and the political sciences (for example, MacDonald et al. 2012). Focussing less on the official political discourse itself, Croft (2006) provides an excellent account of the roles that U.S. media and popular culture played in the construction, or "co-production", and dissemination of the powerful discourse that has come to be known under the shorthand of "America's War on Terror". By contrast, there have been only few attempts to explore the rhetoric, metaphors, and narratives that served to legitimate the so-called "war against terror" from the point of view of literary and cultural studies, and even fewer attempts at exploring the central role that metaphors and narrative strategies have played in what Adam Hodges, in arguably the best book on the topic at hand, aptly calls "the construction of the textual product that is the Bush 'War on Terror' Narrative" (Hodges 2011: 10). There are, however, two excellent exceptions to this rule, namely Hodges's *The "War on Terror" Narrative: Discourse and Intertextuality in the Construction and Contestation of Sociopolitical Reality* and Patrick Colm Hogan's *Understanding Nationalism: On Narrative, Cognitive Science, and Identity*, which features an insightful chapter on "Heroic Nationalism and the Necessity of War from King David to George W. Bush" (Hogan 2009, Ch. 5). Hodges provides a perspicacious examination of "the relationship between microlevel discursive action – in the form of presidential speeches and public discourse – and the shared cultural understanding bound up in the macrolevel Bush 'War on Terror' Narrative" (Hodges 2011: 7–8). While the conceptual and methodological framework that Hodges develops is mainly informed by the approach known as "Critical Discourse Analysis" (Hodges 2011: 7) and the terminology of intertextuality, Hogan draws on the insights and tools of cognitive science in order to shed new light on the "Techniques of Nationalization" (Hogan 2009: 66) and the "Narrative Structure of Patriotism" (Hogan 2009: 167).

Attempting to complement these seminal monographs, the focus of this article will be on a metaphorological and narratological analysis of selected speeches of former President George W. Bush because they can illuminate the central question raised by the editors of this volume, i.e. the question of the relation between narratives and their performative quality, on the one hand, and cultural conflicts on the other. We will go even further and argue that Bush's speeches provide a paradigmatic example of the ways in which narrative constructions and processes can be endowed with performative power, actively moulding, constructing or even creating the cultural and ideological conflicts that they purport merely to reflect or represent. Instead of merely referring to actual conflicts, metaphors and narratives arguably play an active role in generating them and in producing a hegemonic discourse that serves to interpret events in a propagandistic way and to shape a shared cultural understanding of the world as projected in the official narrative. Although Bush's speeches do not exactly make for very entertaining or edifying reading, they arguably provide an excellent case study in the role of narratives as ways of conflict- and worldmaking.

But let us first turn our attention to one of the great contemporary American storytellers, Paul Auster, and briefly look at the scenario that he conjured up in his sombre post 9/11-novel *Man in the Dark* (2008). When sleep refuses to come to the eponymous seventy-two-year-old August Brill, the narrator-protagonist tells himself stories in order to try to keep at bay recent traumatic events, including his wife's death, the murder of his granddaughter's boyfriend as well as 9/11 and the war in Iraq. In the embedded narrative that he is inventing while insomniac, the protagonist finds himself in an alternative world, an America not fighting a war in Iraq, but rather an America ravaged by a terrible civil war that has been going on for four years. Very mysterious men tell him that he has been picked "for the big job" (Auster 2008: 9) of becoming an assassin, the assignment being to kill someone who is said to deserve to die because he purportedly invented a war by writing down a particular story. The dialogue between the mysterious men and the highly reluctant assassin-to-be deserves to be quoted at some length because of the light it can shed on the topic at hand:

> 'Because he owns the war. He invented it, and everything that happens or is about to happen is in his head. Eliminate that head, and the war stops. It's that simple.'
>
> 'Simple? You make him sound like God.'
>
> 'Not God, Corporal, just a man. He sits in a room all day writing it down, and whatever he writes comes true.' (Auster 2008: 10)

The implications of this peculiar dialogue, which, in the context of a novel, is of course highly self-referential and metafictional, are that it is stories that can invent conflicts, crises, and even wars, and what is needed is a different kind of story in order to change the course of events, end a war, and turn a narrative of conflict and crisis into quite another kind of narrative: "The story would end, and the war would be over" (Auster 2008: 72). Although the political undertones and implicit references to the actual crises that occurred in the aftermath of 9/11 are already quite clear at this stage, the references to the war in Iraq, which is mentioned in this dialogue (Auster 2008: 8), become even more explicit in the course of the novel when, showing that "this America, this other America, which hasn't lived through September 11 or the war in Iraq, nonethless has strong historical links to the America he knows" (Auster 2008: 50; see 62–63 for other reality-references). Though the inconclusive dialogues and reflections about "multiple realities and multiple worlds" (Auster 2008: 90) that we find in Auster's novel may confuse many readers almost as much as the characters, these metafictional devices can throw additional light on the ways in which stories can actually generate conflicts and events, reconfigure spaces, and even lead to wars.

As both Auster's novel and the stories disseminated by the Bush administration serve to show, narratives can indeed be one of the most powerful ways of conflict- and worldmaking as well as weapons of mass deception designed to foster crises and provide the mental preparation for a war. The main reason for this is that storytelling not only generates possible worlds, narratives also exert performative power. In her groundbreaking monograph *Shakespeare's Storytellers*, Barbara Hardy pins it down with great precision in talking about "the theatrical power of narrative, its capacity to change events, its control and compounding, its passion and its immediacy" (Hardy 1997: 60). This performative force or even theatrical power of storytelling stems from the reality-constituting, identity-, sense-, space- and indeed worldmaking qualities that characterize narration and narratives.

What do these random examples tell us about ways of narrative conflict- and worldmaking and the performative power of narratives, then? Perceiving imaginary weapons of mass destruction seems to consist in producing not only weapons in the mind, but also stories that can change reality, having far-reaching consequences for a potentially great number of people. Conjuring up an epic conflict or a crisis in Iraq, or any other country, for that matter, can be very much a matter of inventing it: once the diagnosis that there "is" a conflict or a crisis comes to be regarded as a political or economic reality, culturally available crises-plots are activated, assigning not only roles to the participants involved, but also a particular meaning to the events thus designated (see A. Nünning 2010, 2012). The activity of narrative conflict- or worldmaking, including the choice of a particular kind of metaphor and story, is not so much a matter of recognizing actual crises or historical changes "out there", but of imposing order and meaning on a sequence of happenings that could also be emplotted in quite different ways. All of this should give anyone interested in narrative reason to pause, and to take a fresh look at the ways in which events, conflicts and stories are created or made through the complex processes involved in narrative worldmaking.

Although the stories and narratives disseminated by George W. Bush in his remarkably repetitive presidential speeches are neither as complex nor as theatrical as those told by either Auster's narrators or Shakespeare's characters, they certainly demonstrate the performative power of narrative and its unsurpassed capacity to change events and generate ideological conflicts. With regard to the topic of this volume, i.e. the role of narrative constructions and processes in cultural conflicts, Auster's novel and the stories generated by the Bush administration raise a number of interesting research questions. What are the main narratological and rhetorical features of narratives of conflict and crisis like the mini-narration encapsulated in the ominous phrase "weapons of mass destruction"? What are the cultural and political functions that such narratives of crisis can fulfil? What can the study of literature and culture contribute to a better understanding of narratives of conflict and crisis and the cultural work that they do? The main goal of this article is not only to address these questions, but also to make a modest attempt to come up with some preliminary answers.

By drawing on recent work on the cultural life of crises and catastrophes (Meiner and Veel 2012) as well as on concepts from metaphorology and narratology (including, among others, event, configuration, emplotment, cultural plots and perspectives), this article pursues three main aims: first, to analyze George W. Bush's speeches as a paradigm example of narratives of conflict and crisis and to try to illuminate the main metaphorological, narratological and rhetorical features of these stories in particular and narratives of conflict in general. Second, it tries to tease out, and comment on, some of the processes and discourse strategies that go into Bush's narrative conflict- and worldmaking. Third, the essay attempts to explore the cultural and political functions that the story of weapons of mass destruction and other narratives of crisis are designed to serve. Though we cannot provide a comprehensive account of Bush's rhetoric and "politics of fear" (Gore 2008, Ch. 1), we will attempt to demonstrate that a narratological analysis of Bush's speeches can yield valuable insights into the topic at hand, i.e. the many ways in which narratives do not merely reflect or represent cultural, political or military conflicts, but rather serve to create or generate conflicts, crises, events, wars and even worlds. In order to do so, let us begin by examining some narrative ways of worldmaking and the performative power of narrative in greater detail.

2 "Weapons of Mass Destruction" as a metaphorical concept and mini-narration: main features of narratives of conflict and crisis from a conceptual and metaphorological point of view

Anyone who wants to get to grips with such a rich topic as the relation between narratives and conflicts might as well begin with the seemingly simple question of what conflicts and crises actually are. One of the many possible answers would be to argue that conflicts and crises are by no means always simply givens that exist 'out there', i.e. in the real world. On the contrary, they can rather be conceptualized as resulting from signifying practices, from the use of symbolic forms, indeed from particular cultural 'ways of worldmaking', to adopt Nelson Goodman's felicitous term: when people designate a particular kind of occurrence, constellation or event as a 'conflict' or a "crisis" they typically resort to metaphors (see Nünning 2009, 2012). Putting it like this, however, means that we are back to square one, though the question now is 'what is a metaphor?'

In the preface to his seminal encyclopaedia of philosophical metaphors, the editor Ralf Konersmann answers the question of what metaphors are by providing a somewhat unusual definition: "Metaphors are narratives that mask themselves as a single word" (Konersmann 2008: 17; our translation). The subtitle ("Figuratives Wissen") of the preface, which is actually a highly interesting essay on the nature and functions of metaphors, sheds light on another key aspect of metaphors: the phrase "figurative knowledge" emphasizes that metaphors do indeed generate knowledge, albeit of a figurative kind. Konersmann is, of course, neither the only nor the first scholar to draw attention to the fact that metaphors and metaphorical concepts can be conceived of as condensed narratives (Koschorke 2012: 274) and that they produce a special kind of knowledge. Philip Eubanks, for instance, has argued that metaphors project "mininarrations" (Eubanks

1999: 437), and other theorists have also acknowledged the cognitive and knowledge-creating potential of metaphors.

Understanding metaphors and concepts as condensed narratives provides a heuristically fruitful starting point for coming to terms with the topic at hand, i.e. the question of the relation between narrative constructions and processes, and their performative power with particular regard to cultural conflicts. If there is one rhetorical leitmotif that runs through most of the presidential speeches given by George W. Bush, it is arguably the ominous phrase of "weapons of mass destruction", which provides a case in point for how metaphorical concepts can project condensed narratives or mini-narrations. The same holds true for the somewhat peculiar phrase "war on terror", with which Bush designated the rhetorical and military campaign which he himself launched and started as a result of the terrorist attacks against the United States on 11 September 2001.

Although one might assume that the phrase "weapons of mass destruction" only entered the somewhat limited and highly repetitive presidential rhetoric and vocabulary after the terrorist attacks of 9/11, it is worth noting that the former American President used it right from the very beginning of his first term. Without providing any kind of context, coherence, exposition or at least pretext, Bush suddenly announced in his inaugural address: "We will confront weapons of mass destruction, so that a new century is spared new horrors" (Bush 2001a: 3). Although this threatening remark was neither motivated historically at that stage nor rhetorically within the texture of the inaugural address, with the benefit of hindsight it is fairly obvious that this sentence is not just the first official reference to Bush's pet project that would soon turn into an obssession, but also something like the narrative kernel from which the main features of the stories that the Bush administration preferred to tell after 9/11 can be deduced or derived.

The phrase so obsessively used by President Bush, "weapons of mass destruction", is a case in point in that it can be conceived of as both a highly charged metaphorical concept and a condensed ideological narrative of conflict. Though this metaphor is a narrative that masks itself as four words, it entails a narrative kernel with at least two antagonistic roles and a potential plot. Like other metaphors and concepts, the term "weapons of mass destruction" contains a particular narrative that is entailed in the very logic of the term and that is virtually waiting to be spelled out (Koschorke 2012: 270).

This is exactly what Bush began to do in the months after his inauguration, for example in his Address to the Joint Session of the 107th Congress in Washington in February 2001. Delineating his idiosyncratic views on how "to extend and secure our present peace by promoting a distinctly American internationalism" as well as "our values" (Bush 2001b: 32), Bush suddenly turned the audience's attention to what he called the need for "a clear strategy to confront the threats of the twenty-first century – threats that are more widespread and less certain. They range from terrorists who threaten with bombs to tyrants in rogue nations intent upon developing weapons of mass destruction" (32). Bush thus began to forge a link between terrorists, threats, and tyrants as early as seven months before the attacks of 9/11.

As these quotations already indicate, "weapons of mass destruction" can be seen as an abbreviated or condensed narrative of conflict in that weapons are always developed and owned by some party in order to be potentially deployed against an enemy. Using the phrase "weapons of mass destruction" is thus a way of introducing or creating a conflict because the very phrase implies or defines a line of conflict and a potential battle-line between friends and foes. It also served to provide the central motivation and legitimation of the future course of events, especially of Bush's "war on terror", in that it stands to reason that any nation would be well-advised to defend itself against a yet to be defined enemy who might possess such weapons, thus naturalizing and seemingly justifying an aggressive policy that would eventually lead to the wars in Afghanistan and Iraq.

The recurrent reference to "weapons of mass destruction" is a way of launching a condensed narrative of conflict that can be further elaborated or fleshed out in a number of ways. The close link between Bush's obsession with the notion of "weapons of mass destruction" and the narrative of conflict that it encapsulates can be seen in the way in which it generates binary oppositions, conveniently dividing up the world in us vs. them, i.e. the American nation and its enemies, also known as the "evil men" (Bush 2001g: 93), to quote another one of Bush's pet phrases. Although there is a host of examples of his use of binarisms in just about every speech that Bush gave during the eight years of his presidency, his fateful penchant for manichaeisms like "lawful change" vs. "chaotic violence" (93) and either-or-alternatives was probably never more bluntly expressed than in the famous, or rather infamous, speech he gave nine days after 9/11: "Every nation, in every region, now has a decision to make. Either you are with us, or you are with the terrorists. From this day forward, any nation that continues to harbor or support terrorism will be regarded by the United States as a hostile regime." (Bush 2001e: 69) The first two sentences illustrate how the metaphorical concept of "weapons of mass destruction" provides the cognitive and affective rationale for dividing up the world into two antagonistic camps: us vs. the terrorists. Jackson (2005, Ch. 3) has meticulously shown how the discourse of counter-terrorism constructed the enemy in terms of evil, alien, dehumanised and demonised terrorists, pitting them against the equally ideological construct of innocent and heroic "good Americans". The often-quoted second sentence is not just an infamous example of Bush's penchant for binarisms and for defining the protagonists of the unfolding narrative as "us" and, or rather, versus, "them" (Hodges 2011: 47), it also serves to show "that a rigidly binary model is so conducive to displays of intolerance and destructive social emotions. Expressed with classic completeness in the formula 'If you're not with us, you're against us,' this model historically comes to the surface whenever creativity is pushed aside by destruction" (Lotman 2013: 79–80). With the benefit of hindsight, Lotman's observation made many years before 9/11 assumes an uncanny prophetic quality in that Bush's binaristic thinking and rhetoric did indeed forestall creativity and fostered destruction on many levels.

The third sentence in the quotation above provides the kernel of the new national security strategy that has come to be known as "Bush Doctrine" and that has since served to map out and expand the narrative of conflict entailed in the metaphorical concept of "weapons of mass destruction". Already in his Address to the Nation on the September 11 attacks, Bush announced: "We will make no distinction between the terrorists who committed these acts and those who harbor them." (Bush 2001c: 58) In his later speeches, Bush never left anyone in any doubt that he believed that the United States had the right to secure itself against any countries that harbour, shelter, or support terrorist groups, giving aid to them or even supplying them with weapons of mass destruction, as his remarks about the Taliban in his Address to the United Nations General Assembly in November 2001, for example, illustrate (see Bush 2001f: 86, 88).

Although the condensed narrative of conflict implied in the concept of "weapons of mass destruction" provided a highly convenient way of ideological worldmaking that divided up the nations and people into two groups, the definitions of who was to be regarded as friend or foe, good or evil, belonging to "us" or to the "terrorists", turned out to be somewhat arbitrary and subject to historical change. Looking at Bush's speeches in chronological order, one cannot fail to notice how the slot of the enemy, or enemies, is filled differently in the months and years following 9/11. While the former American President tended to be pretty vague about this matter in his early speeches, using general phrases like "those who are behind these evil acts" (Bush 2001c: 58), "our enemies" (Bush 2001d: 61; Bush 2002a: 110) or "enemies of human freedom" (Bush 2001d: 61), he began to be more specific in the weeks and months after 9/11, mentioning both the names of "al Qaeda" (Bush 2001e: 66, 68) and Osama bin Laden (cf. Bush 2001e: 67), while also repeatedly referring to loosely or ill-defined entities like "the terrorists" (Bush 2001f: 84), "a few evil men" (Bush 2001g: 93), "a few dozen evil and deluded men" (Bush 2002c: 127) or "the enemies of the twenty-first century" (Bush 2001g: 98). It was only when, largely for political and strategic reasons, Bush needed a new selling point, that he began to zoom in onto

Saddam Hussein and Iraq, claiming that the United States was "acting to end the state sponsorship of terror" (Bush 2001g: 93).

In the attempts of the Bush administration to fix a designated enemy, the words "terrorists", "terror" and "terrorism" fulfilled several crucial functions. In his brilliant and meticulous philosophical examination of the implications and functions of "the name 'terrorism'", the French philosopher Alain Badiou argues that "the word 'terrorism' has a triple function" (Badiou 2003: 142): It not only determines "the subject who is targeted by the terrorist act" (Badiou 2003: 142), and the subject who commits the act, one might add, and "supports predicates" (Badiou 2003: 143), it also "determines a sequence – the entire current sequence is from now on considered as 'the war against terrorism'" (Badiou 2003: 143). Identifying, designating and naming the purported enemy is thus anything but an innocent or self-evident act in that these ways of worldmaking exert performative power. As Juri Lotman aptly observes in a different context, "the peculiar nature of cultural processes manifests itself when different phenomena are given names and acquire their own reality. This reality in turn invades the original object and transforms it into its own image and likeness" (Lotman 2013: 70). This is exactly what happened in the wake of 9/11 when the former American President's speeches conjured up a particular narrative of conflict, which not just determined the future sequence of events, but also invaded reality as well as Iraq.

In addition to launching a narrative of conflict, the metaphorical concept of "weapons of mass destruction" can also be seen as a condensed narrative of crisis in that it already emphasizes what Bush himself called a "sense of urgency" (Bush 2001g: 95) and a necessity to act before it might be too late. Time and again Bush conjured up the great potential dangers that could result from regimes that possessed weapons of mass destruction and that might pass them on to terrorists, thereby trying to bolster up his claim that "the threat is imminent" (Bush 2003a: 163). The performative power of narratives is underscored by the fact that when Bush himself began using the phrase "our nation in crisis" (Bush 2002a: 111) in his State of the Union Address in January 2002, he did not present an objective diagnosis of the actual state of affairs, but rather stirred up an atmosphere of anxiety and fear associated with the notion of crisis. In the infamous speech he gave in Cincinnati on October 7, 2002, Bush not only outlined what he called "a great threat to peace", he also expressed "America's determination to lead the world in confronting that threat" (Bush 2002f). What is particularly interesting in the present context is the way in which Bush attempted to explain and justify what he called "the urgency of action" by delineating in great detail not only the great dangers and threats that, according to him, come "from Iraq", also referred to as "the threat gathering against us", but also the crisis or moment of decision brought about by this threat. One section of the Cincinnati speech deserves to be quoted at some length because it illustrates the amazing ways in which Bush entirely dispenses with factual evidence, logic, and reason, resorting instead to verbal repetition, counter-factual claims, association and the emotional implications of the crisis scenario that he himself generated through his narrative of conflict and crisis and that also served to underscore the sense of urgency that Bush was so anxious to create:

> Some citizens wonder, after 11 years of living with this problem [i.e. the threat posed by the regime in Iraq], why do we need to confront it now? And there's a reason. We've experienced the horror of September the 11th. We have seen that those who hate America are willing to crash airplanes into buildings full of innocent people. Our enemies would be no less willing, in fact, they would be eager to use biological or chemical, or a nuclear weapon.
>
> Knowing these realities, America must not ignore the threat gathering against us. Facing clear evidence of peril, we cannot wait for the final proof – the smoking gun – that could come in the form of a mushroom cloud. (Bush 2002f)

This daunting and devious narrative scenario serves to show once more that the metaphorical concepts of "weapons of mass destruction" and "crisis" evoke a number of culturally determined connotations, associations and affective implications, the main ones being, besides disease, illness, and a search for remedies, danger and threat, anxiety and alarm, fear and concern (Nünning 2012: 74). Already two months after 9/11, for instance, Bush claimed that "terrorists are searching for weapons of mass destruction, the tools to turn their hatred into holocaust" (Bush 2001f: 84), thus creating an atmosphere of anxiety and fear by linking the threat of terrorism up with the atrocities committed by the Nazis. In his highly manipulative and propagandistic 2002 speech in Cincinnati, Bush evoked the devastating potential consequences that Iraq's alleged weapons of mass destruction might have for the American people, not even refraining from encouraging his compatriots to imagine a terrorist attack with nuclear weapons and the apocalyptic and catastrophic scenarios that might result from the use of such weapons of mass destruction. The rationale behind the Bush administration's preference for focussing on what Al Gore has aptly called "convenient untruths" (Gore 2008: 104) is perfectly obvious with the benefit of hindsight, since the idea "that a 'mushroom cloud' might threaten American cities unless we invaded Iraq to prevent Saddam Hussein from giving a nuclear weapon to the same terrorist group that had already attacked us with deadly consequences" was part of a "highly orchestrated" campaign, as Gore (2008: 104–105) poignantly observed. Bush's frequent use of counterfactual statements or "convenient untruths" also confirm one of the observations made by Martin Amis in a candid review of Bob Woodward's book *State of Denial: Bush at*

War, Part III (Woodward 2006): "Students of history are aware that illusion – or, if you prefer, psychopathology – plays a part in shaping world events" (Amis 2008: 151).

These brief quotes from Bush's "mushroom cloud" speech as well as many other examples serve to show that both the choice of his pet phrases and the condensed narratives of conflict and crisis that they entail and generate are anything but neutral representations of the actual state of affairs. On the contrary, these highly suggestive rhetorical and narrative choices are affectively and ideologically charged strategies that imply that a critical moment or even a turning-point has been reached, that decisions have to be made and that what is needed is immediate action to ward off the dangers and threats associated with the ill-defined enemies and their purported weapons of mass destruction. It may be noted in passing that the identification, or rather diagnosis, of a crisis, however, very much depends on the perspective of the observer or narrator, but being the incarnation of the apodictic politician, Bush always suggested that his way of diagnosing and delineating the state of affairs was the only possible interpretation.

Once a certain situation is metaphorically characterized as a crisis, this kind of definition or diagnosis of a situation automatically implies and immediately activates certain affective implications, cognitive frames and narrative schemata (Nünning 2009, 2012). To start with, "crisis" implies great danger, a threat and general insecurity. In the case of a crisis, the climax and turning point of a dangerous development is reached, or imminent. What Bush managed to achieve with the condensed narratives in his speeches is nicely summed up in the English saying, "We must bring things to a crisis": by conjuring up a crisis through narrative conflict- and worldmaking, he managed to blur the boundary between "illusory threats and legitimate ones" (Gore 2008: 25), to convince more than seventy percent of all Americans that Saddam Hussein was responsible for the attacks of September 11, 2001 (Gore 2008: 26), and to suggest that a moment of decision-making had been reached.

Who and what is sought after in a situation designated as a "crisis" is apparent according to the respective culturally available crisis plots because, when talking about a "crisis", specific actions and developmental patterns are invoked at the same time. Depending on the social realm of action, there are different crises, but the fundamental scheme remains the same, both from a narratological perspective and from the point of view of metaphor theory: what is in demand in a crisis are competent and determined crisis managers, crisis management plans, and purposeful actions. Speaking about a crisis always evokes conventionalized schemata and plot patterns which sketch out the future course of action, while also reinterpreting the recent past in a particular way. For this reason, a crisis diagnosis is always already more than a specific definition of the respective situation and, in retrospect, often appears as a self-fulfilling prophecy, as we will try to show in the next section, which is devoted to a narratological analysis of Bush's rhetorical conflict- and worldmaking.

3 "Weapons of Mass Destruction", "Axis of Evil" and other narratives of conflict and crisis: main features from a narratological and rhetorical point of view

First of all, Bush's speeches, especially those that he gave in the aftermath of 9/11, show that labelling a dangerous situation as a "crisis" or as a "war" is anything but a neutral way of representing what actually happened. On the contrary, the choice of a particular concept or metaphor that serves as a designation for the event(s) in question not only provides a specific definition of the respective situations, determining what kind of event it purportedly is, but also evokes certain narrative schemata, development patterns, and plots. On the one hand, these schemata interpret the events that have preceded the current situation in a highly specific way. Thus, designating dangerous and ominous developments as a "crisis" or a "war" not only implies that something has happened before, it is also a way of interpreting the past in a very particular way. On the other hand, describing a situation as a "crisis" or a "war" is also always a diagnosis from which certain therapeutic perspectives and action scenarios for future developments, can be derived. As soon as we speak about "crisis", a course-of-disease scheme is invoked: "There is an identifiable beginning which is to be understood as a cause and which starts a development which leads to a reasonable ending; disturbances of this structure provoke an extensive awareness of danger" (Bullivant and Spies 2001: 17; our translation).

Consequently, Bush's speaking about or diagnosing an alleged crisis in the aftermath of 9/11 includes not only defining certain action-roles but, as a result of the systematic logic of these metaphorical concepts, also linking past, present and future in a comprehensive plot. With regard to the past, the diagnosis of a crisis implies a negative, more or less teleological development towards a crisis. By contrast, the present in a crisis-diagnosis is perceived and interpreted as a grave danger, a decisive moment and a realm of possibilities. With regard to the possible future developments this results in a spectrum of different potential scenarios, which range from the extremes of death and destruction on the one hand to recovery and the overcoming of the crisis on the other. Before we take a closer look at how George W. Bush managed to project a narrative of conflict and crisis, including a storyworld in which antagonistic forces, ideologies and values are pitted against each other, let us briefly outline what is involved in narrative worldmaking (A. Nünning 2010; V. Nünning 2010).

From a narratological point of view, narrative worldmaking can be examined on a number of different axes: the paradigmatic axis of selection, the syntagmatic axis of combination, and the discursive axis of narrative mediation and perspectivization. Firstly, the selection and emphasis of the chosen events and plot elements leads to a "hierarchization of meanings" (Gutenberg 2000: 118) on the paradigmatic axis, representing one of the procedures of "weighting" (Goodman 1992 [1978]: 10). Secondly, the methods of plot configuration on the syntagmatic axis, i.e. the arrangement, combination, and causal and logical interconnections, are crucial for the processes of narrative meaning- and world-making. Depending on the selected principles of the interrelatedness of plot elements and the favoured macro-structural configuration-types, an occurrence can be transformed into a variety of different stories and narratives. Thirdly, the discursive axis plays a pivotal role in narrative worldmaking because the explicit and implicit constitution of meaning also greatly depends on the narrative mediation and perspectivization. Perspective or point of view deserves special attention as yet another act or procedure of narrative worldmaking in its own right, because it influences all of the processes involved in the making of events, plots, and storyworlds mentioned above.

To begin with, narratives of conflict and crises, just like other stories and types of events, are the result of selection, abstraction and distinction (A. Nünning 2010). Tying in with the colloquial meaning of "significant occurrence" or "significant event", narratology first of all distinguishes between the chaotic and the contingent totality of all occurrences and the event as a particularly relevant and significant part thereof (Stierle 1975). Both the emphatic event-concept of narratology (Schmid 2005: 20–26) and the metaphoric concept of crisis are not concerned with everyday occurrences, but with incidents or changes which are collectively thought to be of great relevance and importance. Thus, the configuration of the kind of significant events that is commonly designated as a crisis or a conflict is based on singling them out from the continuous flow of occurrences and qualifying them as something special or surprising; thus, any conflict and crisis is based on construction, selection, and distinction by an observer.

The narratives conjured up by the Bush administration provide an interesting case in point in that they serve to illustrate how certain occurrences are first of all singled out and then turned into key events and into a story of a particular kind, i.e. a narrative of conflict or crisis. Narrative worldmaking typically begins with selection, which also involves "deletion" and "supplementation" (cf. Goodman 1992 [1978]). As we have already seen, the focus of many of Bush's speeches on 9/11 and the metaphorical concept of weapons of mass destruction is a largely arbitrary way of selecting a particular narrative kernel that implies an antagonism and that lends itself well to elaborating narratives of conflict and crisis.

Moreover, a certain temporal section must be singled out and – not least through such ways of worldmaking as selection, ordering, and weighting – be given meaning, and it is thereby already interpreted in a contingent, but very particular way. Accordingly, the respective story told is the result of a selection of certain moments and qualities from the happening, whose amorphous endlessness is thereby transferred into a limited, structured form which is enriched with meaning. The story contains the selected moments of action in their chronological order, however, without already transferring them into a plot. The latter does not happen until the story is transformed into a particular narrative, or plot, which is the result of arrangement and shaping that occurs on the syntagmatic axis of combination and emplotment.

As far as the processes that go into narrative worldmaking are concerned, it is not just the selection of certain things that happen and the deletion of others, which is important for the analysis of how events, stories, and worlds are constructed, but the narrative arrangement of the selected material into certain narratives plays an equally important role. The significance of what Goodman calls "ordering" (Goodman 1992 [1978]: 12), i.e. the structuring of events through narrative procedures, lies in the fact that processes of configuration must first establish a relationship between the selected elements to turn them into an orderly, meaningful whole: "First, the configurational arrangement transforms the succession of events into one meaningful whole [...]. Second, the configuration of the plot imposes the 'sense of an ending' [...] on the indefinite succession of incidents" (Ricœur 1984: 65). In Bush's speeches, the configuration of the selected events, persons, and situations, which consists in establishing connections, interrelations, and patterns between them, turns them into a particular kind of story, namely a narrative of conflict, generating a particular storyworld.

As far as the emplotment strategies are concerned, it is first of all interesting to note how Bush marks the beginning of what he relentlessly referred to as the "war on terror". Reading his speeches, one is reminded of the first sentence of Ian McEwan's mesmerizing novel *Enduring Love* (1997), in which the seemingly unreliable narrator apodictically observes: "The beginning is simple to mark" (McEwan 1998 [1997]: 1). In all of his speeches relating to what Bush kept calling "the war on terror", the former American President also pretends that the beginning of the ideological conflict is simple to mark: it was the morning of September 11, conjured up by Bush time and again, when terrorists attacked America by turning airplanes into missiles and flying them into the World Trade Center as well as the Pentagon. In many of his speeches Bush emphasized this by using the terrorist attacks as his narrative point of departure or by referring to the temporal distance between 9/11 and the respective present, using such phrases as "September 11th, 2001 – three months and a long time ago" (Bush 2001g: 92), "In the last seven months" (Bush 2002b: 123), "Since September the 11th" (Bush 2002b: 123), or "We're now approaching the fifth anniversary of the day this war reached our shores" (Bush 2006: 380). Leaving aside for the moment that the last quote is one of the countless examples of counterfactual statements to be found in Bush's speeches, it is interesting to note that Bush not only dated everything back to "the horror of that morning" (Bush 2006: 380), but that he also insisted that "the nightmare of September the 11th, 2001" (Bush 2006: 381) constituted the outbreak of "this war" (Bush 2006: 380). According to the official narrative disseminated by the Bush administration, 9/11 constituted the "precipitating event" (Hodges 2011: 43, 49) that served as "the starting point" (Hodges 2011: 43) of the story which Bush kept telling his compatriots and which became "a crucial reference point in the Narrative. It acts as the pivot around which the Narrative is organized" (Hodges 2011: 43). Hammering home the same propagandistic message time and again, Bush kept reminding his audience where the story that he was forging and telling began: "As we fight this war, we will remember where it began – here, in our country", Bush (2003a: 157) maintained in January 2003.

What Bush failed to acknowledge, or even accept as a possibility, however, is that the beginning of any narrative is always dependent on both more or less random decisions and one's point of view, and is thus anything but simple to mark. What is more, even if we accepted the premise that 9/11 marked the beginning of what was turned into a military and ideological conflict through the President's ways of narrative worldmaking, both the nature of what actually happened on 9/11 and the appropriate way to designate the ensuing reactions and events would still have to be defined and negotiated.

In the first couple of days and weeks after the day usually referred to as 9/11, the American President, just like many commentators around the world, was somewhat less sure as to what kind of event the occurrences of 11 September 2001 actually constituted. While he began by referring to what had happened on that fateful day quite accurately as "terrorist attacks" (Bush 2001c: 57), the American President and his advisors soon decided to designate the terrorist attacks as a "war", in fact using the phrase "war against terrorism" (Bush 2001c: 58) already on the eve of what has come to be known as 9/11. Only three days after 9/11, in the speech that Bush gave on what was christened the "National Day of Prayer and Remembrance", Bush introduced the ominous term that would serve to prefigure the future course of events: "War has been waged against us by stealth and deceit and danger" (Bush 2001d: 59). As we all know with the benefit of hindsight, this has turned out to be a fateful choice that had far-reaching consequences because of the legal and ideological implications as well as the narrative schemata that it entailed. Bush already began to sketch out the rough plot of the narrative of conflict and revenge that he generated and fostered with his rhetoric and storytelling in the same speech:

> Just three days removed from these events, Americans do not yet have the distance to history. But our responsibility is already clear: to answer these attacks and rid the world of evil.
>
> War has been waged against us by stealth and deceit and danger. This nation is peaceful, but fierce when stirred to anger. This conflict was begun on the timing and terms of others. It will end in a way, and at an hour, of our choosing. (Bush 2001d: 59 – 60)

As these sweeping statements show, Bush assumed the role of an omniscient narrator who defines the beginning and ending of the story that he is in the process of making up, claiming the sole right to explain and interpret the events that his idiosyncratic narrative of conflict puports merely to reflect, but actually serves to generate. Almost ten days after 9/11, the former American President had officially reframed the terrorist attacks in terms of war: "On September the 11th, enemies of freedom committed an act of war against our country" (Bush 2001e: 66). Bush also inserted this "act of war" into history by referring to "wars on foreign soil" and "one Sunday in 1941", i.e. Pearl Harbor. As Jackson (2005) and Hodges (2011, Ch. 2) have shown, the choice of the concept of war as the official frame of reference and symbolic register had far-reaching consequences, both for the further elaboration of Bush's narratives and for then moulding the actual future course of events and developments. In his perspicacious analysis of the implications of the symbolic register of war, Alain Badiou (2003: 154) even goes so far as to argue that "the American imperial power, in the formal representation it makes of itself, has war as the privileged, indeed unique, form of the attestation of its existence". The choice of the symbolic register of war, rather than that of crime and policing (Hodges 2011: 25), or the complex framework of international law (Duffy 2005), for that matter, not only fostered national unity and American collective identity, it also served to provide some kind of pseudo-legitimation for attacking whatever country or adversary that was designated as a terrorist and an enemy of the United States. It may be noted in passing that Bush was at least wise enough to change a significant detail of the story that he kept telling his compatriots when he addressed the United Nations General Assembly on November 10, 2001, suddenly claiming that the terrorist attacks actually constituted "attacks on the world" (Bush 2001f: 85) rather than just "an act of war against our country".

In his double role as President and omniscient storyteller, Bush also claimed the right to decide what the appropriate reaction to the "war" that the terrorist attacks allegedly constituted was, eventually settling on the curious phrase "war on terror". The fateful choice of the metaphor and symbolic register of war not only entailed framing the events in military terms, it also served to provide a pseudo-legitimation for claiming that a military response was called for (Hodges 2011: 159). In his brilliant examination of the generic and ideological implications of the war metaphor, Adam Hodges (2011: 19) has convincingly shown that the "generic framework of a nation at war provides a highly recognizable template for narrating the 'war on terror'" as well as "a ready-made cultural framework to aid in both telling and interpretating the Narrative" (Hodges 2011: 20). After having identified "a radical network of terrorists, and every government that supports them" (Bush 2001e: 68) as "[o]ur enemy", Bush roughly delineated his notion of the plot that the "war on terror" narrative would have, already ominously indicating that it might well be a long affair without closure: "Our war on terror begins with Al Qaeda, but it does not end there. It will not end until every terrorist group of global reach has been found, stopped and defeated." In the same speech, Bush also told the Congress and the American nation that "[t]his war will not be like the war against Iraq a decade ago": "Americans should not expect one battle, but a lengthy campaign, unlike any other we have ever seen" (Bush 2001e: 69). Though Bush acknowledged that this was an "unconventional conflict" (Bush 2001g: 94), it was his choice of the metaphorical mini-narrative of "war on terror" that served to determine what kind of conflict and story it would be.

By the time Bush addressed the United Nations General Assembly in November 2001, he used the terms "this war on terror" (or "war against terror") and "this new conflict" (Bush 2001f: 87) interchangeably, thus establishing his narrative of conflict and defining the nature of the conflict as a war. As Jarvis (2009: 3) has shown, first there was a "war against terrorism" and then there was a "discourse shift in its framing. That shift [...] related to the linguistic contraction of terrorism to terror." One does not have to be a novelist to realize that the very peculiar term "war on terror" is actually an infelictious misnomer at best, or even, like the phrase "war on terrorism", a "conceptual contradiction" or "a contradiction in terms" (Jackson 2005: 123, 147), but most people will probably be inclined to agree with one of the main characters in Graham Swift's recent novel *Wish You Were Here* (2011), who not only ponders about this phrase, but also about the story that it projects: "There was a war going on, that was the story. [...] A war on terror, that was the general story. Jack knew that terror was a thing you felt inside, so what could a war on terror be, in the end but a war against yourself?" (Swift 2011: 60) The protagonist Jack also realizes that such a phrase is anything but an innocent choice and that it does make a big difference what a conflict, event, or war is called because the choice of the phrase can have far-reaching implications: "What they meant, of course, was a war against *terrorism*. But then it became a matter of who and where, of geography" (Swift 2011: 61). By contrast, waging a war on terror, i.e. against a word or a feeling, is a whole lot more ambiguous and ominous, open to interpretation and reframings.

In his self-appointed role as omniscient narrator, the former American President also provided clear-cut, but apodictic and highly questionable answers to some of the questions that, according to him, "Americans are asking" (Bush 2001e: 68, 69), for example concerning causality and motivation, including the question of "why do they hate us?" (Bush 2001e: 68). Bush even pretended to know all the answers to the questions that he imputed to his compatriots, but which he actually raised himself in order to assert his supreme narrative and performative power to interpret the recent traumatic events. According to Bush the storyteller, the terrorists not only "hate our freedoms", they also kill "to disrupt and end a way of life", which is the American way of life, of course. Although there is almost as little evidence for these pseudo-explanations of the terrorists' alleged motivations as for the weapons of mass destruction that provided the pretext for the preemptive war against Iraq, Bush hammered home the same points, apodictically claiming that "the only way to defeat terrorism as a threat to our way of life is to stop it, eliminate it, and destroy it where it grows" (Bush 2001e: 70).

The answers that Bush gave to his own questions are, however, little more than projections, revealing more about the unreliable rather than omniscient narrator that Bush gradually turned out to be than about the actual causes of the events or the terrorists' motivations and reasons. His insistent claim that terrorism was mainly directed against the core American values and constituted "a threat to our way of life" (Bush 2001e: 70) is mainly self-serving in that it provided the pseudo-justification of what the Bush administration claimed it was doing, i.e. defending American liberty, promoting the values of America and advancing freedom worldwide. When Bush claimed that Al Qaeda's ultimate goal was "remaking the world" (Bush 2001e: 66), he was apparently blissfully unaware of the fact that this was actually what he himself and his narratives of conflict and crises were doing and trying to achieve, i.e. "remaking the world" in America's image.

Reframing the 9/11 terrorist attacks in terms of the concept and metaphor of war not only allowed Bush to develop his own narrative of a "war on terror", but also opened up the possibility of embedding the latter in an overarching master narrative in which America's mission was clearly defined. Ominously wondering "if America's future is one of fear" (Bush 2001e: 72) and even insinuating that some "speak of an age of terror", while broaching this idea himself and thus fostering his policy of fear, the former American President resolutely announced: "As long as the United States is determined and strong, this will not be an age of terror" (72). He went on to explain that "in our grief and anger we have found our mission and moment" (72), delineating what he regarded as the mission and future role that America would have to play as well as the antagonistic forces:

> Freedom and fear are at war. The advance of freedom [...] now depends on us. Our nation – this generation – will lift a dark threat of violence from our people and our future. We will rally the world to this cause by our efforts, by our courage. We will not tire, we will not falter, we will not fail. (72)

This ominous mini-narration, which is actually a thinly veiled clarion-call and rallying-cry, provides another paradigmatic example of the ways in which narratives do not merely reflect or represent conflicts and crises, but rather serve to create, foster, and mould them by embedding and framing them in an overarching master narrative. The same holds true for the hazy predictions that Bush often made about the future course of developments, which also show the self-righteousness that was another one of the many unfortunate features of his deeply moralistic discourse: "The course of this conflict is not known, yet its outcome is certain. Freedom and fear, justice and cruelty, have always been at war, and we know that God is not neutral between them" (Bush 2001e: 73). While Bush kept insisting apodictically on what he called "the rightness of our cause" (73), he just as sweepingly condemned the enemies of the United States, claiming that they "were as wrong as they are evil" (Bush 2002a: 110).

Couching the narrative of conflict that he was creating in terms of an epic battle between the forces of good and evil, or freedom and war, Bush boldly proclaimed that "[w]e know that evil is real, but good will prevail against it" (Bush 2001f: 89). Resorting to what he called "the language of right and wrong" (Bush 2002c: 129), Bush described his view of the nature of the narrative of conflict that he himself was telling time and again in no uncertain terms, while also using his story as a weapon of mass deception and worldmaking: "We are in a conflict of good and evil, and America will call evil by its name" (129). As Spielvogel (2005: 552) has shown, by framing "the war as part of an ongoing struggle between 'good and evil,'" Bush's speeches helped to naturalize that frame and make it commonly acceptable and even hegemonic. Moreover, this manner of emplotting the narrative suggests that the "characters in Bush's 'war on terror' narrative are motivated almost exclusively by moral action" (Spielvogel 2005: 560). The former American President was apparently quite aware of the fact that it was a conscious effort at worldmaking that his narratives and policy-makers were engaged in, projecting a storyworld in which the forces of good and evil are at war. As Badiou (2003: 159) trenchantly and pithily observes, "[w]ith Bush, one has God at one's side, along with the Good, Democracy, and also America (it's the same thing) for tracking down evil".

According to Bush, the mission of the United States in this epic battle of good against evil was ethically defined "to make our world safer" (Bush 2003a: 155) and "to make this world better". Since 9/11, the role of the United Stated was clearly cut out for Bush: "America will lead the world to peace" (Bush 2001g: 99). It did not take Bush very long to make his promise "I will not relent in waging this struggle for freedom and security for the American people" (Bush 2001e: 73) come true, though he quickly began to substitute the more idiomatic word "war" for "struggle" in order to describe what he was in fact waging. Occasionally Bush used euphemistic expressions like "to wage a relentless and systematic campaign against global terror" (Bush 2002b: 116) when he was in fact describing "our military operation" or simply "the war" (Bush 2002b: 117). Though Bush was again a bit more cautious in his wording when he addressed the United Nations General Assembly, whose support he was trying to gather, he apodictically and hypocritically delineated what he regarded as the task and mission of the United States, outlining the script of history that he intended to write with his narratives of conflict, crisis, and war:

> It is our task – the task of this generation – to provide the response to aggression and terror. We have no other choice, because there is no other peace.
>
> We did not ask for this mission, yet there is honor in history's call. We have a chance to write the story of our times, a story of courage defeating cruelty and light overcoming darkness. (Bush 2001 f: 89 – 90)

What writing "the story of our times" or "a hopeful chapter in human history" (Bush 2001g: 92) actually meant was turning Bush's narrative of conflict and crisis, the epic battle of good against evil that he never tired of delineating, into reality by aggressively executing this so-called mission and waging a "war on terror" against amorphous, "shadowy, entrenched enemies" (Bush 2001g: 94) that had yet to be more clearly defined and located. Many of Bush's speeches contain references to his notion of the American master narrative according to whose script he intended to mould the course of history. Bush claimed that America had "a greater objective than eliminating threats" (Bush 2002a: 113), i.e. "to foster the momentum of freedom" (113) and "to seek a just and peaceful world beyond the war on terror" (113): "In a single instant, we realized that this will be a decisive decade in the history of liberty, that we have been called to a unique role in human events." (113) Despite their somewhat limited narrative and rhetorical means, Bush's narratives thus exemplify the performative power of storytelling, its capacity to change events, to create conflicts, and project possible futures.

Although we cannot discuss or delineate either all the emplotment strategies deployed by Bush or the various stages in which his peculiar narrative and rhetorical worldmaking, and indeed the political campaigning at large and the day-to-day decision- and policy-making, were gradually developed, we would like to single out three aspects related to modes of emplotment that can throw additional light on the performative power of narratives and their active role in creating, rather than merely reflecting, conflicts.

Adopting the concept and metaphor of "war on terror" as his particular frame of reference, Bush's stories illustrate that emplotment strategies serve the purpose of overcoming the contingency of historical occurrences, narratively structuring the selected events and shaping them into a certain story: "Emplotment is the way by which a sequence of events fashioned into a story is gradually revealed to be a story of a particular kind" (White 1973: 7). The contextual meaning is not inherent in the historical occurrence or the event as such, but is primarily created through the choice of a concept or metaphor that serves as the main frame of reference. Through processes of narrativization, the events are given not only a certain structural and narrative pattern, but also a meaning and a sense.

Second, emplotment and storytelling in general always involve explanation and interpretation as well, with the the meaning of narratives depending on both explicit discussions of causes and the modes of emplotment chosen by the narrator or author of the story. Only three days after the terrorist attacks of 9/11, Bush already pretended to know what the causes of the events and the motivations of the terrorists were: "They have attacked America, because we are freedom's home and defender" (Bush 2001d: 61). In the speeches that Bush gave between 9/11 and the beginning of the war against Iraq, he generated a plethora of similar self-serving explanations and interpretations, which tell us more about the unreliable narrator himself than about the actual causal connections.

Thirdly, emplotment always involves both relating the parts of the story to the whole and the story as a whole to broader cultural assumptions, models, and master narratives. This can be seen by looking at the ways in which Bush tried to embed his mini-narrations within an overarching master narrative inextricably intertwined with core American values. Like many American presidents before him, Bush began sketching out his particular version of what he called "the American story" (Bush 2001a: 1), the "grand and enduring ideals" and an "unfolding American promise" (1) as early as in his first inaugural address. Unlike most of his predecessors, however, he also right away began to pit this American story against what he called "the enemies of liberty and our country" (Bush

2001a: 3), announcing what the mission of the American nation was, while couching it in terms that sounded more than just like a veiled threat: "America remains engaged in the world by history and by choice, shaping a balance of power that favors freedom" (3). Time and again, Bush reminded his audience that "America has committed its influence in the world to advancing freedom and democracy as the great alternatives to repression and radicalism" (Bush 2006: 382).

The former American President seems to have been much less certain when or how the narrative projected by his mini-narrations of weapons of mass destruction and the war on terror might end. In December 2001, for example, Bush vaguely and ominously announced that "preventing mass terror" would "be the responsibilities of Presidents far into the future" (Bush 2001g: 94). In the same speech, he admitted that the war against terror "may continue for many years" (Bush 2001g: 99), while in the speech tellingly entitled "The World Will Always Remember September 11" he merely predicted: "In time, this war will end." (Bush 2001h: 101) When he started to redirect the public's attention from Afghanistan to Iraq, he gave his story about the war on terror not just a new twist, but also a new momentum by vaguely observing that "[o]ur war on terror is well begun, but it is only begun" (Bush 2002a: 106; cf. Bush 2002c: 127), and by ominously announcing: "What we have found in Afghanistan confirms that, far from ending there, our war against terror is only beginning" (Bush 2002a: 104). Though he was drafting himself the script of the plot that the United States was enacting, Bush grudgingly had to admit that even his omniscience was somehow limited: "The war will take many turns we cannot predict" (Bush 2002c: 127).

Although Bush was wise enough to use vague and rather meaningless generalizations whenever he talked about the estimated duration of the military campaign or made predictions about the future course of events, he never left his audience in any doubt about who would eventually win the war: "But the outcome of this conflict is certain: There is a current in history and it runs toward freedom. Our enemies resent and dismiss it, but the dreams of mankind are redefined by liberty" (Bush 2001f: 89). Even before the United States military forces had begun to attack Iraq, Bush already provided glimpses of what he chose to call "the possibilities of a world beyond the war on terror" (Bush 2001g: 92). Many of Bush's announcements, however, later turned out to be premature, and five years after the terrorist attacks he had to grudgingly admit: "This war will be difficult; this war will be long; and this war will end in the defeat of the terrorists and totalitarians, and a victory for the cause of freedom and liberty" (Bush 2006: 380). What Bush and his comrades in arms failed to acknowledge, or perhaps even to realize, however, is that their apodictic claims about winning the "war on terror" were actually absurd and untenable, because "there is no possible way to win the 'war on terrorism'; it is simply the wrong metaphor", as Jackson wryly observes: "Conceptually, winning a war against terrorism would be akin to winning a war against insurgent warfare; this is because terrorism is a strategy of political violence which will always appeal to certain actors" (2005: 138).

When the Bush administration began to redirect the public's attention from the terrorists in Afghanistan to Iraq and Saddam Hussein's regime and its alleged arsenal of weapons of mass destruction, Bush first used the ominous phrase "axis of evil" that David Frum, one of his former speech writers, had coined. After briefly referring to North Korea and Iran as countries that either have or aggressively pursue weapons of mass destruction, Bush then singled out Iraq for special accusation and abuse. Bush not only claimed and complained that "Iraq continues to flaunt its hostility toward America and support terror" (Bush 2002a: 106), he also maintained that it was "a regime that has something to hide from the civilized world" (106), summing up his accusations in the infamous metaphor that would go down into history as one of the key phrases of the Bush era and that succinctly expresses Bush's obsessions and paranoia:

> States like these, and their terrorist allies, constitute an axis of evil, arming to threaten the peace of the world. By seeking weapons of mass destruction, these regimes pose a grave and growing danger. They could provide these arms to terrorists, giving them the means to match their hatred. They could attack our allies or attempt to blackmail the United States. In any of these cases, the price of indifference would be catastrophic. (106)

By coming up with this infamous spatial metaphor, Bush provides a highly peculiar diagnosis of the state of the world, conveniently dividing up the countries and nations according to his not so subtle distinction between good and evil forces that are allegedly at war. Though the scenarios that Bush projects are expressed in the subjunctive mode, the combination of the metaphorical concept of weapons of mass destruction with the suggestive and ideologically charged metaphor of the axis of evil serves to conjure up a crisis that seems to be so dangerous and urgent that its outcome might well be "catastrophic". In the speeches he gave in spring and summer 2002, Bush kept harping on the same theme, vaguely outlining narrative scenarios in which "the spread of chemical and biological and nuclear weapons" (Bush 2002c: 127) could get into the hands of terrorist groups which might use "ballistic missile technology" (127): "when that occurs, even weak states and small groups could attain a catastrophic power to strike great nations" (127–128). In other words, Bush outlined a plot in which the metaphorical concept of weapons of mass destruction did not only conjure up a state of crisis, but also served to project a narrative that might well end in an apocalyptic scenario.

Moreover, the narrative that he was developing, the binary distinction between "us" and "them" along the axis of evil, and the Bush doctrine allowed the Bush administration not only to gradually redirect people's attention from the terrorist group actually responsible for the 9/11 attacks to what he vaguely called "unbalanced dictators" (Bush 2002c: 128), "mad terrorists and tyrants" (Bush 2002c: 129) and "other countries" (Bush 2002b: 117), but also to practise ruthless worldmaking and world-threatening on a global scale: "Across the world, governments have heard this message: You are either with us, or you are with the terrorists" (117). Such linguistic devices as verbal repetition and parallelism serve to broaden the scope of Bush's narrative to a truly global scale: "We will not allow the world's most dangerous regimes to threaten America or our friends and allies with the world's most destructive weapons" (117). The moral to be drawn from 9/11 and Iraq's recalcitrance to cooperate with the arms' inspectors is that America should never again be foolish enough to believe anything that Saddam Hussein agrees to or promises. In his State of the Union Address to the 108th Congress, for instance, Bush sketched out a future narrative scenario in which Saddam Hussein "could provide one of his weapons to terrorists, or help them develop their own" (Bush 2003a: 162). Encouraging his listeners to "imagine" what the fatal consequences of such an as-if-scenario might look like, Bush was actually once again trying to insinuate that there were links between the events of 9/11, international terrorism, and the regime in Iraq despite the lack of any factual evidence for his largely counterfactual claims:

> Before September the 11th, many in the world believed that Saddam Hussein could be contained. But chemical agents, lethal viruses and shadowy terrorist networks are not easily contained. Imagine those 19 hijackers with other weapons and other plans – this time armed by Saddam Hussein. It would take one vial, one crate slipped into this country to bring a day of horror like none that we have ever known. We have to make sure that that day never comes. (162)

The combination of his earlier claim that "nations are either with us or against us in the war on terror" (Bush 2002d: 135) and the metaphor of the axis of evil provided the rough outlines of both the world that the Bush administration was in the process of making and the script for, and the roadmap towards, the war in Iraq. Though these fairly general narrative schemata gave the former American President a lot of leeway when it came to elaborating and fleshing out the script that he was writing, it provided a convenient yardstick for gradually making the story and world that Bush envisioned more concrete. "To be counted on the side of peace, nations must act", Bush (135) demanded in June 2002, delineating what "every nation actually committed to peace" (135) would have to do to belong to the right camp, including, of course, to "oppose regimes that promote terror, like Iraq" (Bush 2002d: 136). Bush told every nation that they should "choose the right side in the war on terror" (136) and to "be included in the peace process" (136), which was actually a careful preparation of a preemptive war. In his infamous Cincinnati speech, Bush still maintained that "the Iraqi regime has an opportunity to avoid conflict" (Bush 2002f), hypocritically adding "I hope this will not require military action, but it may" (136), despite the fact that his narratives of conflict and crisis had been providing both the pretext and the ideological justification for his pet project, i.e. the "war on terror" that he intended to extend to Iraq. In February 2003, while rhetorically preparing the ideological grounds and paving the way for the war against Iraq, Bush boldly made the counterfactual claim that the United States and other nations were "working on a road map for peace" (Bush 2003b: 171), a white lie that sounds as though it was straight out of George Orwell's sinister dystopian novel *1984*. The same holds true for the President's Address to the Nation on Military Operations in Iraq, in which Bush told "all the men and women of the United States Armed Forces" (Bush 2003c: 175), who had just started to wage war against Iraq, euphemistically described by Bush as "the early stages of military operations to disarm Iraq" (175), that "the peace of a troubled world and the hopes of an oppressed people now depend on you" (175).

When Bush announced that America had "entered the next phase of the war" (Bush 2003c: 175), he again made sure that the conflict plot that he was in the process of outlining and turning into reality at the same time was not only embedded within the American master narrative; he was also anxious to garner whatever support he could muster from history, once again boldly and apodictically repeating his highly questionable claims: "History has called us to these responsibilities, and we accept them. America has always had a special mission to defend justice and advance freedom around the world." (Bush 2002b: 117) This idealized myth of the reluctant soldier called upon to defend core values not only sounds like a version of the "White Man's Burden", with all of its empty imperialistic overtones, it is also explicitly linked up with the claim that "[i]n a time of war, we reassert the essential values and beliefs of our country" (117). By referring to the examples of Abraham Lincoln, Franklin D. Roosevelt and Ronald Reagan, Bush tried to further legitimate his performative narrative of conflict and to reduce the obvious paradox that leading "America into global war" (117) is a somewhat peculiar way of seeking "a just and peaceful world beyond the war on terror" (Bush 2002a: 113; Bush 2002c: 132). The same holds true for his less than logical claim that leading a war is a means for defending and even promoting peace: "We fight, as we always fight, for a just peace – a peace that favors human liberty" (Bush 2002c: 127). And in his State of the Union Address to the 108th Congress in January 2003, Bush even maintained that war was, or had been, forced upon the United States, once again bending logic and reason to the utmost: "If war is forced upon us, we will fight in a just cause and by just means" (Bush 2003a: 163). Even after the military operations had actually started, Bush continued to repeat his half-hearted claim "our nation enters this conflict reluctantly" (Bush 2003c: 176), after having spent almost a year carefully using narratives and lies as weapons of mass deception.

One should note, however, that Bush, like many other political propagandists who have purported to look mainly at the past or at the present, in fact does so with an eye to the future. The brief and peculiar ways in which he selected and referred to key events in American history like Pearl Harbor or the "Cold War" show that he was less interested in providing an accurate view of the historical record than in unabashedly exploiting what Evgeny Morozov in his eye-opening and sobering examination of the digital age aptly calls "usable pasts, myth-like stories that draw on historical events, not in order to remember the past but, rather, to make sense of the present and the future" (Morozov 2013: 51). Rewriting history in terms of his favoured master narrative of the United States advancing and promoting democracy, freedom, and liberty is one of the narrative means of trying to influence the future course of events by pitting diametrically opposed possible futures against each other. As we will see, Bush was actually narrating futures when he purported to delineate historical events or to assess the present state-of-affairs, thus creating strongly teleological narrative logics.

The President's penchant for projecting threatening narrative scenarios and binary oppositions noted above is especially obvious in the way in which he delineates possible narrative futures, typically pitting two diametrically opposed narrative scenarios against each other. Boldly maintaining that his policy was allegedly designed to "deliver our children from a future of fear" (Bush 2001f: 85; Bush 2001g: 92), which he actually kept conjuring up himself, Bush somewhat randomly claimed that "[w]e choose the dignity of life over a culture of death" (Bush 2001f: 85), as though these were the main or only options. In his infamous Address to the United Nations General Assembly, Bush provided the most comprehensive juxtaposition of two future developments of events and narrative scenarios, pretending that the UN as well as each and every nation would have to make a choice between them:

> Events can turn out in one of two ways: If we fail to act in the face of danger, the people of Iraq will continue to live in brutal submission. [...] With every step the Iraqi regime takes

> toward gaining and deploying the most terrible weapons, our own options to confront that regime will narrow. And if an emboldened regime were to supply these weapons to terrorist allies, the attacks of September the 11th would be a prelude to far greater horrors.
>
> If we meet our responsibilities, if we overcome this danger, we can arrive at a very different future. (Bush 2002e: 146)

What Bush chose to ignore is that there were myriads of other options and perspectives, options which he preferred not even to consider. The main reason for this was that they did not fit into the dichotomous storyworld and the alternative that he was projecting, which he summed up like this: "We must choose between a world of fear and a world of progress" (Bush 2002e: 146). In other speeches, Bush spoke about "a world at peace" and "a world of chaos and constant alarm" (Bush 2003a: 158), apparently without realizing that his narratives, rhetoric, and politics of fear just created such a world of alarm and constant low-level anxiety. Pitting two different worlds or narrative futures against each other underscores our central hypothesis that the stories that Bush disseminated not only exerted performative power, but were also a way of conflict- and worldmaking in a very literal sense. Time and again Bush not only presented his peculiar version of what he regarded as America's history, mission, and values; his teleological storytelling also extended to projecting future scenarios and worlds.

The same structural patterns can also be observed in the ways in which the use of point of view privileges a particular perspective and world-model. Not only does the observer's spatial and temporal perspective of perception already play a decisive role in the choice of certain elements of the event, but his ideological perspective, i.e. his values and norms, is important as well. The same is also true for the processes of composition through which a story becomes a narrative of a particular kind, as well as for the verbalization which creates the text or the representation of the story. Working within the binary rhetoric of us vs. them, Bush always adopts an American point of view, apparently taking it for granted that there was no other way of conceptualizing or framing the events in question.

Over and beyond the structural and narrative features discussed so far, Bush's kind of conflict- and worldmaking is also characterized by a number of other rhetorical characteristics that throw light on how he dispenses with traditional notions of logical reasoning and any kind of storytelling that shows an interest in factuality and causality. In the president's speeches, causality, reason, and logic are largely substituted by alliteration, analogies, apodictic claims, and counterfactual statements. The way in which Bush tried to forge a link between the terrorist attacks of 9/11 and Iraq is a particularly interesting case in point. Instead of providing either empirical, factual evidence of the alleged connection between al Qaeda and Saddam Hussein or a convincing causal or narrative explanation, Bush resorted to other means to insinuate that such connections existed. He, or rather his speech-writers, showed a particular penchant for such poetic devices as alliteration, assonance, and consonance, which serve to provide or suggest links between words through the repetition of the same sounds. Typical examples include the incredibly repetitive use of such semantic combinations as "the Taliban and the terrorists" (Bush 2001g: 92), "terrorists and tyrants", "tyranny and terror", or "terrorists and totalitarians" (Bush 2006: 379). Instead of providing evidence or logical reasoning, Bush preferred to resort to "analogical comparisons" (Hodges 2011: 34), alliteration, and syntactic parallelisms: "When we fight terror, we fight tyranny" (Bush 2001h: 101). For want of any real evidence, Bush's speeches used such rhetorical devices in order to give the "convenient untruths" (Gore 2008: 104) that his counter-factual narratives promoted at least the semblance of plausibility, creating connections where none existed in the real world by way of alliteration, as countless examples testify: "We will defend the peace against threats from terrorists and tyrants" (Bush 2002c: 127).

It is thus through the linguistic and rhetorical texture of his speeches rather than through actual causality, empirical evidence or at least coherent narrative strategies that the Bush administration via the President's voice managed to forge links between the terrorist attacks and a tyrant like Saddam Hussein. Though Bush failed to provide any convincing evidence for the actual existence of Iraq's alleged weapons of mass destruction, he managed to redirect people's attention from the terrorist network that had actually been responsible for the attacks of 9/11 to a regime in Iraq that had nothing to do with them.

Moreover, the thorough assault on logic and reason (cf. Gore 2008) characteristic of Bush's narrative conflict- and worldmaking can be seen in the amazingly apodictic terms in which his narratives are couched and in the many counterfactual statements that many of his speeches contain. Almost every speech that Bush gave about the topics at hand contains apodictic and unwarranted claims like "our cause is just" (Bush 2002a: 104). As far as counterfactual statements are concerned, a case in point is Bush's peculiar claim that "America and Afghanistan are now allies against terror" (Bush 2002a: 103), which is arguably as untrue today as it was when Bush gave the State of the Union Address to the 107th Congress in January 2002. In the same speech, he surprisingly proclaimed that "we are winning the war on terror" (103), which has turned out to be a somewhat premature announcement. In his State of the Union Address to the 108th Congress, Bush continued in the same vein, once again making one of his many unfounded claims despite plenty of proof to the contrary: "The war goes on, and we are winning" (Bush 2003a: 156).

As this brief analysis of some of the main narrative and rhetorical features of Bush's speeches shows, this kind of narrative worldmaking constitutes not just a remarkable "assault on reason", as the felicitous title of Al Gore's book has it, but also a mind-boggling assault on logic and causality. The analysis has also served to confirm a number of other insights of the book, in which Gore provides a comprehensive and devastating analysis of Bush's "Politics of Fear" (Gore 2008: 23), not just corroborating Gore's eponymous assessment, but also illuminating how Bush managed to plant "the seeds of war" (Gore 2008: 175) by harping on the same line of the alleged weapons of mass destruction and then gradually fleshing out the condensed narrative of conflict encapsulated in that phrase through his narrative ways of worldmaking. Although we now know beyond a shadow of a doubt that there was no evidence whatsoever for those weapons, the stories disseminated by Bush, his administration, and his followers served to create the impression that Saddam Hussein was indeed responsible for the terrorist attacks of 9/11.

4 Creating narrative ontologies and patriotic xenophobia: on the community-, conflict-, space-, and worldmaking functions of narratives of conflict and crisis

Although most of the narratives of the Bush administration about weapons of mass destruction, the axis of evil, and the war on terror have antagonism and conflicts as two of their salient semantic implications, one might wonder to what extent these were antagonisms, conflict and ideological struggles "of the mind", or of the imagination, rather than factual ones, before the performative power of storytelling turned them into reality. The urgency and insistence with which Bush and his followers tended to harp on the same conceptual, metaphorical, and narrative themes indicates that great efforts were made to represent the state of affairs in terms of conflict and crisis. Elizabeth Ermarth's shrewd observation about the representation of social order in nineteenth-century narratives applies equally well to the language of fear and religion and the narratives of conflict and crisis used by the Bush administration. The conflicts and crises in question were "not a reality to be reflected but a problem to be solved" (Ermarth 1997: 125). Rather than just taking the dominant legitimizing and patriotic rhetoric of Bush's narratives of conflict and crisis at face value or even mistaking such narratives and tropes for a simple reflection of political relations, one might look more closely at the functions that the narratives analyzed above served to fulfil. There are at least six such functions that can be identified, although many of them are syncretized in specific texts.

In the first place, by reducing the complexity and elusiveness of the actual state of affairs and events, Bush's narratives served to impose form upon a chaotic reality. Their most obvious function is thus to impart some sort of structure to an amorphous geographical and political entity, and thus to serve as unifying devices. Despite their inevitably reductive character, such narratives as those analyzed above could fulfil heuristic or cognitive functions in that they purport to reflect and represent recent events, while actually emplotting and framing them in an ideologically charged way. As conceptual tools, metaphors and narratives resemble models. Imposing form upon an untidy reality, they serve as models for thought, as conceptual fictions people live by (see Lakoff and Johnson 1980). To identify the functions of such narratives and metaphors entirely with those of models, however, is to miss the significant cultural, ideological, and political functions they can also perform. Equating them with models ignores the creative uses of metaphors and narratives in the representation of events, objects, and situations. In contrast to models, which *represent* structural relations, metaphors *impose* structures; they "often do creative work" (Turner 1987: 19), and this holds true for narratives as well. Like metaphors, narratives can largely determine the way in which a given domain is perceived and understood in the first place, with the symbolic register of war examined above being a perfect case in point. The second reason why metaphors and narratives are more than just conceptual or cognitive models is that the evoking of emotion is an important aspect of metaphorical and narrative processes. Of far greater interest for the cultural historian are those functions that shed light on the "representational politics" (Ermarth 1997: 125) that metaphors and narratives can fulfil in specific contexts.

In addition to their power to impose structure, a second function of the stories of the Bush administration consisted in providing contemporaries with simplified, but more or less coherent narrative explanations and normative frameworks for reinterpreting recent events and political developments. As mental models, narrative fictions provide powerful tools for making sense of the traumatic experience of 9/11 and the events that happened in its aftermath. By actually commenting upon the events and relations they purported merely to reflect or to represent, Bush's stories served as a means for explaining complex historical processes and political constellations. As we have tried to show above, the structure and logic inherent in the stories in question reduces the complexity of the actual political relations and transforms a chaotic series of events into simple patriotic and propagandistic stories, projecting a very euphemistic and highly simplified master narrative of American and world history in an abbreviated form.

Some of the most important aspects of narratives are thus the explanatory functions and teleological projections they serve to fulfil. Both narratives and explanations, and narratives and conflicts are mutually interdependent in that the ways in which people narrate, or narrativize, a conflict depends upon how they explain it, and vice versa, as Albrecht Koschorke (2012: 244) rightly observes. By rewriting history and turning current conflicts into readily intelligible stories, such narratives as those told by Bush and his followers not only helped to explain and make sense of the past; the pseudo-explanations proffered by the reductionist "war on terror" narrative also served to license the military project against Iraq by couching it in terms of a master narrative of a fight for freedom and other American values.

Thirdly, the narratives of the Bush administration therefore also fulfilled important normative, legitimizing, and licensing functions because they not only authorized and propagated ideologically charged views of the relations between America and its enemies, but also provided rationalizations and justifications of the "war on terror". In doing so, the narratives, just like metaphors, implicitly project what Eubanks (1999: 424, 426) aptly calls "licensing stories": "for us to regard any mapping as apt, it must comport with our licensing stories – our repertoire of ideologically inflected narratives, short and long, individual and cultural, that organize our sense of how the world works and how the world should work" (Eubanks 1999: 426).

Fourth, the narratives and their rhetoric of American values and national character, with its juxtaposition of freedom-loving Americans and various groups of highly stereotyped enemies, were an important propagandistic and ideological means of nurturing the culture's dominant fictions, creating not only cultural conflicts, but even "[t]he Ideological Struggle of the twenty-first Century", to quote the subtitle of Bush's address to the American Legion National Convention that he gave in Salt Lake City on 31 August 2006. Even if we are prepared to assume, for the sake of the argument as well as for simplicity, that neither the President nor his speech-writers were as stupid as one may often be inclined to think, it is still absolutely amazing that Bush would refer to the war in Iraq, or the war on terror, as "the first war of the 21st century" (Bush 2006: 379). The functions discussed so far can be seen in the way in which Bush claimed the sole right to define and interpret both the nature of the conflict and the two parties which are at war, once again confirming the insight that his narratives created and shaped the conflicts that they purport merely to delineate or represent. This results in a strong 'manichean' outlook on world politics, as the following passage reveals:

> The war we fight today is more than a military conflict; it is the decisive ideological struggle of the twenty-first century. On one side are those who believe in the values of freedom and moderation – the right of people to speak, and worship, and live in liberty. And on the other side are those driven by the values of tyranny and extremism – the right of a self-appointed few to impose their fanatical views on all the rest. (Bush 2006: 380)

Anyone reading Bush's speeches and analyzing their functions with the benefit of hindsight may be forgiven if he or she gets the impression that his rhetoric itself can be seen as an example of a sustained attempt of "a self-appointed few to impose their fanatical views on all the rest" (Bush 2006: 380).

Fifth, Bush's narratives also serve as an important means of fostering and maintaining loyalty, creating narrative communities by emplotting the American nation in a propagandistic and patriotic way. This emotional and patriotic function is particularly obvious in the case of Bush's narratives because they imply a feeling of fellowship, a sense of togetherness and unity. The stories told and disseminated by the Bush administration serve to show that there are always certain culturally available plots and nationally specific ways in which narratives represent and shape events, tell stories, and make worlds. In one of the best narrative or narrativist theories of culture to date, Wolfgang Müller-Funk has argued that cultures differ not only with regard to the subjects and themes they are particularly interested in, but also with regard to their favoured modes of storytelling, their forms of constructing narratives (Müller-Funk 2008 [2002]: 53). From this point of view, cultures are not so much "imagined communities" (sensu Anderson), but "narrative communities", i.e. communities forged and held together by the stories the members tell about themselves and their culture as well as by conventionalized forms of storytelling and cultural plots. Müller-Funk has therefore made the valuable suggestion to conceptualize cultures as "narrative and memorial communities":

> Without any doubt it is narratives that form the basis of collective, national memories and that constitute politics of identity and difference. Cultures should always also be conceived of as narrative communities which are distinguished from each other by their reservoir of narratives. (Müller-Funk 2008: 14; our translation)

Lastly, and arguably most importantly, the stories of the Bush administration were thus central to the formation and maintenance of collective identities. The images, metaphors, and stories projected were instrumental in what one might call the imaginative forging of the mental infrastructure, because not only a nation, but "any imagined community, is held together in part by the stories it generates about itself" (Arata 1996: 1; Anderson 2008 [1983]). Heavily drawing on cherished "stories Americans live by" (McAdams 2013 [2006]), Bush's stories served as an important means of maintaining an advantageous American self-image and of forging American national identity, something which is neither natural nor stable, but discursively constructed: "In an important sense, we are dealing with the formation of cultural identities understood not as essentializations [...] but as contrapuntal ensembles, for it is the case that no identity can ever exist by itself and without an array of opposites, negatives, oppositions" (Said 1993: 60). Though proceeding from a different starting point and focus (language and writing rather than narratives, metaphors, and ways of worldmaking), working within a different disciplinary context (political science rather than literary and cultural studies), and using a different methodology (critical discourse analysis rather than narratology), the political scientist Richard Jackson comes to similar conclusions about the functions that the discourse of counter-terrorism and the language of the "war on terrorism" fulfilled. In his highly perspicacious monograph *Writing the War on Terrorism: Language, Politics and Counter Terrorism*, Jackson very convincingly demonstrates that the language of the so-called "war on terrorism", far from being "an objective or neutral reflection of reality", should be conceived of as

> a deliberately and meticulously composed set of words, assumptions, metaphors, grammatical forms, myths and forms of knowledge – it is a carefully constructed *discourse* – that is designed to achieve a number of key political goals: to normalise and legitimise the current counter-terrorist approach; to empower the authorities and shield them from criticism; to discipline domestic society by marginalising dissent or protest; and to enforce national unity by reifying a narrow conception of national identity. (Jackson 2005: 2)

As this quote, in which he summarizes part of the overall argument of his book, already indicates, Jackson not only does an excellent job at teasing out the political goals and functions (113–120) that this ideological discourse has so successfully served to fulfil since the attacks of September 11, 2001; he also sheds new light on the ways in which the language of the "war on terrorism" paved the way for the military and political practices of the "war on terrorism". Though not working within a Goodmanian, worldmaking or narratological framework, Jackson also emphasizes the fact that language and discourse are neither innocent nor neutral, but should rather be seen as powerful ways of creating "a whole new world" (Jackson 2005: 96), i.e. "a world of unimaginable dangers and unspeakable threats" (120). The performative, reality-constituting power of narratives, however, does not only reside in such ways of worldmaking as selection, deletion, ordering, supplementation, weighting and framing, but also in the fact that language and practice mutually reinforce each other, i.e. that "writing the threat of terrorism is co-constitutive of the practice of counter-terrorism" (119): "practice reinforces meaning and vice versa; the language and institutions soon become co-constitutive of the reality of the war against terrorism" (162; also 119). In short, Jackson's much more comprehensive examination of the forms and functions of the public language of the "war on terrorism" confirms, from the point of view of a renowned political scientist, what we have tried to show from a narratological and metaphorological angle: that the generative and poietic power of narratives consists not just in emplotting events in a particular way and in disseminating propagandistic and patriotic stories, but also, and even more so, in discursively constructing an atmosphere of anxiety, danger, threat and "supreme emergency" (98 f.; also Ch. 4), moulding conflicts, forging collective identities, and making cultural and even geopolitical worlds.

5 Narratives as weapons of mass deception and mass destruction: the performative power of narrative worldmaking revisited

As shown through our analysis of their metaphors, rhetoric, and narrative strategies, Bush's speeches provide a paradigmatic example of the ways in which narrative constructions and processes can be endowed with performative power, actively creating or constructing the cultural and ideological conflicts that they purport merely to reflect or represent. The stories that Bush never tired of telling about weapons of mass destruction, the "axis of evil", and the "war on terror" serve to show how narratives can function as cultural ways of conflict- and worldmaking, not just in a metaphorical, but also in a very literal sense. The ideologically charged narratives told by the Bush administration did not only serve to disseminate concepts, metaphors, and narratives that Americans and many other people have become accustomed to live by, but they have also shaped the actual geopolitical realities or worlds we live in today.

Narrative ways of worldmaking do not merely reflect, but also partake in and shape, the narrative communities and the hierarchies of norms and values that distinguish cultures from one another and can create cultural conflicts. Conceptualizing narrative fictions as both cognitive forces in their own right and as cultural ways of worldmaking, a yet to be fully developed cultural narratology should explore the ways in which the formal procedures of narrative worldmaking outlined above reflect, and influence, the unspoken mental assumptions and cultural issues of a given period. Cultural narratology recognizes that, since "ideology is located in narrative structures themselves" (Helms 2003: 14), analyses of the semanticization of narrative forms can shed light on unspoken assumptions, attitudes, ideologies, as well as values and norms prevalent in any given text, genre, and period. Once narrative forms are understood as socially constructed cognitive forces, narratives become valuable sources for cultural history and studies of conflicts because analyses of "their narrative forms provide information about ideological concepts and world views" (Helms 2003: 14). Such an approach promises to shed new light on the performative power of narratives to make worlds, to disseminate worldviews, and to shape conflicts, three key aspects and functions of narratives about which we know only too little and which narrative theory has up to now largely ignored.

Although it is still unclear how the historical developments ushered in by the rhetorical "war on terror" and the concomitant real wars against Afghanistan, Iraq and international terrorist networks will continue, with the benefit of hindsight we can conclude that the metaphors and stories conjured up and popularized by the Bush administration about weapons of mass destruction and the axis of evil have not only been worldmaking in a metaphorical sense, but have really had performative, worldmaking power in a very literal sense. Rather than just mirroring or representing real conflicts, Bush's metaphors and narratives of conflict moulded and sequenced events in such a way that they created and fomented the conflicts and crises that they purported merely to represent, thus shaping actual conditions of today's real world. A year after the President's notorious State of the Union address given on 29 January 2002, Julian Borger in an article in *The Guardian* observed that the phrase "axis of evil" "has not only defined the battle-lines of the twenty-first century, it has helped shape the world we now inhabit" (Borger 2003).

From the point of view of a critical cultural narratology, one might add that the metaphors and narratives of conflict disseminated by the Bush administration have not only served to foment cultural conflicts and shape prevalent interpretations of the past, present and future, they have also had performative and worldmaking effects in that their hegemonic status has largely blocked or shaded alternative accounts, interpretations, and narratives. As Hodges succinctly puts it, "instead of being seen as one among several possible interpretations, the 'war on terror' discourse becomes naturalized as a widely accepted, 'common sense' way for viewing and talking about 9/11 and America's response to terrorism" (Hodges 2011: 7). Many of the critical and sobering observations that Evgeny Morozov recently made about the reductionist accounts proffered by what he dubs "internet-centrism" apply equally well to the detrimental effects that Bush's rhetorical narratives of conflict and of the "war on terror", and their ideological implications, have had. They have not only "mangled how we think about the past, the present, and the future", but have also "erroneously convinced us that there are no other ways to talk about these issues without downplaying their importance" (Morozov 2013: 62). Moreover, what has been gained in ideological and political efficacy "has been lost in analytical clarity and precision" (Morozov 2013: 62).

Furthermore, the reductionism of both Bush's binaristic rhetoric and worldview, and of the narratives of conflict that the metaphorical concepts of "weapons of mass destruction" and "war on terror" have projected, has prevented a more nuanced analysis and critical debate about the complex issues that the volume at hand explores, masking rather than highlighting the active and generative role that narrative constructions and processes have played, and continue to play, in cultural and political conflicts. Alain Badiou's comments about the word "terrorist" as an "intrinsically propagandistic term" (Badiou 2003: 145) also pertain to the no less propagandistic phrases that provide the core of Bush's highly limited semantic and ideological universe. The concept of "weapons of mass destruction", or "war on terror", for that matter, too, "has no neutral readability. It dispenses with all reasoned examination of political situations, of their causes and consequences" (145). Though these propagandistic phrases are largely "devoid of all content" (153), this apparent semantic lack does not diminish their ideological and political efficacy in any way. On the contrary, it rather increases their malleability and usefulness, which mainly consists in "designating the 'terrorist' enemies of the United States" (151), shaping as well as allegedly justifying cultural, political and military conflicts, and defining the battle-lines for years to come. Even though Badiou (158) has convincingly shown in his critical philsophical analysis of the key words of the phrase "the war against terrorism" that "more or less nothing intelligible remains", it would thus be a serious mistake to underestimate the performative and worldmaking power that Bush's propagandistic rhetoric and his favourite metaphors and narratives have had. What Hodges rightly points out about the consequences of the war metaphor also holds true for Bush's narrative of the war on terror as a whole: "In the case of the Bush administration's response to terrorism, the implications of the war metaphor for characterizing 9/11 have produced very real consequences" (Hodges 2011: 30).

On a much larger and politically much more important scale than fictional worldmaking, many of the stories generated and disseminated by the Bush administration since 9/11, especially those about the alleged production of weapons of mass destruction in Iraq, thus underline the fact that narratives can be a very powerful, and potentially dangerous, way of conflict- and worldmaking. Though we now know that these narratives failed to correspond to either reality or truth, they even had the capacity to emplot events and shape interpretations of what purportedly happened in such a way as to construct conflicts and to change the course of history. The reality-changing potential of these stories also depended on their correspondence to the culturally available schemata, metaphors and plots that contemporary American society lives by (McAdams 2013 [2006]), i.e. whether they appear sufficiently plausible to the majority of people. This example also serves to show that powerful narratives can themselves be both weapons of mass deception and weapons of mass destruction. The same holds true for other stories generated by the Bush administration, the "War against Terror(ism)" being the most powerful and destructive case in point. When ideologically charged stories or metaphors come to be regarded as a factual account of the actual course of events or as a political argument, what an irresistible argument it always seems!

This also holds true, however, for less aggressive and ominous stories than those disseminated by the Bush administration, e.g. for Barack Obama's "Yes, we can" version of the "American Dream" narrative. Though reading Bush's speeches seems to suggest the contrary, narratives can arguably also be ways of conflict-solving. In order to solve a conflict and change the story, however, you need a new storyteller or narrator. And yet, as we have seen since October 2008, it is arguably not quite as easy to stop a war as Paul Auster's novel *Man in the Dark* quoted in the first section of the article suggests. This idea remains fascinating, though, and the journalist Jason Horowitz gave one of his articles in *The Washington Post*, from January 2010, the hopeful title: "Obama speechwriter Ben Rhodes is penning a different script for the world stage" (Horowitz 2010).

Even though this hopeful announcement turned out to be somewhat premature, since Barack Obama neither managed to end the war in Iraq nor to live up to the reputation of someone who has been awarded the Nobel Peace Prize, he has certainly managed to show how new narratives, or alterations of well-established narratives, can perhaps contribute to reframing, and potentially even solving, conflicts. As Dan McAdams (2013 [2006], Ch. 10) has shown, Bush and Obama offer "competing stories of redemption", but with regard to the "war on terror" narrative, the uncanny similarities between their respective versions arguably outweigh their differences. The degree to which President Obama has been caught in, and constrained by, the "war on terror" narrative so carefully crafted by his propagandistic predecessor serves to underline the performative power that narratives can exert and to show how difficult it can be to end a war that, according to hegemonic narrative worldmaking, has been defined as open-ended. The most prominent case in point in this regard is perhaps the hotly debated speech that President Obama gave on the future of the war on terror at the National Defense University on 23 May 2013, in which he attempted to make significant alterations to the infamous "war on terror" narrative launched and popularized by the Bush Administration. President Obama's important speech is, however, also a case in point of the worldmaking power of narratives in that it serves to show how politicians and a nation at large can be caught in a story that it has been told to live by and how difficult it is to reframe a hegemonic narrative, let alone step out of it or turn over a new page. Emphasizing that "America is at a crossroads", President Obama rightly observes: "We must define the nature and scope of this struggle, or else it will define us. [...] Beyond Afghanistan, we must define our effort not as a 'global war on terror' – but rather as a series of persistent, targeted efforts to dismantle specific networks of violent extremists that threaten America" (Obama 2013). Reframing "the nature and scope of the struggle" in this way, pointing out that "this war, like all wars, must end", and wisely adding that "the next element of our strategy involves addressing the underlying grievances and conflicts that feed extremism", Obama provided some contours and parameters of a new story that may, perhaps, serve to show that narratives might also be a way of solving conflicts and problems. But that would be an entirely new story and require another article.

Works cited

Aldis, Anne, and Graeme P. Herd (eds.) (2007) *The Ideological War on Terror: World-Wide Strategies for Counter-Terrorism* (London: Routledge).

Amis, Martin (2008) *The Second Plane* (London: Vintage).

Anderson, Benedict (2008 [1983]) *Imagined Communities: Reflections on the Origins and Spread of Nationalism* (London: Verso).

Arata, Stephen (1996) *Fictions of Loss in the Victorian Fin de Siècle* (Cambridge: Cambridge UP).

Auster, Paul (2008) *Man in the Dark* (London: Faber & Faber).

Badiou, Alain (2003) "Philosophy and the 'War against Terrorism,'" in *Infinite Thought: Truth and the Return to Philosophy* (London and New York: Continuum), 141–164.

Birkenstein, Jeff (ed.) (2010) *Reframing 9/11: Film, Popular Culture and the "War on Terror"* (New York: Continuum).

Borger, Julian (2003) "How I created the axis of evil", in *The Guardian*, 28 January 2003. www.guardian.co.uk/world/2003/jan/28/usa.iran (accessed 4 March 2014).

Brady, Sara (2012) *Performance, Politics and the War on Terror: "Whatever It Takes"* (New York: Palgrave Macmillan).

Bullivant, Keith and Bernhard Spies (2001) "Vorwort", in *Literarisches Krisenbewußtsein: Ein Perzeptions- und Produktionsmuster im 20. Jahrhundert*, ed. Keith Bullivant and Bernhard Spies (München: iudicum), 7–18.

Bush, George W. (2001a) "The First Inaugural Address, January 20, 2001", in *Selected Speeches of President George W. Bush. 2001–2008*, http://georgewbush-whitehouse.archives.gov/infocus/bushrecord/documents/Selected_Speeches_George_W_Bush.pdf (accessed 2 August 2016), 1–5.

Bush, George W. (2001b) "Address to the Joint Session of the 107th Congress, February 27, 2001", in *Selected Speeches of President George W. Bush. 2001–2008*, http://georgew

bush-whitehouse.archives.gov/infocus/bushrecord/documents/Selected_Speeches_George_W_Bush.pdf (accessed 2 August 2016), 23–35.

Bush, George W. (2001c) "Address to the Nation on the September 11 Attacks, September 11 2001", in *Selected Speeches of President George W. Bush. 2001–2008*. http://georgewbush-whitehouse.archives.gov/infocus/bushrecord/documents/Selected_Speeches_George_W_Bush.pdf (accessed 2 August 2016), 57–58.

Bush, George W. (2001d) "National Day of Prayer and Remembrance Service, September 14, 2001", in *Selected Speeches of President George W. Bush. 2001–2008*, http://georgewbush-whitehouse.archives.gov/infocus/bushrecord/documents/Selected_Speeches_George_W_Bush.pdf (accessed 2 August 2016), 59–61.

Bush, George W. (2001e) "Address to the Joint Session of the 107th Congress, September 20, 2001", in *Selected Speeches of President George W. Bush. 2001–2008*, http://georgewbush-whitehouse.archives.gov/infocus/bushrecord/documents/Selected_Speeches_George_W_Bush.pdf (accessed 2 August 2016), 65–73.

Bush, George W. (2001f) "Address to the United Nations General Assembly, Nobvember 10, 2001", in *Selected Speeches of President George W. Bush. 2001–2008*, http://georgewbush-whitehouse.archives.gov/infocus/bushrecord/documents/Selected_Speeches_George_W_Bush.pdf (accessed 2 August 2016), 83–90.

Bush, George W. (2001g) "Address at the Citadel, December 11, 2001", in *Selected Speeches of President George W. Bush. 2001–2008*, http://georgewbush-whitehouse.archives.gov/infocus/bushrecord/documents/Selected_Speeches_George_W_Bush.pdf (accessed 2 August 2016), 91–99.

Bush, George W. (2001h) "The World Will Always Remember September 11, December 11, 2001", in *Selected Speeches of President George W. Bush. 2001–2008*, http://georgewbush-whitehouse.archives.gov/infocus/bushrecord/documents/Selected_Speeches_George_W_Bush.pdf (accessed 2 August 2016), 101–102.

Bush, George W. (2002a) "State of the Union Address to the 107th Congress, January 29, 2002", in *Selected Speeches of President George W. Bush. 2001–2008*, http://georgewbush-whitehouse.archives.gov/infocus/bushrecord/documents/Selected_Speeches_George_W_Bush.pdf (accessed 2 August 2016), 103–113.

Bush, George W. (2002b) "Promoting Compassionate Conservatism, April 30, 2002", in *Selected Speeches of President George W. Bush. 2001–2008*, http://georgewbush-whitehouse.archives.gov/infocus/bushrecord/documents/Selected_Speeches_George_W_Bush.pdf (accessed 2 August 2016), 115–123.

Bush, George W. (2002c) "West Point Commencement, June 1, 2002", in *Selected Speeches of President George W. Bush. 2001–2008*, http://georgewbush-whitehouse.archives.gov/infocus/bushrecord/documents/Selected_Speeches_George_W_Bush.pdf (accessed 2 August 2016), 125–132.

Bush, George W. (2002d) "Middle East Peace Process, June 24, 2002", in *Selected Speeches of President George W. Bush. 2001–2008*, http://georgewbush-whitehouse.archives.gov/infocus/bushrecord/documents/Selected_Speeches_George_W_Bush.pdf (accessed 2 August 2016), 133–138.

Bush, George W. (2002e) "Address to the United Nations General Assembly, September 12, 2002", in *Selected Speeches of President George W. Bush. 2001–2008*, http://georgewbush-whitehouse.archives.gov/infocus/bushrecord/documents/Selected_Speeches_George_W_Bush.pdf (accessed 2 August 2016), 139–147.

Bush, George W. (2002f) "Remarks by the President on Iraq", in *The White House*, 7 October, 2002. http://www2.gwu.edu/~nsarchiv/NSAEBB/NSAEBB80/new/doc%2012/President%20Bush%20Outlines%20Iraqi%20Threat.htm (accessed 2 August 2016).

Bush, George W. (2003a) "State of the Union Address to the 108th Congress, January 28, 2003", in *Selected Speeches of President George W. Bush. 2001–2008*, http://georgewbush-whitehouse.archives.gov/infocus/bushrecord/documents/Selected_Speeches_George_W_Bush.pdf (accessed 2 August 2016), 149–164.

Bush, George W. (2003b) "Remarks on the Future of Iraq, February 26, 2003", in *Selected Speeches of President George W. Bush. 2001–2008*, http://georgewbush-whitehouse.archives.gov/infocus/bushrecord/documents/Selected_Speeches_George_W_Bush.pdf (accessed 2 August 2016), 167–173.

Bush, George W. (2003c) "Address to the Nation on Military Operations in Iraq, March 19, 2003", in *Selected Speeches of President George W. Bush. 2001–2008*, http://georgewbush-whitehouse.archives.gov/infocus/bushrecord/documents/Selected_Speeches_George_W_Bush.pdf (accessed 2 August 2016), 175–176.

Bush, George W. (2006) "Address to the American Legion National Convention: The Ideological Struggle of the 21st Century, August 31, 2006", in *Selected Speeches of President George W. Bush. 2001–2008*, http://georgewbush-whitehouse.archives.gov/infocus/bushrecord/documents/Selected_Speeches_George_W_Bush.pdf (accessed 2 August 2016), 377–391.

Christie, Kenneth (2008) *America's War on Terrorism: The Revival of the Nation-State Versus Universal Human Rights* (Lewiston, NY: Mellen).

Croft, Stuart (2006) *Culture, Crisis and America's War on Terror* (Cambridge: Cambridge UP).

Duffy, Helen (2005) *The "War on Terror" and the Framework of International Law* (Cambridge: Cambridge UP).

Ermarth, Elizabeth Deeds (1997) *The English Novel in History 1840–1895* (London and New York: Routledge).

Eubanks, Philip (1999) "The Story of Conceptual Metaphor: What Motivates Metaphoric Mappings?", *Poetics Today* 20.3, 419–442.

Evangelista, Matthew (2008) *Law, Ethics, and the War on Terror* (Cambridge: Polity Press).

Frank, Michael (2014) *Narrating Terror: The Cultural Imaginary of Terrorism in Public Discourse, Literature, and Film* (Habilitation, University of Constance).

Goodman, Nelson (1978/1992) *Ways of Worldmaking* (Indianapolis, IN: Hackett).

Gore, Al (2008) *The Assault on Reason* (London and New York: Bloomsbury).

Gutenberg, Andrea (2000) *Mögliche Welten: Plot und Sinnstiftung im englischen Frauenroman* (Heidelberg: Winter).

Hardy, Barbara (1997) *Shakespeare's Storytellers: Dramatic Narration* (London and Chester Springs, PA: Peter Owen).

Helms, Gabriele (2003) *Challenging Canada: Dialogism and Narrative Technique in Canadian Novels* (Montreal et al.: McGill-Queen's UP).

Hill, Andrew (2009) *Re-Imagining the War on Terror: Seeing, Waiting, Travelling* (New York: Palgrave Macmillan).

Hodges, Adam (2011) *The "War on Terror" Narrative: Discourse and Intertextuality in the Construction and Contestation of Sociopolitical Reality* (Oxford: Oxford UP).

Hogan, Patrick Colm (2009) *Understanding Nationalism: On Narrative, Cognitive Science, and Identity* (Columubus: The Ohio State UP).

Holloway, David (2008) *9/11 and the War on Terror* (Edinburgh: Edinburgh UP).
Horowitz, Jason (2010) "Obama speechwriter Ben Rhodes is penning a different script for the world stage", in *The Washington Post*, 12 January 2010, http://www.washingtonpost.com/wp-dyn/content/article/2010/01/11/AR2010011103758.html (accessed 2 August 2016).
Jackson, Richard (2005) *Writing the War on Terrorism: Language, Politics and Counter Terrorism* (Manchester: Manchester UP).
Jarvis, Lee (2009) *Times of Terror: Discourse, Temporality, and the War on Terror* (New York: Palgrave Macmillan).
Konersmann, Ralf (ed) (2008) *Wörterbuch der philosophischen Metaphern* (Darmstadt: Wissenschaftliche Buchgesellschaft).
Konersmann, Ralf (2008a) "Vorwort: Figuratives Wissen", in Konersmann 2008, 7–21.
Koschorke, Albrecht (2012) *Wahrheit und Erfindung: Grundzüge einer Allgemeinen Erzähltheorie* (Frankfurt/M.: Fischer).
Kuypers, Jim A. (2006) *Bush's War: Media Bias and Justifications for War in a Terrorist Age* (Lanham, MD: Rowman & Littlefield).
Lakoff, George, and Mark Johnson (1980) *Metaphors We Live By* (Chicago: The U of Chicago Press).
Lotman, Juri M. (2013) *The Unpredictable Workings of Culture* (Tallinn: Tallinn UP).
MacDonald, David B., Dirk Nabers, and Robert G. Patman (eds.) (2012) *The Bush Leadership, the Power of Ideas, and the War on Terror* (Farnham: Ashgate).
Mahajan, Rahul (2002) *The New Crusade: America's War on Terrorism* (New York: Monthly Review Press).
McAdams, Dan P. (2013 [2006]) *The Redemptive Self: Stories Americans Live By* (Oxford: Oxford UP).
McEwan, Ian (1997/1998) *Enduring Love* (London: Vintage).
Meiner, Carsten, and Kristin Veel (eds.) (2012) *The Cultural Life of Catastrophes and Crises: Facts, Forms, Fantasies* (Berlin and New York: De Gruyter).
Morozov, Evgeny (2013) *To Save Everything, Click Here: Technology, Solutionism and the Urge to Fix Problems That Don't Exist* (London and New York: Allen Lane).
Müller-Funk, Wolfgang (2002/2008) *Die Kultur und ihre Narrative: Eine Einführung*, second edition (Vienna and New York: Springer).
Müller-Funk, Wolfgang (2012) *The Architecture of Modern Culture: Towards a Narrative Cultural Theory* (Berlin and New York: De Gruyter).
Naftali, Timothy (2010) "George W. Bush and the 'War on Terror,'" in *The Presidency of George W. Bush: A First Historical Assessment,* ed. Julian E. Zelizer (Princeton, NJ: Princeton UP), 59–87.
Nünning, Ansgar (2009) "Steps Towards a Metaphorology (and Narratology) of Crises: On The Functions of Metaphors as Figurative Knowledge and Mininarrations", in *Metaphors Shaping Culture and Theory. REAL – Yearbook of Research in English and American Literature* 25, ed. Herbert Grabes, Ansgar Nünning and Sibylle Baumbach (Tübingen: Narr), 229–262.
Nünning, Ansgar (2010) "Making Events – Making Stories – Making Worlds: Ways of Worldmaking from a Narratological Point of View", in Nünning, Nünning & Neumann 2010, 191–214.

Nünning, Ansgar (2012) "Making Crises and Catastrophes: Metaphors and Narratives Shaping the Cultural Life of Crises and Catastrophes", in *The Cultural Life of Catastrophes and Crises: Facts, Forms, Fantasies*, ed. Carsten Meiner and Kristin Veel (Berlin and New York: De Gruyter), 59–88.
Nünning, Ansgar, and Vera Nünning (2010) "Ways of Worldmaking as a Model for the Study of Culture: Theoretical Frameworks, Epistemological Underpinnings, New Horizons", in Nünning, Nünning & Neumann 2010, 1–25.
Nünning, Vera (2010) "The Making of Fictional Worlds: Processes, Features, and Functions", in Nünning, Nünning & Neumann 2010, 215–243.
Nünning, Vera, Ansgar Nünning, and Birgit Neumann (eds.) (2010) *Cultural Ways of Worldmaking: Media and Narratives* (Berlin and New York: De Gruyter).
Obama, Barack (2013) "Remarks by the President at the National Defense University", *The White House* http://www.whitehouse.gov/the-press-office/2013/05/23/remarks-president-national-defense-university (accessed 2 August 2016).
Ralph, Jason G. (2013) *America's War on Terror* (Oxford: Oxford UP).
Ricœur, Paul (1984) *Time and Narrative*, Vol 1 [1983], transl. Kathleen McLaughlin and David Pellauer (Chicago, IL and London: U of Chicago Press).
Roger, Nathan (2013) *Image Warfare in the War on Terror* (Basingstoke: Palgrave Macmillan).
Said, Edward (1993) *Culture and Imperialism* (London: Vintage).
Schmid, Wolf (2005) *Elemente der Narratologie* (Berlin and New York: De Gruyter).
Schopp, Andrew, and Matthew B. Hill (eds.) (2009) *The War on Terror and American Popular Culture: September 11 and Beyond* (Madison, NJ: Fairleigh Dickinson UP).
Shafir, Gershon (2013) *Lessons and Legacies of the War on Terror: From Moral Panic to Permanent War* (London: Routledge).
Spielvogel, Christian (2005) "'You Know Where I Stand': Moral Framing of the War on Terrorism and the Iraq War in the 2004 Presidential Campaign", *Rhetoric and Public Affairs* 8.4, 549–569.
Stierle, Karlheinz (1975) "Geschehen, Geschichte, Text der Geschichte", in *Text als Handlung* (München: Fink), 49–55.
Swift, Graham (2011) *Wish You Were Here* (London: Picador).
Turner, Mark (1987) *Death is the Mother of Beauty: Mind, Metaphor, Criticism* (Chicago and London: U of Chicago Press).
Wade, Marianne (2010) *A War on Terror? The European Stance on a New Threat, Changing Laws and Human Rights Implications* (New York: Springer).
Welch, Michael (2006) *Scapegoats of September 11th: Hate Crimes & State Crimes in the War on Terror* (New Brunswick, NJ: Rutgers UP).
White, Hayden (1973) *Metahistory: The Historical Imagination in Nineteenth Century Europe* (Baltimore, MD and London: Johns Hopkins UP).
Woodward, Bob (2006) *State of Denial: Bush at War, Part III* (New York: Simon & Schuster).

Index

https://doi.org/10.1515/9783110556858-014